ON ANARCHISM

ON ANARCHISM

DISPATCHES FROM THE PEOPLE'S REPUBLIC OF VERMONT

DAVID VAN DEUSEN

FOREWORD BY JEFF JONES
OF THE WEATHER UNDERGROUND

Algora Publishing
New York

Library of Congress Cataloging-in-Publication Data —

Names: Van Deusen, David, 1973- author.
Title: On anarchism: dispatches from the people's republic of Vermont /
    David Van Deusen.
Description: New York: Algora Publishing, 2017. | Includes bibliographical
    references.
Identifiers: LCCN 2017036132 (print) | LCCN 2017040821 (ebook) | ISBN
    9781628943054 (pdf) | ISBN 9781628943030 (soft cover: alk. paper) | ISBN
    9781628943047 (hard cover: alk. paper)
Subjects: LCSH: Deliberative democracy—Vermont. | Deliberative
    democracy—United States. | Anarchism—Vermont. | Anarchism—United
    States. | Democracy—Decision making.
Classification: LCC JC423 (ebook) | LCC JC423 .V343 2017 (print) | DDC
    320.5/709743—dc23
LC record available at https://lccn.loc.gov/2017036132

Cover illustration by Xavier Massot.

Printed in the United States

This work is dedicated to the past & present members of the Green Mountain Anarchist Collective, NEFAC, Anti-Racist Action, the CCC, Vermont AFL-CIO, United Electrical Workers, Vermont State Employees' Association-AOT, the Vermont Workers' Center, the Vermont Abenaki Tribes, those who have bravely marched with the Black Bloc, anti-fascist Motorcycle Clubs everywhere, all who continue to struggle for a more free and just Vermont, the memory of the Green Mountain Boys, and the International Freedom Battalion (who today fight valiantly with arms in Syria for the establishment of a libertarian-socialist society in Rojava).

Table of Contents

FOREWORD: RED AND BLACK IN THE GREEN MOUNTAIN STATE

You don't have to climb onto the back of David Van Deusen's Harley to enjoy the ride you are about to take in these pages. Van Deusen's long trip starts with his first time running with the Black Bloc at the 1996 Democratic Convention in Chicago and goes through his life as anarchist activist and scholar, union organizer, environmentalist, town official and unwavering supporter of indigenous Abenaki land rights and tribal self-determination in the Green Mountain State.[1]

David's life is consistent, militant and principled. These are admirable qualities, more important than ever in today's political climate: we need all the examples we can get of people standing up to racism and white supremacy, manifesting solidarity with the victims of imperialism. David identifies as a revolutionary: that is, he believes in and works for a complete transformation of our society as presently constituted. What's more, he believes this transformation is possible. And reading the story of his Movement life and work, and his many partners along the way, has strengthened my own hope for this transformation, and it will strengthen yours.

As the story unfolds, the theory becomes practice. But it starts with a vision. A co-authored Black Bloc manifesto published in 2000, shortly after the Battle of Seattle, identifies the emerging principles of insurrection. The authors identify the increasing loss of communal and

---

[1] Van Deusen served two terms as a Selectman in his town (endorsed by the socialist Vermont Liberty Union and Vermont Progressive Parties) and three terms as First Constable. He also worked with the Nulhegan Abenaki Tribe and the Vermont Sierra Club from 2010–2012 to help establish their first Nulhegan-owned tribal forest in over 200 years. This forest, which is also a working sugar bush generating common revenue for the tribe, exists to this day in the Northeast Kingdom of Vermont.

human values in our country caused by "the experiential emptiness of intensified neo-capitalist commodification of pseudoreality and its necessary results of mass alienation, anxiety and boredom." If that statement seems complex, it is nevertheless worth parsing. It's an almost perfect description of early 21-century America that a decade and a half later brought Donald Trump to the presidency on a neo-fascist platform of racism, xenophobia, misogyny and transparently empty promises appealing to the nihilism of a significant part of his base.

David and I met through his family early on in his journey. At the time, he was living an off-the-grid and outlaw life in a Southern Vermont anarchist collective. He seemed to appreciate my history in Students for a Democratic Society, some very militant days running with Lower East Side anarchists in late '60s, and the Weather Underground. We were born into different generations, but our paths have been parallel for many years, including fighting white supremacy, defending the planet and trying to build an alliance between environmentalists and the labor movement.[2] David is a true warrior, especially for the people of Vermont.

If there are issues to be addressed from these pages, they center on the role of a militant left in a time of hard right ascendancy. When hundreds of neo-Nazis, KKK members and other white nationalists marched in Charlottesville, Virginia earlier this summer, attempting a show of force for a revitalized white supremacist movement through a Unite the Right rally, they faced opposition that was confrontational and determined. The subsequent debate in the media and the left about the proper response is valid. But let's not forget that we must confront and challenge attacks on people of color, women, immigrants and progressives targeted by the right. As African-American leader and thinker Cornell West said on Democracy Now! describing a moment in Charlottesville when some 20 religious and anti-racist leaders were surrounded by several hundred rightists, "the antifascists...they saved our lives."

David's writings help us understand the history, practice and theory of someone who has spent the past two decades standing up to the racist right, in its many forms. These pages include stories about confronting the quasi-vigilante Minutemen, an earlier neo-Nazi manifestation that formed along the southern U.S. border. When they tried to set up shop in New England, in 2006, with the claim that the

---

2 Between 2010–2012 Van Deusen formed an active partnership between the Vermont Sierra Club and the Iron Workers Local 7 in support of new green energy projects and securing of union jobs on said projects.

U.S. needed civilian volunteers to interdict immigrants and political refugees crossing the border from Quebec, David was there with anti-racist militants from across Vermont and New England. Faced with real opposition, the Minutemen soon vanished.

That was 11 years ago. A disturbing aspect of this particular story, however, is how pervasive the racist and anti-immigrant ideas and violence of this energized neo-fascist movement has actually become since it became official U.S. policy under Trump. I know from my work with John Brown Lives! in the Adirondack North Country today that the border with Canada has again become a safety valve for immigrant families who still follow the Drinking Gourd, escaping the deportation net cast by Trump-era federal agents. In reality, immigration to the US is exactly the opposite of what the wall-builders believe. Historically, people come to the U.S. to be safe, not to do harm. Now they have become victims and look north for refuge. Thanks to groups like the Green Mountain Anarchist Collective, there are still safe pathways for them to follow.

While the role of militancy emerges dramatically from these pages, so does the role of unity — and the question: on what terms?

Returning to the Black Bloc manifesto of 2000, I am particularly intrigued by point number seven. This was after the Battle of Seattle, a transformative moment in Movement history that both David and I missed. The protests against the neo-liberal, global corporatist World Trade Organization drew an unexpected but welcome unity that included a new alliance between environmentalists and trade union activists. This particular manifesto reflected the Black Bloc's attempt to understand and provide direction — a tough call for avowed anarchists — to the re-energized movement. "The generational maturity of the children of the 60s and 70s has now come to fruition," they wrote. "This is a fact that should not be overlooked as we intend to build on and further destroy where our mothers and fathers left off." I take this as a positive reference to the ideas and militant actions of our earlier days opposing the Vietnam War and supporting the Black liberation movement.

The actions of militant anarchists and others at the 1996 Democratic Convention in Chicago came 28 years after our own protests on those same streets. The formation of Weatherman was still a year away. Between those two protests, our generation confronted similar issues of militancy, organization, ideology and tactics, followed for some by years of apology and remorse, while others stood firm. For me, the most important lessons, repeated in successful movements and revolutions around the world, are resistance and unity. That is, in the strategy advanced by Fidel Castro more than half a century ago as the Cuban Revolution gained ground: "the ideal thing is unity" around basic principles and the strategic issues of the day.

This is not so easy, especially when confronted by entrenched constituencies tending toward compromise. So, the other strong thread that emerges from David's writing and practice are the stories he tells, and the practice he describes, from an exciting range of groups and people who have found common ground in the Green Mountain State.

The title of this book refers to the anarchist writings; anarchist here being of the broader family of socialism. In Vermont, home to Bernie Sanders, you can be a socialist and get elected, both to the United States Senate and, in David's case, to local office. You can also be a labor leader. You can ride with anti-racist bikers, advocate for Vermont's independence and support the legitimate national aspirations of the state's first citizens, the Abenaki Tribes. These writings begin with an outlaw life lived at the end of a dirt road in Southern Vermont. They describe a political and personal journey that weaves inside and outside of the political system.

The journey is not over yet.

Jeff Jones, Albany, NY
October, 2017

CHAPTER 1: HISTORY

THE RISE AND FALL OF THE GREEN MOUNTAIN ANARCHIST COLLECTIVE[1]

Members of the Green Mountain Anarchist Collective

"The chains of authoritarianism and capitalism can only be shattered when they are broken at many links. Vermont is our home, and it serves as the one link that we can access, but it is only one. Any victory here would only be partial. Deliverance to the Promised Land will only come when many more than us rise up against that which holds the multitude in bondage."

—The Green Mountain Anarchist Collective, From 'Vermont Secession'

Montpelier, Vermont, 2015 — Established in 2000, in a cooperative household located at the termination of a wooded dirt road in Southern Vermont, the Green Mountain Anarchist Collective (GMAC), for a time, did its part in carrying forth Vermont's long tradition of radical, leftist politics. Founded in Windham County by Natasha Voline, Johnny Midnight, Xavier Massot, and (myself) David Van Deusen, the collective was birthed with strong Situationist, leftist, and militant inclinations. The original GMAC nucleus lived together (along with

---

1 2017 note from the author: The article was first published in Infoshop News and Anarchist News in 2015. The article was peer reviewed and published in the Interface Journal in 2016. This essay articulates my views and memories of the collective. Other collective members will inevitably have different takes on the same subject matter.

comrades Imelda R, Bridget M, and Ted K), and operated as a kind of outlaw community, connected to the broader area counter culture based in and around Brattleboro. Together, they functioned on a cash & barter basis, opening phone and utility accounts under assumed names. They adorned the walls with stolen Salvador Dali works. Torr Skoog and Liam Crill, of the Boston band The Kings of Nuthin (whom Massot befriended shortly after he emigrated from his native France), were occasional visitors.

Half of the household's income came from the black market, the rest from a single student loan and occasional manual labor (once being paid to build a bird aviary for Kermit W — the rumored son of Egypt's Nasser]. Two household members were wanted by the law (one facing some years in prison the other on minor charges); another was an artist; two were brought up in strong union households; a few experimented in poetry; the household included two guitars and a five piece drum set in the living room. All present shared an interest in furthering a more creative, life affirming, and non-capitalist future. When not cutting their-own wood to feed the stove (which was typically the case), they "borrowed" a half cord at a time from unoccupied vacation homes scattered throughout the area. Trips to town often involved beer at the Common Ground (a co-op founded by local communes in the 1970s), or $5.40 double whiskeys at Mike's (a rough-around-the-edges working class tavern on Elliot Street). However, town, being 15 miles away, largely remained un-visited. Instead, target shooting off the back porch with .22's & SKS's, making firecrackers out of black powder, listening to The Clash & Johnny Cash, trying to get a half junked 56' Chevy working, long conversations, chess, strong marijuana (very strong marijuana), vigorous debate, and intensively reading from the Situationist, Existentialist, Anarchist, and Marxist cannons filled the time until a more direct political involvement came to be.

When this group founded the Green Mountain Anarchist Collective, it was agreed that its first task would be to provide support and tactical innovation to the Black Bloc and growing revolutionary anarchist movement; a movement which was gaining steam in the immediate aftermath of the Battle of Seattle (1999). What marked GMAC as different from some anarchist or leftist collectives, was that it was anchored in a deeply rural community with a strong tradition of local democracy (Town Meeting), and this broader community (Vermont) itself was premised upon an armed uprising prior to the American War for Independence (Vermont conducted guerrilla warfare against the royal colony of New York which, by 1770, was actively engaged in an effort to appropriate the lands east of the historic NY border). These facts, as much as the artwork of Dada, Russian Futurists, or the writings of Debord, Bakunin or Marx, came to form the radical world view of this collective, while also influencing the content of its own writings. In brief, the Green Mountain Anarchist Collective, at its best, helped to give voice and organized action to the anarchist and leftist prescriptions concerning the problems of modern capitalism, while also framing such radical paths of progressive change in an old world language particular to Vermont; their revolutionary cannon being one part Debord, one part Bakunin, and two parts Ethan Allen & the Green Mountain Boys. That said, the full realization of this revolutionary language did not appear upon conception. Rather, GMAC evolved as the scope of its community organizing experiences expanded.

The Political Premise

From the start, the collective, which was never a mass organization but rather a tightly knit cadre, held an anarchist-leftist political position influenced by Situationist concepts. It argued that twenty-first century capitalism, along with class oppression, represents an abstraction of organic existence, one which seeks to have the individual (and by extension the group) subordinate its notion of reality to the artificial singularity of 'capital' as a universal commodity (with all aspects of contemporary existence being understood as commodities). However, the contemporary nature of 'capital', for the most part, no longer being linked to a universally recognized (tangible) signifier (be it gold, silver, or even paper money), makes 'capital' into a kind of 'Holy Ghost' of the current Western World. In such, capital, and therefore contemporary capitalism, becomes akin to a post-religious and all reaching grid of perception. By achieving this, capitalism maintains its economic primacy while also reaching into a realm previously reserved for religious or mystical understanding; it becomes an epistemology, ontology, and a means by which a kind of daily survival is perpetuated. Such is the singularity of this form of capitalism that its internal logic dictates a colonization not only of foreign markets (as with conventional later-stage capitalism), but also the colonization of the individual's subjective thoughts, desires, perceived needs, etc.. And here, upon success, a kind of artificial objectivity is created where objectivity is, in reality, void. Thus the danger of a more stable oppressive social/economic/cultural super structure becomes apparent.

GMAC also held that this model of individual and mass perception perpetuates a unequitable, unfulfilling, and oppressive class system whereby the many are subordinate to the few insofar as this new campaign to commodify the subjective mind serves the same basic role as the colonization of foreign territories did during the nineteenth and twentieth centuries; namely the creation of new frontier accessible to the primary and secondary exploitive relationships to capitalist markets. The few who economically benefit from this new colonization (and the resulting buying and selling of false or perceived want), for their part, also become subordinate to the abstract system which ostensibly serves their material (minority) economic interests. Furthermore, by society focusing mass amounts of time, energy, and resources into the creation of such needs (advertising, public messaging, etc.), and then manufacturing the objects of these needs, requires the equivalent amount of social energy being taken away from tasks which could serve the real interest of humanity. As such, GMAC argued that human growth and political/economic equality (not to mention sustainability) would come only through the success of a militant revolutionary movement which would seek to overthrow not only the political and economic structures which support the status quo, but also the predominant new culture (referred to by GMAC as anti-culture) which allows for the absurd to become accepted fact. Therefore, the revolution required to deliver a victory against the new capitalism would not only take militant action against the state, but also a counter-cultural effort against that which is perceived to be; this victorious revolution would concern itself not only with guns and butter, but also with music and art. GMAC further argued that both the physical and cultural resistance must be emanated from the bottom up (in line with radical democratic principles), in order to reflect the realized goals of a non-alienated, equitable, post-revolutionary society, whereby the individual (and group by extension) could realize its creative potential through a collaborative nexus of free expression, experimentation, and basic cooperation. And finally, in that it would take the many to overcome the few (or in relation to the anti-culture, to overcome the striving totality), and because it is the many who suffer most in the current exploitative paradigm (and are its natural foe), GMAC understood the need for this revolutionary process to be an expression of the majority economic stratum: the working class.

The collective, while starting largely as a support cell for the militant movement outside Vermont, soon became deeply engaged in local efforts to bring about radical change in the Green Mountains. These efforts tended to be grounded in the labor movement, but also, at times, ventured into the struggle of the small farmers. As GMAC became more and more vested in the local struggle against capitalism (and for a direct democracy), they also became more drawn to Vermont's unique cultural posits which tend to run counter to the larger consumer culture of the United States. And with such cultural difference, GMAC sought to build a bridge from the distant memory of rural insurrection, over the demons of modern capitalism, to the realization of a socialist community entrenched in the ideals of an expanded Town Meeting democracy: a kind of Guy Debord and Jean Paul Sartre meet yeoman farmers with aspirations.

The Black Bloc and Beyond

From its inception, the Green Mountain Anarchist Collective recognized the historic importance and potential for change in the growing anti-globalization movement. Here, GMAC posited that this movement was inclined to question not only the negative symptoms of the failure of the modern age, but also was inclined to look for the root cases; the mother disease which birthed said systems. And here GMAC believed the likely conclusion of any such mass diagnosis would be the unveiling of capitalism (with all its current mutations) as the essential prime mover. Given that organized labor and the mass environmental groups were increasingly engaging in this movement (along with small radical cadres from hundreds if not thousands of cities), the collective saw the potential for a shift in popular consciousness. However, GMAC also asserted that capitalism, increasingly fortified by not only the obvious chains of oppression, but also with the unseen chains binding individuals through the colonization of the mind, possess the ability to create many false crossroads aimed at fooling or misdirecting the people. Therefore, a concerted and militant effort would have to be inserted into this movement in order to help create the conditions necessary for a kind of mass clarity; the reality of Bakunin's instinct to rebel. And finally, it was argued that in the face of an increasing singularity of oppression, physical resistance is not only a right, but a necessity. On the other hand non-violence, and non-violent resistance, although not completely rejected by GMAC, was viewed with distrust by the collective. Specifically, GMAC questioned whether or not nonviolence, if not balanced by a parallel physical militancy, would increase the likelihood of submerging resistance into a quagmire of strictly symbolic action which does little to threaten a status quo already relatively secure it its expanding singularity. Where militant and direct resistance can be jarring, disruptive, and challenging, pacifism, to GMAC, was understood as a sort of hollow self-therapy; a million may walk down the road carrying a sign, and thousands my block an intersection for a few hours, but at the end of the day these actions, alone, do not alter the experience of those passively viewing the actions, or even those taking part. Such activities typically carry little risk in the more developed capitalist world; the lack of risk, to the uninitiated popular mind, often sugars out into a lack of interest; to those at the pinnacle of power, it reads as little threat. In brief, an apostate that lives in the wilderness threatens no believer.

GMAC did however make a distinction between non-violence as a tactic and non-violence as an ideology (pacifism). As a tactic, the collective saw a conditional role. As an ideology, it viewed it as borderline insane. GMAC accepted that a tactic should be utilized and judged based on contextual analysis and successful results. As an ideology, it viewed it as a very mature and brilliant appendage to the anti-culture; as a kind of false opposition to that which is. Once resistance becomes self-limiting and non-lethal to its other, the other has taken a long step toward the perpetuation of an alienating social system whereby the chains are no longer seen, and whereby the key is lost to the collective memory.

In the pamphlet "On The Question of Violence and Non-Violence as a Tactic and a Strategy in The Social Protest Movement" (Black Clover Press, Vermont, 2001), the Collective wrote:

> Clearly there are many circumstances in which non-violent tactics are not only advisable, but also the only effective course possible... this commitment to non-violence... is fundamentally based on pragmatism... while finding its material existence through the implementation of tactics. However, non-violence should, under no circumstances, be understood as a strategy in and of itself.

And further:

> Ideological non-violence is the negation of [the working class's] shared history of struggle. It denies their dreams of freedom by its shear absurdity and stifles certain forms of their self-expression through its totalitarian and insanely idealistic demands. In a word, strategical non-violence is the negation of class consciousness; it is irrelevant at best and slavery at worst. In itself, it represents the conscious and/

or unconscious attempt of the more privileged classes to sterilize the revolutionary threat forever posed by a self-confident, self-conscious and truly revolutionary working class.

With these premises in place, GMAC understood the rise of the Black Bloc as a chance to further cultivate one aspect of the resistance movement. It was towards the Black Bloc that GMAC therefore turned.

If ideological pacifism represented a kind of hollow self-therapy, GMAC understood the violent and assertive actions of the Black Bloc as a kind of mass shock-therapy; one capable of further shaking the foundation of popular belief and acceptance. Here it should be noted that GMAC did not advocate for an unreasoned, isolated, or suicidal Black Bloc. Rather, it campaigned for one that served its role within a larger movement of resistance which, ironically, was not ready to fully embrace militant tactics. For GMAC, the Black Bloc represented one dynamic and necessary aspect of a diverse struggle waged on many fronts and through divergent means; the totality of these differing approaches, together representing a kind of mutually dependent arising of revolutionary potential. But again in order to realize the full effectiveness of the Black Bloc, GMAC understood it necessary to analyze, critique, and modify its tactics and organizational structure in order to address ostensible failings experienced by the Bloc in historic street actions (failings that GMAC feared would intensify as state police and intelligence agencies studied Black Bloc manifestations). Hence, in its early years the collective worked to strengthen the capabilities of the Black Bloc. This emphasis led it to the writing and wide circulation (within anarchist and leftist circles) of the pamphlet *Communique on Tactics and Organization* (Kersplebedeb Press, Montreal QB, December, 2000).

This pamphlet identified indecision, deficient mass mobility, lack of coordinated planning, and a cavalier security culture as the immediate causes of its limitations in effectiveness. Looking to history (specifically anarchist history) GMAC then sought to recommend a democratic internal command structure within the formation, as well as the utilization of more complex use of tactical maneuvers. To quote from the tactics communique:

> [O]ur experiences have... illustrated certain short comings that we thus far are yet to overcome. Specifically our lack of democratic tactical command structure has hindered our abilities to act with more punctuating speed and tactical ferociousness... [W]e [therefore]

propose that the present use of elected affinity group spokes people be expanded to that of acute tactical facilitator... The role of this person should be to help facilitate the organized movement of their immediate section as recommended by [a] general tactical facilitation core.

This first edition of the pamphlet was met with a mixed reception among anarchist groups. Some charged that GMAC's position risked a shift towards a more centralized Leninist command structure. While others, such as the Boston based Barricada Collective, and Ohio based Columbus Anti-Racist Action, agreed with the need to move to a re-organization of the Bloc. Those that viewed the work favorably tended to agree with GMAC's assertion that the temporary election of militant leaders was in line with the historic practices of the CNT and FAI anarchist militias during the Spanish Civil War (1936–1939). The Barricada Collective published this version of the pamphlet in 2001, in their magazine, also called Barricada.

An on-going correspondence between GMAC and Columbus ARA led to the meeting between the groups in Ohio, in the winter of 2001. It was agreed that further changes should be made in the pamphlet to strengthen the abilities of the Black Bloc. A second revised edition of the pamphlet was produced and circulated in July of 2001 (Columbus ARA Press, Columbus OH). Key recommendations included: the Black Bloc should elect a temporary officer core empowered to make tactical decisions, especially concerning movement and engagement with state forces during street actions; the Bloc should hold a force of one third in reserve to be called into action at the demand of the officer core during acute times of need; and finally, individual affinity groups should be organized into larger clusters responsible for the integrity of different areas of the Bloc (front, back, right, left, center), and that each affinity group focus on a specialized need concerning the Bloc's core (offensive, defensive, capitalist property destruction, recon, first aid, morale, public outreach, etc.).

Upon its release by Black Clover Press (and distribution by AK Press), this revised pamphlet was met with mixed opinion; those skeptical of formal organization remaining opposed, those recognizing the value of increased organization tending to be in support. In general, the Northeastern Federation of Anarcho-Communists (who the Barricada Collective was affiliated with) supported the recommendations. GMAC joined this federation, as its Vermont affiliate, in 2002.

In 2001, GMAC members Xavier Massot and David Van Deusen also (largely) wrote and edited the book *The Black Bloc Papers*

(Insubordinate Editions, Baltimore MD, 2002). The book sought to provide a comprehensive collection of Black Bloc communiques from North America, while situating the phenomenon within a cultural-social-economic context of creative resistance.

In the book's introduction, Xavier Massot posits:

> Getting away from the instinctive fear of not having enough is the next real bridge to cross for humanity. Our ancestors had to find ways to survive. The world today knows how to live, yet refuses to do so in an equitable manner. A work ethic is a great thing, that is undeniable, but to work for the sake of working is nothing but a slow cop-out suicide... Let's eliminate the role of society as murderer and rapist. If we're going to [mess] up, let's do it ourselves without unnecessary abstractions guiding and answering our treachery.

In Chapter I, David Van Deusen writes:

> Within... a [revolutionary] counterculture it is only natural that certain people will carry the ball in this [militant] direction. And it is here that specific people and collectives will organically key in on revolutionary political action akin to that presently demonstrated by the Earth Liberation Front cells on the one hand and the Anarchist Black Bloc on the other. Here it cannot bide its time and wait for the perfect moment. It must lash out at its other as a basic means of political expression. It must transcend its relative passivity through violent resistance of its own repression as well as the repression directed against the poor and working classes as a whole. And in such, it achieves an honesty that progressive impostors cannot readily provide.

And again from Massot:

> A lot of people object to the Black Bloc on both sides of the protest fence... I understand their grievances and I disagree with all of them... I am, however, certain that it's healthy to physically confront authorities who physically uphold a rotten system and to remind the rest of the populous that such things can be done.

The work additionally sought to further highlight the need for internal reorganization as advocated in its previous pamphlet. Although originally slated to be published by AK Press, this first edition was eventually produced by Insubordinate Editions, Baltimore MD, in 2002, and covered Black Bloc activities in North America from 1999–2001. An expanded online version of the work was published by Breaking Glass Press, Lawrence KS, in 2010 (covering the years 1988–2005). In 2014, Little Black Cart, Berkeley CA (an imprint of Ardent Press) published a third edition of the work.

In the same year that the Black Bloc Papers was being written, GMAC member Van Deusen (the author of this article) produced an additional pamphlet entitled "On The Question of Violence and Non-Violence as a Tactic and Strategy in The Social Protest Movement" (Black Clover Press, Montpelier, VT, 2001; distributed by AK Press).

It's important to recognize GMAC's militant—rather than merely intellectual roots and motivation. Prior to the founding of the collective, future members took part in Black Bloc actions across the United States. These included the marches against the Democratic National Convention (Chicago, 1996); Millions For Mumia (Philadelphia, 1999); the protests against the International Monetary Fund and World Bank (A16-Washington DC, 2000); and the demonstration against the Republican National Convention (Philadelphia, 2000). GMAC also took part in the Quebec City uprising against the Free Trade of the Americas Agreement (FTAA) in 2001, and the Siege of Lewiston (against a failed fascist organizing drive-Maine-2003). It was through GMAC's Black Bloc experiences that it drew its conclusions concerning the need to enhance the Bloc's tactical abilities. During later, post pamphlet actions, it further sought to incorporate the changes it recommended into street experiments.

Leading up to the massive protests against the Free Trade of the Americas Agreement summit in Quebec of April, 2001, GMAC was asked by Columbus ARA to facilitate the clandestine border crossing of this group. At the time, Columbus ARA was recognized as one of the most militant organizations in North America, and there was concern that they would be barred from entering Canada if they sought to cross the border through traditional means. GMAC, with wide logistical support from rural Vermont residents (otherwise unaffiliated with the organized aspects of the movement), was successful in this effort, crossing the frontier on foot, through thick forests in the cover of darkness. The crossing location, which necessitated a rugged overnight hike over a mountain and through deep spring snow, was recommended to them by a friendly 65 year old radical (RH, a former member of the revolutionary Free Vermont commune movement of the 1970s) who previously used the same route to help undocumented workers (from Central American warzones) pass through the boarders, unseen, in the 1980s. Columbus ARA and GMAC were therefore able to play a militant role in the urban conflict which ensued over two days of rioting in Quebec City. There an ARA and GMAC member suffered minor wounds as a result of police weapons. However, none from this affinity group suffered arrest, and the Black Bloc made a strong showing, as evident in sections of a security fence being torn down, a bank being torched, and police being effectively fought back through the use of clubs, stones, and petrol bombs on numerous occasions.

After the Quebec City actions, membership in the collective became fluid. GMAC's first generation of membership broke down in the summer of 2001 while people traveled. Massot went west and then back to Brattleboro. Van Deusen moved to Columbus, Ohio, for a good part of a year, and worked with ARA. Johnny Midnight left the collective altogether (moving on to become a union electrician). The second generation of GMAC began to form in 2002 when Van Deusen, along with "Lady" of Columbus ARA (and now GMAC member), moved to a rural area in North Central Vermont (near the capital city of Montpelier). Van Deusen and Lady established another collective household, this one, although being less than ten miles from town, being more remote than the first (requiring a snow machine to gain access to the last mile for half the year). From this base, new members emerged and brought with them their unique perspectives. HR, a resident of the Northeast Kingdom (NEK), was a radical largely involved with food security issues. Will Dunbar, who at the time also lived in the Kingdom (in another collective household), was an early member of the Second Vermont Republic (a Vermont separatist organization which he resigned from in order to join GMAC) and was rumored to be attached to the Iconoclast Liberation Front. Will was also instrumental in the founding of the Northeast Kingdom Music Festival. SW and JM moved from Philly (where they were members of the Northeastern Federation of Anarcho-Communists-NEFAC) to Montpelier and were interested in retaining their political activity. KW, a Montpelier native, came to the group through her personal relationship with numerous members and her political activism (KW did counter-recruitment against military service among high school students, and soon would become the Chief Steward in a new radical labor union). NR, (a labor activist previously from Michigan) and AL (a Montpelier native) joined after becoming engaged with the collective largely through a union organizing effort. HB was going to the University of Vermont (Burlington) and was a member of the Student Labor Action Project. People joined, and people left.

It should also be recognized that the collective did not think of itself as geographically-based (unless that geography is expanded to include all of Vermont). When the majority of members lived within a dozen miles of Montpelier, it still recruited members in the Northeast

Kingdom and even in Burlington. For a time Massot (who would go through periods of being a member and not being a member) maintained an affiliation while remaining in Southern Vermont (even though the majority now lived in the North). Suffice to say that GMAC always viewed itself as a statewide anarchist organization; one that believed its campaigns and energy should be focused on affecting progressive and revolutionary change on Vermont as a whole; not in a single municipality or community as such. While there doubtlessly are criticisms that could be lodged at GMAC, failing to see the forest for the trees is not one of them.

In the summer of 2001, even while the collective was going through a period of inactivity, a representative of GMAC along with an ally from ARA made an appearance at the Renewing Anarchist Traditions conference, held at the Institute of Social Ecology, Plainfield, VT. The appearance was made in order to seek out a meeting with a trusted member of a Boston NEFAC collective, ML. ML was trusted by the collective (and ARA) because of his past (pre-political) personal relationship with Massot, dating back to when Massot lived in Boston. There, GMAC, which already carried out one successful clandestine border crossing in the spring, offered a contingency plan by which GMAC would facilitate other extra-legal border crossings for U.S. NEFAC members if and when such actions became advisable due to changing political circumstances. It is worth noting that even prior to the terrorist attacks on September 11th (later that same year), GMAC was concerned that the George W Bush administration was heading in a direction towards a clampdown on civil liberties. Here, the relative effectiveness of the Black Bloc, and NEFAC's role in organizing such Blocs, made NEFAC a potential target for a state crackdown. GMAC asked that the offer, and the contact protocols, be made discreetly known to trusted NEFAC members. Before GMAC/ARA made its approach to the Institute for Social Ecology (to relay this offer) the license plate on their 1978 Ford van was removed in case of police/state intelligence gathering.

In September, 2001 the terrorist attacks caught everyone off guard, including the collective. Massot was in France. Van Deusen and (soon to be a member) Lady were together in Western Canada (and were only able to slip back into the US, some days later, after they made their way to an isolated road crossing between Quebec and Vermont favored by GMAC). The political aftermath of this attack changed the social landscape. The state used this as an excuse to launch a massive crackdown on civil liberties, to aggressively go after dissident groups, and the American public seemed to pause; suddenly the tens-of-thousands turning out for anti-globalization rallies dwindled to a few thousand. It would not be until the rise of the mass anti-war rallies in 2003 that the numbers and energy would return to the streets. But regardless, for the next year after 9/11, members of GMAC remained dispersed, and direct political activity became immersed in the broader anarchist movement (not with a clear GMAC identity attached to it). The only unique GMAC activities during this time were the publication of written material (as discussed elsewhere in this work). However, by September, 2002, when Lady and Van Deusen established the new base near Montpelier, and as a new generation of members began to come to the collective, GMAC would become active again as its own political entity. This time it would affiliate with the Northeastern Federation of Anarcho-Communists (which had member collectives in Quebec, New England, and throughout the broader Northeast region). As NEFAC's Vermont affiliate, GMAC continued to engage in militant street actions, and increasingly in radical grassroots organizing.

GMAC joined NEFAC for a couple reasons. First, it understood the need to better coordinate the militant resistance to capitalism across the region. It also was impressed by NEFAC's apparent ability in organizing Black Blocs. And finally, it agreed with the undertone of member collectives who argued in favor of political organizing beyond mass protests (an assertion increasingly supported by GMAC — but not understood as an either-or proposition). Even so, GMAC was surprised when at a 2002 conference held in Baltimore, Maryland, elements of the federation strongly argued that they should deemphasize their engagement with mass Black Bloc actions at large anti-globalization protests, and instead to focus the federation's collective energy towards labor and community organizing. While GMAC delegates recognized (and agreed with) the need to engage in community and labor organizing, it opposed the decision to partially disengage from large scale Black Bloc actions. GMAC argued that the role of the revolutionary anarchist organizations should be to embody the principles of being both the most relevant and the most militant. GMAC also argued that the relative success of high profile Black Blocs resulted in not only an advance in popular consciousness concerning resistance to capitalism, but also acted as a prime recruiting mechanism, drawing militant and committed revolutionary youth into the federation. However, by a democratic vote of NEFAC delegates, GMAC's position was defeated. GMAC, as an affiliate of the federation, remained in NEFAC and respected the strategic decision of the organization, even if it continued to believe it was the wrong decision.

This refocus by NEFAC, along with the changed domestic political reality following the 9/11, resulted in a temporary regression concerning the use and growth of the Black Bloc as an effective street tactic in North America. This regression would not begin to reverse itself until after the U.S. invasion of Iraq in 2003.

Building The Movement

Back in Vermont, GMAC members, in November 2002, walked picket lines of striking United Radio, Machine, and Electrical Workers of American (UE) outside the gates of the Fairbanks Scale factory, in St. Johnsbury (NEK), Vermont. (Note that this strike was receiving acute support from the Vermont Workers Center, and to a lessor extant the social-democratic Vermont Progressive Party.) The union factory workers had a long history of militancy (during their previous strike picketers overturned a bus filled with scabs). When a delivery truck sought to drive into the factory grounds, UE members and GMAC participants attempted to block the vehicle. This situation soon led to violence between picketers and deputy sheriffs. One GMAC member exchanged head-butts with one cop and took a face full of pepper spray as a result. Still, the blockade was not relinquished until union leaders gave the order. When police came to arrest the (now blinded) GMAC member, union leaders intervened, making an arrest impossible. The following week GMAC returned to the picket line to the applause of the union workers. The union went on to win the strike, securing better pay and working conditions on the shop floor.

In January, 2003, GMAC led the militant organizing effort aimed at shutting down a planned fascist organizing effort in Lewiston, Maine. Working with local radicals, other NEFAC collectives, and ARA chapters, the collective (under the direction of Lady) helped organize a 500 strong protest contingent, 100 of these being organized into a Black Bloc. In the front line of the march was GMAC along with Vermont comrade, JW (a former member of the Love and Rage #10 Collective, co-founder of the Vermont Workers Center). Utilizing methods supported by GMAC's tactics pamphlet, this Black Bloc was able to push through police barricades, and lay siege to the armory (where the fascist meeting was being held) without suffering a single arrest. (Note that while this militant confrontation was taking place, an anti-racist unity event was also being held. This event drew 5000 local residents.) NEFAC's deemphasizing of Black Bloc tactics only related to their use at high profile national events. It did not apply to small scale actions, especially those aimed at confronting fascism.

Lady, in her written report back to NEFAC stated:

> We were expecting the... pig force of Lewiston to be able to utilize their special training for our arrival, and the following precautions were to be employed by them: the confiscation of flag or sign poles, backpacks, cameras that weren't given previous press clearance (because you know how terrorists like to hide bombs in cameras?!), and random searches. No protesters were permitted to be in radius of the National Guard Armory, and were going to be directed to two 'park and rides half a mile down another street. Roads were going to be blocked off, and ID's checked upon rerouting traffic to the park and rides... Deciding to use Black Bloc tactics was an advantage on our part. With this situation at hand, the contingent of Antifa decided to employ Black Bloc tactics (it is specifically important here that we decided to march in formation, and elected a tactical facilitation core)... By wearing black, masking up, and marching in a tight rectangular formation with banners on all sides, we looked intimidating to the pigs. The first road block consisted of three cop cars and six or so pigs. All but one stood there staring, while the "ranking officer" approached us. The banner was lifted right over his head, and wouldn't you know—he found himself right in the middle of the Bloc. Piece of cake. (Here, this worked well. In another situation, where the police are our primary combatants, we should never allow an enemy in our midst except to physically deal with them.) The next barricade consisted of two city dump trucks and a few cop cars. It looked tough and could have been, but we never paused and just kept moving forward. The drivers of the trucks were working people. One driver waved to us, while the other backed up just a little. We moved on through...When we passed the [non-Black Bloc] protesters who were stuck at the park and ride, we enthusiastically invited them to join us. A Bloc of only 50 quickly turned into about 300 when seemingly everyone from the two park and rides joined us!

Not all of GMAC's activities were centered in street conflicts. As previously eluded to, from late 2002 on GMAC devoted substantial time and organizational resources to grassroots campaigns. Seeking to achieve a broader impact in its efforts, the collective typically worked in cooperation with other democratic/leftist community organizations. In 2002, GMAC decided to commit itself to providing limited support to a farmer organizing campaign known as the Dairy Farmers of Vermont (DFV). This group, founded by Progressive farmer

Dexter Randle, and organizers Anthony Pollina and Peter Sterling, was seeking to gain the affiliation of farms representing a minimum of one third of all raw milk produced in the state. (Note that Deter Randal went on to be a Progressive Party State Representative for the Town of Troy, Anthony Pollina went on to received 21% of the vote for Governor in 2008 and became a Progressive Party State Senator in 2010. Sterling would later head the pro-single payer organization Campaign For Healthcare Security and in 2017 was made Chief of Staff of VT Senate Pro Tem Tim Ashe-Progressive.) Upon reaching this number, DFV intended to seek to collectively bargain for a sustainable price for said milk from the processors. Failing this, the group was exploring the possibility of opening a farmer owned processing plant which could provide payments that could be sustaining to family farms. DFV operated internally through democratic principles.

GMAC, recognizing the significance of mobilizing Vermont's farmers towards resistance to current capitalist expressions, provided DFV with volunteer hours on a regular weekly basis. GMAC's support tended to be low level activities (stuffing envelopes, answering phones, research, etc.), but necessary ones never-the-less. In the end DFV, who achieved its membership goals, was stonewalled by the processors, but did manage, for a time, to open and operate a farmer controlled processing plant in the Northeast Kingdom.

In 2003 GMAC worked with representatives of the state's largest labor unions (AFL-CIO, National Educators Association, Vermont State Employees' Association-VSEA), and other mass organizations in forwarding a project called the Peoples' Round Table Organizing Committee. This campaign, largely the brainchild of Ed Stanak—the president of the Vermont State Employees Association (VSEA), and IWW supporter, and eventually the 2012 Progressive Party candidate for Attorney General--sought to build a united left platform from the grassroots of all the major popular VT organizations, and to further this platform through mass action and political participation. However, GMAC learned from this effort that the specific leaders of the various mass (VT) organizations, no matter how well intended, do not necessarily reflect active support from below. While a limited number of public (platform building) meetings were held throughout the state, and while a draft platform was produced (after countless nights and hours of delegate meetings), the campaign largely proved to be lacking in the necessary buy-in and active support from the tens of thousands of members whom the organizing delegates ostensibly represented. Even so, the political sentiment which underlined this effort, a decade later, was to see fruition in the political sphere —the 2011 passage of VT single payer healthcare legislation being one example of such progress (legislation which was later derailed by Democratic Governor Peter Shumlin). But again, for the moment, GMAC reflected on the fact that it spent significant time on this project but saw very little immediate political successes in return. It is worth noting that the Director of the Vermont Workers Center (an organization founded in 1998 by members of the Love and Rage Revolutionary Anarchist Federation), James Haslam, warned GMAC of this potential outcome from the start. However, it was a lesson GMAC needed to learn on its own.

In that same year (2003), GMAC became heavily engaged in the Montpelier Downtown Workers' Union (MDWU, UE Local 221). The campaign, initiated by the Vermont Workers Center and the United Radio, Machine, and Electrical Workers of America (UE), sought to build an experimental geographic based labor union throughout the unrepresented sectors of Vermont's capital city. The objective was to build a democratic, bottom up union that provided workers with a collective voice. GMAC recognized that a successful conclusion to the project could lead to the model spreading to other towns and cities in Vermont, and beyond. GMAC hoped to help create the example of a democratic workers' organization that could both positively impact the realities for workers on the shop floor, as well as one that could give a broader political expression to workers' struggles in general. Although the campaign ended in defeat, GMAC saw the potential of such an effort and became an outspoken supporter of the union, producing and distributing (to Montpelier workers) the handbill entitled Union + Town Meeting = Democracy.

At the time, GMAC argued:

> Montpelier could be just a beginning... [I]f the workers of towns... come together into strong organizations, and these organizations build strong ties between each other, the Vermont working class as a whole would no longer be at the heels of politicians who have to answer to the bosses... If this time comes, these strong and democratic organizations... in collaboration with farmer's organizations... and taking into account the general will as expressed through more than 200 Town Meetings, would now be in a position to put forth a united and legitimate voice of all these working persons who make Vermont what it is.

GMAC made this campaign its priority for the next two years, eventually counting its members as a majority on the union's Steward

Committee (including, among others, SW & NR), along with the elected Chief Steward, KW. At its height, the union claimed 100 members, out of a labor pool of 800, employed in two dozen shops in Montpelier (population: 7800). In a number of shops (including State Street Market, Charlie O's Tavern, Rivendell Books, and J Morgan's/ Capital Plaza Hotel) union membership, for a time, represented a majority. Other shops where the union claimed members included, but was not limited to, Shaw's Supermarket, M&M Beverage, Rite Aid Pharmacy, Vermont Compost, Onion River Sports, Karma Imports, and Vermont Center For Independent Living. Contracts were eventually achieved at the Savoy Theater and Mountain Herbal Café.

While the winning of union-labor contracts was one goal of the organization, it was not the intended end point. Later in 2004 the Union implemented a citywide grievance procedure, facilitated by Steward-workers, that all Montpelier employees had access to (not just dues paying members). Although not enforceable through a contract (which the exception of the two afore mentioned shops), it was remarkably successful in winning a majority of its grievances through public pressure and direct action. Here the effective leadership and advocacy of Chief Steward and GMAC member KW should be recognized. It is also of note that the Steward Committee and the citywide grievance procedure was supported by the formation of a Workers Defense Squad. This grouping was co-chaired by GMAC member David Van Deusen, and included rank and file members of other area labor unions (including the Carpenters, the Iron Workers, AFT, etc.).

From 2004 on, major policy decisions were made at Worker Town Meetings through a directly democratic process. This method of internal decision making highlighted the fact that the underlying principles of the union reflected the anarchist practice of bottom up, participatory democracy.

In the spring of 2004, while the MDWU was still fully operational, GMAC hosted a NEFAC conference at the Socialist Labor Hall in Barre, VT. Also in 2004, the Philadelphia affiliate of NEFAC was engaged in a similar effort in the South Street district of that city. At the same time, the Montreal affiliate was engaged in some organizing efforts aimed at workers in its city. GMAC made an official proposal to NEFAC that it adopt the geographic, bottom-up union model as the strategic focus of the organization for the coming year. Recognizing that the Vermont experience concerning the MDWU was predicated on the prior example of the Workers Center, GMAC proposed that in NEFAC areas of operation where no similar organization existed, that the first step be to create the equivalent (as the Love and Rage # 10 Collective proved to be an achievable task by a small group of radicals). This proposal was voted down, in essence, by the federation. NEFAC hence declined to adapt this (or any other) truly coordinated regional campaign, and instead continued to function more as a loosely affiliated network of autonomous collectives than as an organization with a platform of united and rational revolutionary action. While the early years of NEFAC brought the affiliates together through common mobilizations at large anti-globalization Black Bloc actions, since 2002 the federation increasingly lacked such common purpose. NEFAC, at least in name, ceased to exist in 2011.

In 2005, after failing to win a recognition effort in a larger city hotel/restaurant, and recognizing that overall membership had not reached a self-sustaining level, the Workers Center and UE made the joint decision to conclude their involvement with the project. GMAC, or rather a faction of GMAC, briefly sought to keep the organization present through the affiliation of MDWU with the Industrial Workers of the World. However, this move only put off the ultimate decline of the union, which concluded in its entirety before the start of 2006. The chances of GMAC reinvigorating the union was further limited by the fact that key GMAC members at the time, former union leaders, also decided to move on. While failing to win a sustainable geographic union, the effort did prove that the concept was plausible. During its life, the union also gained wide coverage in the Vermont media, and became widely known to the public. The chances of a similar effort building on the successes and failures of the MDWU experience should not be discounted out of hand.

Following the demise of the MDWU (and printed in the Northeastern Anarchist), SW reflected:

> We lost the Montpelier Downtown Workers' Union. And the fact is, most organizing drives fail. The cards are stacked against us. At many facilities, workers will go through 3, 4, or even more union drives before attaining success. If organizing at work is truly important to you there are plenty of unorganized places to organize. So don't let one failure get in the way of continuing to fight and eventually winning... Revolutionary socialist anarchism as a political philosophy is based on the fundamental hope that the majority, the working class and all oppressed people, can be the agents of change that will bring about a federated, democratic, and free society of self-managed communities and workplaces... If we, as the majority of common people, are going to do this, we will need to build confidence as a class, and to learn how to

work together for our defense and for the advancement of our common interests.

From 2002–2007, the years in which GMAC was most active and acutely engaged in Vermont politics, the collective also supported the anti-war movement, continued its anti-fascist/anti-extreme right efforts, and continued its support of the worker co-op movement and ongoing labor struggles. In terms of its anti-war work, GMAC took part in demonstrations, attended two People's Assemblies Against the War, and proposed and passed a resolution calling on Vermont soldiers not to engage in offensive combat operations in Iraq.

One amusing incident took place in Boston, at a December 10th, 2004 workers' rights mach. In support of this rally (which was sponsored by organized labor), the Vermont AFL-CIO brought down a bus full of Vermonters. Among them was GMAC members (then largely members of the MDWU). Also on the bus was Peter Clevelle. Clevelle, a good and likable man, was then a long time (social democratic) Progressive Party Mayor of Burlington (Vermont's largest city) and that year was the Democratic Party candidate for Governor (opposing incumbent Republican Jim Douglas). Once in Boston, the members of GMAC found the local anarchist contingent organized by the area NEFAC affiliate. Once the march was underway, under the night sky, a mustached man in a suit and tie emerged from the march of 15,000, and conspicuously walked under NEFAC's black flag. Anarchists, largely with their faces covered by black bandanas, began to give the suited man suspicious looks. None too concerned, the man loudly stated, "I thought I would march with my anarchist friends for a while!" The suited man continued under the black flag, all smiles, for maybe 10 minutes, then moved on to another place in the march. One Boston NEFAC member asked, "Who was that guy?" And GMAC member SW, without skipping a beat answered, "That was Peter. He is very possibly the next Governor of Vermont", to which a Boston NEFAC member muttered something akin to "Vermont is a strange #$! place." (Clevelle lost to Douglas in that election.)

In addition to union organizing, some members of GMAC became active in the worker co-op movement. In 2004, GMAC member Will Dunbar, with comrades outside of GMAC, opened up the worker owned Langdon Street Café in Montpelier. The café, which was also a bar, drew the participation of a number of people with connections to the Bread and Puppet Theater group. Langdon Street served for a number of years as a community meeting place and venue for radical (participatory) art, as well as organized leftist political talks. The upstairs of the café was occupied by an anarchist book store (Black Sheep Books-also a co-op —co-op members included anarchist writer Cindy Milstein and others with various affiliations to the Institute for Social Ecology). During its years of operation, the cafe often functioned as the meeting location for the AFL-CIO's Washington County Central Labor Council, as well as Workers' Center events. The café remained in operation from 2004 until 2011.

In 2006, GMAC helped build a successful protest against the rightwing anti-immigrant group, the Minutemen. The collective recognized that the leftward trajectory of Vermont could be furthered not only by effective grassroots organizing but also by creating a broad environment that was free of organized fascism and extreme rightwing groups. Keeping Vermont free of organized fascists thus remained a priority for the collective. The Minutemen, for their part, previously acted as an armed anti-immigrant vigilante group with a focus on the southern border with Mexico. In 2006 these right wing militants had hopes of building local chapters along the northern border with Canada. Towards this end, a Massachusetts based Minuteman chapter announced plans to patrol the border between Vermont and Quebec (in the Town of Derby) with the hopes (and expectations) of identifying local supporters. GMAC, hearing this news, coordinated efforts with the Burlington chapter of the International Socialist Organization (ISO), local unaffiliated anarchists from the Northeast Kingdom, and even the separatist Second Vermont Republic. In the end, 50 Vermonters turned out in the rain to protest this racist group and to demand that they leave Vermont. The Minutemen, numbering only 3–5 out-of-staters (flatlanders as they are referred to by Vermonters), panicked, failed to show up, and instead decided to walk a bike path in the nearby city of Newport (near the border) for an hour or two before calling it quits.

GMAC and a number of its recruited supporters attended the rally with pistols under their coats and rifles ready in their vehicles.[2] The motivation here was never to see a repeat of what happened in Greensboro, North Carolina in 1979, when the Klan shot and killed 5 activists at a rally opposing racism. But unlike 1979, GMAC (and its allies) would have the home turf advantage, would be prepared, and in any event this precaution proved unnecessary. Instead of a shootout with pistols, GMAC and the protestors marched to the border where they met with friendly anti-Minutemen protesters in Quebec.

---

2 To be very clear, GMAC members and overt supporters were armed at this rally, but they numbered just a small fraction of the 50 protesters. I do not make any claims here that these other protesters were armed.

These included NEFAC members from north of the border. There handshakes were exchanged, songs of solidarity sung, and a soccer ball was kicked back and forth across the official line separating these nations.

Later that night, a number of local anarchists (unaffiliated with GMAC) located the motel where the Minutemen were staying. Accompanied by a member of GMAC, these anarchists laid in wait. By the end of the night, one Minuteman suffered a bloodied nose, and another, their apparent leader, had his truck vandalized. The next day the Minutemen left Vermont, never to return. They recruited no one from the Green Mountain State.

All told, the Green Mountain Anarchist Collective remained very active in numerous aspects of Vermont's social movement through much of the 2000s. Its increasingly deep relationships led to GMAC members joining the Steering Committee of the Vermont Workers Center, and becoming members of the NWU/United Auto Workers, the Teamsters, the United Electrical Workers, and the AFL-CIO in general. A member of GMAC, Van Deusen, served as a District Vice President within the Vermont AFL-CIO, and, again, KW, another GMAC member, was elected as Chief Steward of the MDWU, UE Local 221.

In addition to organizing active and militant street protests, GMAC continued to engage in struggle through the written word. In 2002 the collective launched the publication Catamount Tavern News. This newspaper, for a time, was the only statewide print publication in Vermont, and was the only Vermont media source with a Quebec Affairs Desk (first based out of Quebec City, and later staffed by MD — an ex-NEFAC member — out of Montreal). The paper was published seasonally from 2002–2009. By 2009 it claimed 50 distribution points across the state, and had a circulation of 1,500 (considerable given a state population of just over 600,000). In 2008 it affiliated (as a worker owned operation) with the Teamsters Local 1L, making it the only unionized newspaper in Vermont. In addition to writers from GMAC, it also published works by James Haslam (Director of the Vermont Workers Center), Traven Leyshon (President of the Washington County Central Labor Council AFL-CIO-and later Secretary/Treasurer of the Vermont AFL-CIO), Brian Tokar (well-known environmentalist), Cindy Milstein (from the Institute of Social Ecology), and leftist-economist Doug Hoffer (who was elected as Vermont State Auditor from the Vermont Progressive Party in 2012). The publication also printed interviews with a number of notable Vermonters including farm organizer Peter Sterling, longtime activist Anthony Pollina, and Iraqi Veterans Against The War member Drew Cameron. While the focus of the paper was on the worker and farmer struggles specific to Vermont (as well as cultural issues), it also provided coverage of national protests & Black Bloc actions, stories about the social movement within Provence Quebec, reports from within New Orleans in the immediate aftermath of Hurricane Katrina, a report from the streets of Paris during the 2008 French Protests, and a report concerning the EZLN/Zapatista efforts from within Chiapas, Mexico.

CT News Mission Statement, which was printed in every issue, made clear the following:

> We intend on helping to build a Vermont wherein regular and frequent town meetings, in cooperation with democratic worker and farmer unions, are the basic decision making bodies of the Green Mountains. In addition, we intend on helping to build this society based on the principles of equality, wherein all persons have, among other things, access to decent housing, healthy food, acceptable healthcare, quality childcare, meaningful jobs, and higher education. This is Freedom & Unity.

Initially the newspaper was edited by Lady. Later, GMAC member SW became editor. In its final years, GMAC co-founder David Van Deusen assumed this role. The paper, with some success, strove to bridge the usual gap between concepts of revolutionary social transformation and regular non-initiated wage workers. It sought to achieve this through the publication of articles and material that further reflected the interest of regular Vermonters. With this in mind the newspaper, at various times, covered the Vermont Golden Gloves boxing tournament, included a regular hunting and fishing column (written by Joana "Black Jack" Banis), a column on the harvesting and use of wild plants, a crossword puzzle, and (recognizing the necessity of the cultural struggle against contemporary capitalism) printed poetry and artwork. During its years of print, it was not uncommon for its contents to be read and debated in working class taverns, especially in Brattleboro (taverns being common distribution points for the paper). GMAC members Lady, Will Dunbar and Xavier Massot played key roles in the operations of the paper, as did fellow travels (who never joined the collective) such as JR. Lady, its first editor, made the crossword puzzle, Dunbar served as a staff writer and distributor for the Northeast Kingdom area of Vermont, Massot as Obituaries Editor, and JR (a self-proclaimed socialist) as staff photographer and Image/Design Editor.

Throughout the years of its publication, GMAC members would often bring copies for distribution at labor and Workers' Center events which were handed out for free. A persistent presence at these events was Congressman and later Senator Bernie Sanders. GMAC always made a point of handing a newspaper to Bernie, and Bernie always graciously accepted.

While Catamount Tavern News was perhaps the most visible written organ of GMAC, the collective also made regular contributions to NEFAC's regional English language newspaper, Strike, and to its quarterly magazine, The Northeastern Anarchist. Even so, the collective's seminal written political expression must be judged as the pamphlet entitled *Neither Washington Nor Stowe: Common Sense For the Working Vermonter* (Catamount Tavern Press, Vermont, 2004]. The first edition, composed and printed while still engaged with the MDWU and DFV, reflected the later maturity of the group. While concerning itself with the core transformation of society from a modern capitalist one to a libertarian socialist one, the work largely spoke the language of the common Vermonter. From the pamphlet:

> Because of this remoteness our Green Mountains often feel a century away from Boston, and a million miles from New York. Yet we are still tangled in the treacherous web of Washington politicians and the wealthy elite from Wall Street, to Texas, to Stowe. We are our own people, yet we are compelled to mimic the same bureaucratic structures in our government and economic dead ends in our communities that strangle the common working person from California to Maine.

And later, while seeking to frame the domestic challenge faced by Vermonters:

> There are, in fact, two Vermont's: One of wealth and privilege, and one of hard work and sweat. If Vermonters have any chance of success against the forces of Washington and Wall Street, the battle must start in our own backyard against the business and political elite of Montpelier and Stowe. We must guard against the sly maneuvers of both the conservative and the liberal status quo in Vermont, and fight to win more power for ourselves in our towns and workplaces. Could our efforts ever cultivate a harvest hardy enough to withstand the strong, cold winds of Washington and Wall Street if we do not till our fields first? Can you start a good sugaring season without first cleaning out your sap buckets? The answer is no. There will be no victory over the enemy without before there is victory over the enemy within. Fore it is the privileged and powerful locally

and their dupes who will stand as the first serious line of defense for the privileged and powerful classes in general. So do we bow our heads, mutter curses under our breath, and continue to subsist on the scraps they throw to us — or do we dare to struggle and dare to win against the local elite?

Drawing on Vermont's deep revolutionary, anti-establishment, and rural tradition, this pamphlet sought to explain the post-revolutionary society as an extension of the Town Meeting system which remains embedded deeply in Vermont consciousness. The work further drew on contemporary examples such as the Dairy Farmers of Vermont and Montpelier Downtown Workers Union to explain how worker and farmer control over the means of production (and the achievement of a non alienated society) is not only possible, but, perhaps, the logical progression of such movements. In brief, GMAC called for the reorganization of Vermont (and the broader world) through a greatly empowered network of Town Meetings, an expanded and democratic federation of labor organizations, and countywide farmer groups. Staying true to GMAC's early assertions, the pamphlet also called for continuing support and expansion of radical cultural projects such as the Bread & Puppet Theater. Economically, Washington Nor Stowe advocated for the elimination of the commodity driven paradigm, in favor of a stable, more cooperative labor hour means of exchange, along with strong socialist rights concerning a persons' basic social wellbeing. This pamphlet, first produced in 2004, was revised and reissued in 2007, and a modified version was published in 2014. The work, which was distributed through the Green Mountains, concludes with:

> As working class and farming Vermonters, we owe it to our cultural past, the future of our grandchildren, and ourselves to seek the fulfillment of our common dreams and aspirations. We can no more accept a future where our mountains are further masked by the two dimensional trappings of capitalism, then we could a world without seasons. Before consumerism, bureaucracy, and centralization obscure our culture of independence and equality, we must come together in order to reassert that which is just. For this we must continue to build the popular organizations that will inherit our hills, and we must build them so as they face the proverbial south. And for us, that is toward direct democracy, socialism, and creativity. In a word, we are a people who continually look toward the end of winter, and friends with a little hard work the spring will find us.

The Fall & Legacy

During its active years, the collective, which had no more than 20 members (total), cooperated with a number of leftist organizations. GMAC often lent support to the ongoing efforts of the Workers Center. On occasion it would work with organizations such the Dairy Farmer of Vermont, the United Electrical Workers, the AFL-CIO, and even the International Socialist Organization. It further maintained friendly relations with activists within the Vermont Progressive Party. Although GMAC would later criticize and distant itself (see the article: *Vermont Secession: Democracy and the Extreme Right*, Catamount Tavern News, spring, 2007), it even worked with the Second Vermont Republic (as outlined above) in issuing a joint statement against the racist Minutemen. These efforts were often met with skepticism by other revolutionary anarchists (often by those same anarchists who previously opposed GMAC's militant assertions concerning the Black Bloc). However, based on its analysis of contemporary capitalism and its revolutionary commitments, GMAC argued that a broad-based mass movement from below was necessary. For GMAC, the revolution was both a physical and cultural challenge that unfolded overtime, but could explode in an instant. As such, engagement in mass and visible street actions, as well as engagement in mass organizing efforts, were understood as the key to success.

To recognize that a small insular collective, alone, is incapable of throwing off the chains of social/cultural/ economic oppression is to come to one of three conclusions: (1) that revolution is in fact impossible; (2) that a uniquely new mass movement must be built from the ground up; or (3) that revolutionaries must work with those mass organizations already in existence in order to influence a left turn in their direction. The Green Mountain Anarchist Collective emphatically rejected the first of these conclusions, finding history to tell a different story. GMAC then sought to synthesize the second and third of these conclusions into concerted series of actions. In short, GMAC worked with existing organizations, where possible, to build new expressions of class struggle that would be more grounded in anarchist principles than its parent groups—e.g., the support for the Dairy Farmers of Vermont and Montpelier Downtown Workers Union (although it could be argued that the Vermont Workers Center, excluding the question of Black Blocs, was as far left as GMAC). Finally, GMAC saw no compelling reason not to work with existing mass organizations in a defensive capacity aimed at overcoming further attacks of capitalist and reactionary interest against working people: e.g., its collaborations with the ISO and SVR in opposition to the Minutemen, with organized labor against acute attacks of the boss against workers, and with numerous coalitions calling for a withdrawal of U.S. troops from foreign occupations.

The Green Mountain Anarchist Collective never officially disbanded. However, by 2006 the only original member remaining in the collective was Van Deusen (although Massot later became an active contributor to Catamount Tavern News). After Van Deusen ran for and was elected as First Constable by his Vermont town (2007), NEFAC, in general, expressed concerns that being elected to office (especially an office associated with limited local law enforcement powers) ran counter to the political principles of the federation. As a result, Van Deusen resigned from NEFAC, and began to distance himself from GMAC. For a time, through the continuing efforts of Will Dunbar and HB, the collective continued on. Even so, no longer engaged in a defining strategic project, the collective soon drifted into inactivity. The one GMAC project that had a solid, if limited life beyond 2007, was Catamount Tavern News which was printed into 2009 (although, by that time, it no longer claimed to be a publication of GMAC). Since GMAC's decline (post-2007), former members have occasionally come together (lending the GMAC name), but only for reissuing or revising previously written works. The time of the Green Mountain Anarchist Collective engaging in political action, as a distinct organization, has past.

So how should one asses the legacy of this anarchist organization from the rural and rugged landscapes of the Green Mountains? On the one hand, GMAC's most ambitious political project, the Montpelier Downtown workers Union, failed to achieve lasting success. The Peoples' Round Table Organizing Committee did not achieve immediate political victories. Even the Dairy Farmers of Vermont (which GMAC played a small supporting role in) was compelled to close down its farmer controlled milk processing plant in 2008. On the other hand, GMAC spent considerable energy helping to build the Vermont Workers Center. And today, the Workers Center is the most effective and powerful grassroots organization in the State (largely responsible for creating a political environment whereby minimum wage was increased to above $10). GMAC also played a strong role in shutting down the Minutemen's Vermont organizing drive. The war and military occupations that GMAC resisted are either over or winding down. There is no Free Trade of the Americas Agreement. And politically, Vermont continues to evolve according to a leftist trajectory, largely counter to the direction of the rest of the nation. GMAC did not achieve these victories on its own. But GMAC, along with thousands (if not tens of thousands) of other Vermonters, and millions of north Americans, did its part. It resisted and experimented in new ways through which revolution could be hinted at. GMAC, as part of a broader, diverse, bottom-up movement, achieved politically successes. But of course, the battle, let alone the class war, is far from won. Capitalism, although threatened along the periphery, remains essentially intact. And yet still, the resistance continues to grow in these parts of the Northeastern woods commonly referred to as Vermont. After all, history, radical change, and even revolution ebb and flow with the organizations, groups, classes, and individuals that are periodically sparked into flame by the necessity of fight. The Green Mountain Anarchist Collective, for seven years, took risks, fought battles, and reflected on its wins and losses; it did its part, no more, no less. To quote Xavier Massot, as composed in his afterword for the *Black Bloc Papers*:

> The times are calling, and have been for a while, for a change in the running of human affairs. This is common knowledge, and no argument can undo this obvious conclusion. The only point against active protest is the desire for survival and safety on the part of those who would risk change, but this is a boring and ultimately futile and self-deceptive avenue, selfish and used up. It is true that the young have more life to live and that old have other things to worry about, but the space will get filled. It always gets filled, with an endless supply of woes to prod people to action... It is dawn here in the woods of northern New England. I'm gonna go to sleep and hopefully dream of nicer things than the ridiculous mess which is choking the human race's potential for greatness — justice for starters.

CULTURE AND NOTHINGNESS[3]

"The bow bends; the wood complains. At the moment of supreme tension, there will leap into flight an unswerving arrow, a shaft that is inflexible and free."

— Camus, *The Rebel*

We stand at the threshold of a new millennium. In itself this is no more than an arbitrary marker of time. But, the actual circumstances, both psychological and material, both social and political, denote this arbitrary time as one of the most dynamic in history. The age of wo/man has come face to face with itself through its exhaustion. Both realism and nihilism have been unmasked as the oppressors that they are. Fascism has proven itself homicidal and suicidal in its dark absurdism. Authoritarian communism has reached the apex of its empire of free slaves and has collapsed under its inherent hypocrisy. Finally capitalism is facing its own death not from its failures, but from its success. What stands at the threshold is the world of the rebel; the age of anarchism. But the realization of anarchism must be justified by the means through which it is achieved, and this achievement must be arrived at

---

3 2017 note from the author: A version of this essay was first published in Kinetic, an Ohio underground newspaper, in 2001. No longer possessing a copy of this publication, I cannot recall what city the paper was published out of. I first started to work on this essay in 1999 (shortly after the Battle of Seattle), while living in Seville, Spain. Further revisions were made while living in Marlboro, Vermont, in 2000.

consciously by a free people. Those of us who are already awake must not only sound the horns, but learn the melody that will best express the full aspirations of the people who stand to be liberated. The music will inspire the millions, and together we will establish a brother and sisterhood of humankind. The walls will fall.

What now concerns us is a proper understanding of what it means in the modern age to carry forth the anarchist revolution (which by definition is a qualitative revolution), what is the necessary direction of contemporary anarchism, what relation does it hold in hold in modern society, and what are its means and ends? The anarchism of the new millennium is a far cry from the early proclamations of Bakunin and Kropotkin. Nor are the experiences of revolutionary Ukraine (under Nestor Makhno) or Spain (1936–39) directly relevant in the modern neo-capitalist state. Its propositions as with its approach must adhere to the times. The revolution is not purely a question of economy, nor is it set on a fixed single course. Rather, the revolution must be more than quantitative, and must be respective of the possibility of many roads and many conclusions. The road to revolution can no more be expected to rest on a single set of tracks or to arrive at the same station. On the other hand, its final destination, although at variance, will reach the common land of dignity, freedom, equality, and justice. So what can be said about this revolutionary trajectory that does not relegate it to what it is not? Many things, as long as they are all viewed as probabilities and suggestions among a pallet of others. It is with the above in mind that I will now proceed in this modest essay. To begin with I will discuss the historical-cultural roots of oppression and rebellion, the modern context in which society is situated, the contemporary forms of anarchism which are evolving to meet this challenge, and the cultural process by which revolution occurs. It is to the former that I first turn.

Part I: The Dawn of Nothingness

> I watched with glee while your kings and queens
> Fought for ten decades for the gods they made.
> —The Rolling Stones, "Sympathy for the Devil"

The history of human society is, in part, a history of two great conflicting cultures: that which rests upon the recognition of the inherent value of existence, and that which is in reaction to a perceived nothingness. Existence and nihilism; the great matriarch and patriarch of all the world's culture. The later more rightly must be understood as the foundation for an anti-culture. For its underlying nothingness must ultimately strip unabstracted reality from its modes of expression. Therefore, social history is fundamentally a struggle between culture and nothingness. However, the former originally gave rise to the later through its capacity for imaginary creation, and now the later must give way for the conscious realization of the former.

The human capacity for creative expression allowed wo/man to develop narratives which constitute fables, whose metaphor has the ability to unleash other creative faculties through a process of reflection. For an undeterminable amount of time these fables remained as a legitimate expression of natural existence. They constituted creativity and sparked imagination. This creative capacity also allowed humans to manipulate their environment in order to alleviate a degree of natural oppression and alienation experienced in relation to the elements. In select regions this led to the agricultural revolution and the establishment of permanent settlements. Towns, then cities formed.

With the formation of these cities the tribal chieftains became more separated from the population. Here they began to take the form of a nobility class. This occurred in direct relation to the growing complexities of urban development. In turn these new complexities acted as the motivation for the formation of a bureaucracy. This marked the formation of a class responsible for the administration of the nobility's directives. Together the nobility and the bureaucracy constituted the upper and lower levels of the greater ruling class. One can imagine this ruling class, isolated from the still prevalent cyclical existence of the people and effectively insulated from organic humanness within the walls of their fortresses, began to sense a new form of estrangement. Here, cut off from their roots, perhaps this class grew anxious. The human existence which their chieftain and common ancestors intimately knew likely became more and more an inaccessible memory. It is conceivable that natural existence itself became estranged. Within the citadels life may have lost its inherent value in the murky waters of abstraction and isolation. This would have sparked existential fear, and thereby the first true nihilists would have emerged onto the field of history. In this void this class may have observed the urban structures of their developing cities, their own power as a ruling class, and posited that if nothing exists in an ultimate sense, that is if nothing possesses intrinsic value, then they must make value. This tendency may have been complicated by the recognition that those old common fables could and must serve a purpose toward this end. For if meaning must be forced, and particularly by the hand of the ruling class, then certain devices would have to be utilized in order to guarantee the utmost control of the population. If and when this point was reached the people could rightly be understood as different creatures than their former chieftains and their aides. The people would have still enjoyed that close bond with the earth. They would have lived in cyclical time and accepted the value of natural existence as an unconscious fact. Thus moves which denounced the basic understandings of these people would result in undesired tension. Here the ruling class would be wise to develop a sly path. They could have found a dark purpose for those common fables whose truths were no longer understood by the rulers. They would have the means and motivation to twist them into abstraction by forcing an unnatural literalness upon them. They could have used them as justifications and tools of their control over their former equals. Religion was created. In a word, the position of God and State was solidified as ignorance, oppression, and nihilism incarnate. Dogma was born.

Perhaps these tyrants lost their connection with unabstracted existence through their insulation as a cosmopolitan ruling class; their royal tapestries obscuring the stones from which their walls were built. To combat this abstraction more abstraction could have been employed. Efforts may have been engaged to unify a perceived nothingness by the means of the iron grip of their ego unleashed. If they could perceive no meaning, then meaning would have to be imposed. This morbid task, once begun, dictates a project which cannot be accomplished in any short time or even in the course of a few centuries. To attempt to forge a unity of pseudo-existence through will necessitates that such unity reach everywhere in order for it to constitute itself as a quasi-reality. This quest would have to be expansionist and totalitarian from the moment that it was conceived. It had to place itself everywhere and in doing demand unwavering obedience from all people.

Granting these premises, at first the ruling class would have utilized these fables as tools to their own elevation and semi-consciously as fortresses providing insulation from their demons. They created codified religions out of these fables and here stupefied the masses into the dazzling hell of existential distortion. They created a religion to give moral sanction to their psychotic campaigns. They embarked upon a misguided attempt of achieving a forced unity of content and fake immortality of its source (themselves). And with this, the great masses of the earth would have been blessed with the countless horrors of never-ending imperial wars and untold suffering brought forth through the construction of great monuments; wars paid for by their blood and monuments constructed by their coerced labor.

These wars were, and are, inevitable. For a forced unity must manifest itself everywhere for it to appear to be true. It cannot tolerate obvious external contradiction. This means the continuing subjectification not only of the domestic farmworker, craftsperson, and emerging mercantile population, but also foreign peoples who may or may not still be engaged in an organic hunter-gatherer social structure. This ongoing subjectification must be understood as primitive imperialism. Likewise, the construction of monuments was, and is, unavoidable as a smokescreen against the underlying emptiness and mortality of such escapism. In these ways the multitude of humankind was handed a future of sweat, pain, and death tailored to appear as greatness.

During the formative years the ruler put their faith into their illusion and tried to believe this construction was real, but that belief was only partial. The ruler still maintained access, though limited and repressed access, to their original motivations. Nevertheless the underlying motivations were repressed through the continuing distraction of materialistic hedonism and ritualistic illusion. But, at least at first, these forms of self-hypnosis and foolery were only partially effective; they were not yet complete.

With the rise of class divisions in a post agricultural/more urban society, although the predominant culture had already been transformed into anti-culture, this monster was still tethered by memory. It was prevented from achieving the elevation which its totalitarianism demanded. It could not yet take on the full illusion of existence. But, as the generations passed by, their original purposes were forgotten. The lie became the truth, and the truth heresy. The false idols then began to stir. Freed from the shackles of their makers they began to take on an eerie life of their own. They demonstrated self-moving qualities through, yet often beyond, its one time masters. With this the illusory monster became animated. All was bent to it: the economy its blood; the ruling class its arms; the state its sword; art its clothing; religion its soul; the masses its slaves. It moved beyond the control of its parts. The makers unequivocally threw themselves at the feet of the distortion they brought into being, and believed. They dedicated themselves to it. They indoctrinated and killed for it. They gave it life.

In turn the people were increasingly prevented from experiencing life without abstraction. More and more everything was seen through the grid of this construction; a construction whose manifestation implies nothingness; a construction which is nothingness masked by a narrative and made up in the clothing of an Emperor King of metaphysical proportions. They were alienated by abstractions. In this, countless facets of life within the borders of these civilizations became subordinated to this grand fallacy. Art occasionally was able to poke a hole through this death shroud and allow bits of existential light through, but all too often art only served to reinforce this illusion. However, its totality, fundamentally being false, was never able to surmount that ultimate grip over its slaves.

Part II: The Instinct to Rebel

> There's nothing in the streets
> Looks any different to me
> And the slogans are replaced, by-the-bye...
> Meet the new boss
> Same as the old boss.

> — The Who, "Won't Get Fooled Again"

Wo/man's instinct to rebel continually eluded capture and persisted as a fugitive in a false world. In this capacity it acted as the ever present reminder of something more substantial. For the alienation from complete experience barred upon humankind like the weight of the world upon Christopher's shoulders. The underclasses, however they might be defined at certain moments in our long history, sought ways to counteract or dispel this unseen weight. The anti-culture had to continually struggle to maintain its dominance.

At first struggle was effectively limited by the anti-culture diverting popular animosity towards the particular ruling class. The people were made to believe that the problem lied in the particular regime. They did not yet see that the particular regime was only the temporal facilitator of a broader system of oppression which operated through them, but also beyond them. Thus their mental energies, insofar as politics was concerned, were squandered on interchangeable functionaries acting the part of absolute ruler. This animosity was prevented from maturing by fluctuations in the make-up of the ruling class hierarchy. For the ruling class inevitably developed competing factions all vying for the leadership position. Here the illusion was reinforced since that the changing of the guard tends to relieve popular tension by shifting its focus. The people rejoiced in the death of the old oppressor. Hope was put in the new oppressor.

These internal and external conflicts continued alongside technological advances. Any society which makes a holy shrine out of abstracted super ego is bound to achieve success within the cognitively contingent fields. Actually, technological progress was due in part to imperialism. For technology was a necessary weapon towards expansionist goals. It needed better arms to establish itself over the others. It needed better productive methods to produce the necessary weapons. Transportation and navigation became more developed in order to link its projections and to accumulate more power through wealth. In turn its mobility brought it into contact with foreign ideas which it was able to synthesize into its own. It accumulated all that allowed it to expand. This development sparked an economic sub-dialectic, the kind that Marx, Engels, and Bakunin recognized (and which they assumed to be primary).

The predominant anti-culture (under usual circumstances) requires the functioning of an administrative ruling class which itself requires the state apparatus. Likewise, the ruling class requires a monopoly over the means of production. Therefore, as technological advancements accumulated, the means of production also evolved in kind.

As this trend historically developed, a new class emerged out of the old order and constituted itself somewhere between the lower and ruling class. This class grew in political power as the developing economy inherently favored it. It developed a conflicting class interest opposed to the ruling class. In addition it differed from the old guard in that its primary concern was defined by that which gave it substance. It was brought into being by developments within the economy and in turn this class became neurotically enthralled with capital accumulation. For them, the old distorted fables which to that point constituted the justification for and general parameters of the social construct, held little interest. They desired to strip away the fat and go right for the raw wealth. Here a struggle ensued where this new class came into open combat with the old order in a bid for control over the means of production. Eventually it asserted itself as the new rulers and subsequently modernized the economy in such a way that technological progress not only continued, but grew exponentially. The rising economic dialectic necessitated more than the ascension of a new faction to the heights of power: it necessitated the emerging of a new class altogether; the bourgeoisie; the capitalists.

This insurrectionary class was also subject to the subconscious pressures of alienation brought on by the anti-culture. In this they attempted to frame their struggle in revolutionary terms. They justified their actions as a liberating deconstruction of the old order, which to them may have appeared as the liquidation of the illusory base of society. They killed the holy sanctioning of the nobility and in its place constructed a more seemingly tangible unity; the unity of capital. However this too was, and is, a false unity in that it must imperialistically project itself as an abstraction over and against natural lived experience.

With capitalism, the underlying nihilism of anti-culture managed to persist by deflecting potential elemental change by way of subterfuge. Just as in older times the particular ruling class of a particular state was made into a scapegoat, it now placed all responsibility upon particular religious and economic modes which were present at the time of rebellion. Its basic foundation was neither liquidated nor even seen. It simply absorbed the revolt and in doing made it its own.

This new social order replaced religion with the economy. Although this immediately resulted in the bolstering of the anti-culture it was a progression in that it brought the underlying meta-foundations of the broader social fabric closer to the surface. The anti-culture became more tangible. Its justification was no longer placed in the inaccessible fortress of heaven. Its justification came to clearly rest in the world. Production and profit became its sacraments. And here the misery of the under classes no longer could be as easily deflected by stories of Job. The nature of their misery slowly became apparent. The myth became transparent.

Part III: The Rise of Capitalism

> The men at the factory are old and cunning
> You don't owe nothing, so boy get runnin'
> It's the best years of your life they want to steal...
>
> —The Clash, "Clampdown"

As the anti-culture moved into its later phase of industrialization/capitalism it shifted its mode of operation to that of a seemingly different type. Its functions became more tangible as the totality of God and State more or less were substituted for Economy and State. The primary mode of homogenization ceased to be that of religion and overt political empires and was instead sought through universal commodification of material goods (both raw and refined) as well as labor itself. This forced an abstracted unity which was inherently bent to serve the greed driven interests of the new ruling class. To the bourgeoisie went the spoils and privileges of nihilistic servitude.

These new modes of anti-culture expression managed to develop alongside certain more archaic forms. Political empires and religious zeal were still utilized as tools of micro and macro world manipulation when the new ruling class viewed them as both convenient and effective. However, these feudal holdovers no longer represented the direct priorities of the new oppressors, and thus increasingly gave way to the economic language of capitalism.[4]

This particular system liberated the surf only to place him/her within the confines of a new slavery known as wage labor. For as long as the basic social goods were effectively transformed into commodities, and as long as these commodities were further transformed into capital, the masses were forced into compromising life situations in order to obtain the totalitarian representation of this new form of anti-culture; namely capital —money. In this society the ruling class maintained a functional monopoly over capital and was thus able to control its movement in such a way as to coerce the under classes into various self-denying relations in order for them to subsist. Individuals were recruited into demeaning circumstances of factory life and were thereafter compelled to waste their potential on the sick goal of producing wealth for the benefit of the bourgeoisie. For many the dawn-till-dusk of agricultural labor was replaced with the sixteen hours of factory drudgery. The anti-culture proved its potency and its ability to evolve with the times.

This phase of cultural nihilism was inevitably met with fierce resistance from the increasingly self-conscious exploited classes. Without heaven to confuse the matter in shades of divinity, the masses began more clearly to observe the nature of their own oppression. The instinct to rebel found an objective foothold in the contradictions of capitalist production.

Here the political movement of authoritarian communism took form. The worker observed the impoverished existence of his/herself and that of the under classes generally juxtaposed to the extravagant wealth of the ruling class. It was further moved by this contradiction,

---

4 Here it must be noted that this tension between capitalist modes of anti-culture and religious modes of anti-culture still persists today. While capitalism, or more accurately neo-capitalism, is the dominant world system, the older, more archaic forms revolving around various religious fundamentalisms still linger and struggle. Even so, the religious fundamentalism of today is not a return to the past, but instead it's a last attempt to resist the forces of the present. Neo-capitalism, and not religious extremism, is the dominant force of anti-culture today.

more so than during feudal times, due to the neurotic emphasis put on capital (wealth) by the ruling class of this new era. Capital (as the universal representation of commodities) was, and is, the great binder of the forced (and fundamentally false) totality of nihilistic unity. This marks a radical divergence from the former modes under feudalism in that the prior era maintained a promise of human equity in the religiously defined afterlife.[5] Thus material discrepancies in class and individual living standards did not hold the obvious importance that it does in the age of capitalism. In short, the motivating factor of poverty was obscured in former times due to the religiousification of anti-culture under the vise of an equitable God and ultimately equitable afterlife. Under capitalism the justification and concrete modes of the anti-culture were placed solidly upon the earth. The real poverty of the under classes were then freed from the confines of metaphysical speculation and were in turn allowed to act as powerful and direct motivating factors. The under classes during this era began to develop a vocabulary of rebellion which aimed at the transcendence of their worldly suffering.

Part IV: Authoritarian Communism As An Incomplete Resistance

> "If a victory is told in detail, one can no longer distinguish it from a defeat."
>
> —John Paul Sartre[6]

The later phases of classical capitalism were marked by the rise of authoritarian communist movements of resistance. Although such forms of communism clearly represented a threat to the particular modes of the anti-culture (capitalism), they failed to truly shake the foundation of meta-society on a fundamental level. At best

---

5 This essay does not seek to speculate on the ultimate truth of said afterlife. Rather what concerns us here is an understanding of how these beliefs were contextually used to serve the purposes of the ruling class and the anti-culture to further systems of control in the here-and-now.

6 2017 Note from the Author: Sartre had a long and complex relationship with the Communist Party of France and communism in general. Early in the Nazi occupation of France, the Communist Party rejected Sartre as a political partner. However, during the course of the resistance Sartre and the Communist Party worked closely together as part of the broader resistance. After liberation, Sartre briefly formed a leftist party separate from the Communists, but later he came to work in unity with them on certain issues. During this time Sartre was more or less a supporter of the Soviet Union. However, Sartre publicly withdrew his support for the Soviets following the 1956 entrance of Soviet troops into Hungary. From that time forth, Sartre and the USSR remained at political odds. Even so, Sartre spent much of his later intellectual life seeking a philosophic reconciliation between Existentialism and Marxism.

authoritarian communism was, and is, only capable of alleviating certain portions of material deprivation and of pushing the proverbial envelope somewhat closer to an existential reckoning by way of illuminating its own shortcomings through historical developments.[7]

Under communism, the bourgeoisie is replaced by the Party; the commodity and capital replaced with hierarchical political ideology. A continuing anti-culture still represses unabstracted lived experience, and still seeks to impose a perceptual grid across natural reality. This must be understood as symptomatic of a continuing presence of the underlying social nihilism (i.e., a continuing social paradigm founded upon a philosophical nothingness). This is the case in that the historic ideology of authoritarian communism implies a tight practical hierarchy which can only be justified if it is forced to impose itself against a perceived something. In this case authoritarian communism claims that something is in fact a lingering capitalist consciousness which is still prevalent following the political revolution. Such a capitalist consciousness is a projection contra a perceived nothingness, which in itself represents an underlying nihilism. This nihilism must ultimately act as the grounding for such a social/psychological construction. Any projection which is motivated by such assumptions must itself assume its base prepositions. Likewise, any ideology, no matter how quantitatively divergent, which attempts to place itself over such a consciousness must become a new perceptual grid through which value can be proclaimed. This is the necessary end result of any successful system of such total aspirations. In this sense any forced communist consciousness must also be understood as a strike out against a perceived nothingness. And any program motivated by such factors must be understood as a new development in the continuing manifestation of the ongoing anti-culture. In short, the something that such a communism seeks to assert itself over only retains the relevant power over mass consciousness that such an ideology assumes if it is believed to in fact exist as a legitimate and organic expression of reality as such; in other words, if it is assumed not to be an answer to a perceived nihilism, but as a fundamental historic mode of human social expression.

If on the other hand this something (capitalist consciousness) is viewed as a superfluous social construction based on a perceived nihilism, with the effect of alienating the human experience from a

---

7 This is not meant to degrade or downplay the reality that anarchism also emerged as a mass movement at this time. However, it was authoritarian communism which won revolutions, not anarchism. The age of anarchism would have to wait for conditions to be right for itself to come into its own.

more desirable organic existence, then it would not be necessary to reconstruct a new communist consciousness among the previously indoctrinated masses. Rather, with such a realization, it would only be necessary to deconstruct the false precepts which prevent the oppressed from accessing a more organic and meaningful natural reality in order for that more fulfilling social consciousness/existence to become both accessible, practical, unabstracted, and ultimately tangible. To deny this is to imply that capitalism (or feudalism for that matter) retains a more fundamental meta-social position than its underlying nihilistic underpinnings allow for. To argue such a point is to reinforce the basic nihilism which underscores all oppressive social systems.

Even under authoritarian communism a belief in the fundamental non-platform of nihilism remains the underlying factor in social, political, and economic organization. Unabstracted natural experience still remains elusive and a general alienation, if not material poverty, remains as the collectively felt tethering of the masses. Nothing persists. Unabstracted existence is repressed. The anti-culture continues.

The Bolshevik Revolution of 1917 and the subsequent 72 years of authoritarian communist rule in what became the USSR and (later) the surrounding region is a prime example of how anti-culture nihilism is able to absorb such a threat, and manage to persist. Much may have changed under communism, but a complete liberation was not found. Nevertheless, the rise of the authoritarian communist movement marked a progression towards popular rebellion in that the exploitive properties of nihilism were made more obviously apparent. Stripped of the capitalist sanctity of class superiority and capital, the anti-culture was forced to forge ahead increasingly in its naked brutality towards the goal of complete homogenization; i.e., the perceptual conquest of nothingness and the final domestication of existential fear.

Part V: Capitalist Colonization & Neo-Liberalism

> "The totalitarian-ideological class in power is the power of a topsy-turvy world: the stronger it is, the more it claims not to exist, and its force serves above all to affirm its non-existence." —Guy Debord, *Society of the Spectacle*

Where authoritarian communism failed to take the political reigns, the anti-culture began to shift its particular modes of operation in order to stave off developing insurrectionary threats. At first this was done through a process of political and economic imperialism which allowed for the continuation of the capitalist system (though be it in a modified form). For as the various domestic under classes of the primary capitalist states became increasingly rebellious in the face of their experienced repression, the particular ruling classes of particular states recognized the need to redirect their economy in such a way as to diminish internal oppression in exchange for increased external exploitation. With this the ruling class was able to lessen domestic strife and thus decrease rebellious sentiment while maintaining its profit margins by squeezing much more out of foreign populations. Of course this move, while somewhat addressing the issue of domestic poverty, did little to address the issue of domestic mass alienation.

This trend continued to develop, and was slowly modified in such a way that its obvious oppression of foreign peoples became more and more subtle in order to stem the developing tide of colonial rebellions; i.e. wars of national liberation. Occupying armies within the boundaries of an overt political empire were replaced with flowery worded economic treaties which managed their rape and plunder under the cover of wine and roses. This marked the age of neo-liberalism and is (of course) the paradigm of the present age.

Neo-liberalism alone is inadequate in ultimately turning back the revolutionary tide. Even under such conditions the domestic gap between the haves and have-nots as found within primary capitalist states is huge and growing. Natural animosity still exists between the under classes and the ruling class. Thus the anti-culture is driven to further lengths in order to provide for its continued dominance.

In this capacity anti-culture continues to confuse the focus of the domestic rebel and obscure the vulnerability of its system by attempting the modification of its particular incarnation in such a manner that the oppressed are compelled to actively take part in their own oppression. In this the commodification of society reaches new heights in its imperialistic quest for dominance.

Part VI: Radical Commodification & Consumerism

> Here comes Johnny Yen again
> With the liquor and drugs
> And the flesh machine
> He's gonna do another striptease
> Hey man where'd you get that lotion?
> I been hurting
> Since I bought the gimmick...
>
> —Iggy Pop, "Lust For Life"

With radical commodification, the most trivial things acquire an abstract value. The abstracted values themselves acquire abstracted value. Objects and ideas are put on the selling block and are spoon fed to the masses regardless of practical utility. Technology becomes bent towards this end. A process of commercialization takes hold which is indicative of the radical commodification process. In this capacity commercialization must be understood as indoctrination aimed at propagating popular belief in the commodification of objects and ideas. In this spirit commodities are made increasingly useless, but at the same time they are made increasingly available to the poor and working class. Here they serve as a distraction from reflection (a reflection that is at this time the nemesis of the anti-culture). When one product becomes boring and/or lacking personal and social utility, a new one is made available which promises to be the allusive supplier of the fun, happiness, and basic needs which the formerly acquired product failed to deliver. And again, where that product is unmasked as the lie that it is, a new one surfaces; ad infinitum.

Consumerism is the most contemporary attempt of the anti-culture to reassert itself in a form which: 1.) deflects popular discontent through a quantitative metamorphosis of the social/political/economic particularities of the modern age; and 2.) attempts to subvert popular discontent while fostering a false unity by turning the oppressed classes into willing accomplices in the ongoing crimes committed against them.

In the first case this new capitalism shifts the obvious brutality of classical capitalist exploitation by rearranging itself into a more subtle form. At times it incorporates the trade unions of the developed world into its ranks in such a way as to allow basic reforms which improve the conditions of wage slavery while never addressing the fundamentally degrading relations between boss and worker, capitalist and slave, nihilism and existence.[8] Profit is still pursued against the general utility of society, if only in a less crude form. The workers in the primary capitalist states are thrown crumbs in the form of limited healthcare, limited wage increases, and limited executive representation. In turn this strategy allows the under classes to accumulate more spending power[9], which is utilized again towards the profiteering goals of the economic ruling class of the modern bourgeoisie. For the bourgeoisie can now radically upgrade their profit margin in terms of mass consumer products. The

---

8 This is not to imply that trade unions are devoid of revolutionary potential. It is only to say that the task of radicalizing such forces is made more difficult by continuing onslaughts of anti-culture subversion.

9 Although real wages have been diminishing in much of the developed world for some decades now (but so too has the retail price of unnecessary consumer goods).

capitalist maintains and in fact increases gross capital accumulation by manipulating both ends of the economic system — production and mass consumption.

In the second case, this system attempts to co-opt the under classes by creating false needs which the anti-culture alone is able to fulfill.[10] These commodities are directly made to exist as representations of itself; as emissaries to the perceived world on behalf of the anti-culture. They are monopolized by the system and then distributed in mass as shallow rewards for popular subservience. Their very emptiness is a mark of their reliance upon an anti-culture. Their actual non-utility is testified to by the mass of indoctrination which is required in order to convince the people of their need. Commercialization, itself a commodified industry, is the form which this intense indoctrination materializes.

With this the under classes are put to the task of producing these items, indoctrinating for these items, and then are allowed access to these items in exchange for their physical and mental labor. Actual attainment necessitates an unmasking of the general boringness inherent in them, and therefore, new false needs are immediately developed and then transferred to the masses, through the masses, by way of newly developed commodities. Products remain "new and improved" as long as they do not reach the saturation level of distribution. When this occurs a new "new and improved" item is unveiled through the propaganda machine known as advertising.

This process resembles that which the anti-culture uses to deflect popular discontent during feudal times by which the shifting of the makeup of the ruling class blunted insurrectionary sentiment by way of a shifting of the focus of animosity. The primary difference here is that the under classes are now compelled to take a step by step active part in their own subterfuge as petty mental laborers and producers. Here the under classes are actively convinced that happiness can only be obtained through commodity acquisition. The unmasking of the emptiness of one commodity does little more than open the space for the emergence of the next commodity. The discussion is framed within the parameter of the anti-culture.

With the realization of this form of nihilistic social construction, anti-culture is made both more complete than at any prior historical period, and also more vulnerable to fundamental disclosure and eventual rejection. The former is true in that anti-culture now has

---

10 Of course other social/economic systems are technically capable of producing such products. However it is only an absurd system which would consider actually doing to at the expense of so much more.

begun to colonize the very inner reaches of human dreams, relations, and desires through its commodification of the non-essential, non-work related, intensely personal, and private spheres (i.e. leisure, entertainment, personal identify, social identity, love). While it is true that this was also done during previous times through religion, this modern incarnation must be understood as more complete in that it now has managed to objectify and therefore materialize itself through the individual temples of four billion (potential) believers. Without the question of mysticism to bring structural notions into occasional question, as sometimes occurs in a religiously based society, it can now more formally codify itself in a system which integrates its material constructs with the subjective state of one's inner thoughts. All is commodified and calculable in a formula which reduces everything to the abstract materiality of capital — money. Ideas themselves become reduced to a commodity and in such become both objective and assimilated within the framework of anti-culture.

As anti-culture becomes more prevalent it also becomes more fundamentally vulnerable. No longer are the masses (within the developed capitalist states) primarily motivated towards a revolutionary disposition due to poverty. Now they begin to become agitated by social discrepancies and an intense personal and social alienation brought on by this encroaching nihilism. Where once a person could retain meaningful degrees of freedom within the framework of a more organic private life, the emissaries of commodification and navigators of objectification have more than begun their missionary tasks colonizing this new terrain. Where during the times of Marx the individual began to feel less than human through the oppressive conditions of their coerced labor, they now come to feel less than human at all times. And with this, something has to give.

The weakness of this system of anti-culture is that it can only maintain its proclaimed metaphysical completeness and perceived social legitimacy if it is manifest at all times in all relevant places. However, such an anti-culture, though representing a quasi-social reality beyond the acute control of its ruling class, cannot fully disarm the capital based irrationalities of its constructs (that being the ruling class). This ruling class, cast from the absurd values of this system, consistently refuses to relinquish their practical monopoly over capital which its elevated status relies upon. And because of this glaring fact, the poor and working class cannot reach an economic position where the process of consumption, which radical commodification and commercialism relies upon, is adequately maintained on a secure, constant, and all pervasive level. Systematic gaps necessarily occur among these classes, and with these the systematic subterfuge of consumption of false needs/commodity acquisition cannot consistently cover up the absurdity and lack of social utility which this form of anti-culture dictates.

An increasing number of poor and working class persons can be expected to call this system into question as such gaps of process occur. Also, the very pervasive nature of this process of commodification-consumerism increases the mental pressures of the lower classes by intensifying alienation. Many people can be expected to reject such modes of anti-culture in exchange for a supposedly more liberating, socially equitable, humanly fulfilling, and less psychologically stressful means of social existence. Admittedly, in some cases this will take a repressive and/or reactionary path (i.e. authoritarian, fundamentalist religious, and/or fascist subcultures). But such false roads prove themselves time and again as both socially inadequate and often brutally repressive. They will become transparent and be seen as the dead ends that they are. And here the alienated and exploited masses can be expected to be brought back to the allure of a potential society both free of the oppressive modes of the particular form of present anti-culture, and of the very precepts which give such a nihilism its historic context and imperialistic sanction.

This developing trend aimed at the grassroots eradication of neo-capitalism can be further expected to develop along basic lines which challenge the precepts of alienation in that it is to a great extent motivated by alienation. With this it is forced to challenge the very basis of anti-culture in that it is the subtle underpinning of such which gave rise to the context in which their collective misery stands. Furthermore, the under classes are now more able to realize this underlying fact in that they cannot as easily be confused by religious suppositions (as during feudal times), nor can they be as easily pacified by cosmetic changes among the makeup of the ruling class upper echelon (also during feudal times), or even quantitative changes in the basic goods of social subsistence (as under authoritarian communism). Now the poor and workers within the primary capitalist states are, in part, motivated to action against the standing order by the very process through which they are forced to perceptually experience their life. It is their alienation which drives them and separates them from something their instinct to rebel continually alludes to.[11] The actualization of themselves as individuals and as a class, and all the lost potentiality which their insurrectionary sentiments point to, become the goal which their emerging desires are aimed at. Not a thing remains sacred; not the artificial hierarchy of social constructions, not the fear of nothingness. With this, all notions of social progress become fair game and open to dissection. All that can ultimately stand is that which proves itself non-alienating and free; that of the realization of a world of inherent value and the social role of humans as sentient beings also free to pursue that which their own potentials allow for as fully actualized persons through cooperation and material equity.

Part VII: The Anarchist Rebellion

> Got to give us what we want
> Gotta give us what we need
> Our freedom of speech is freedom or death
> We got to fight the powers that be!
>
> Public Enemy, "Fight The Power"

The modern manifestation of the anti-culture is backed into a corner that it will find increasingly hard to operate from. Due to internal contradictions its particular manifestation seems incapable of maintaining the status quo while at the same time allowing for the necessary shifting of form into that of a homogeneous consumer society. The talons of bourgeois greed are sunk too deeply within all facets of the anti-culture to allow for a transition to a more equitable consumerism; one that could 'socialize' the illusion of meaning through a constant process of consumption. Hence the anti-culture appears vulnerable to radical approaches from the ranks of existence minded revolutionaries.

In a word, commodification and consumerism fail to address its weakness as a super-alienating force within the developed world's non-ruling classes, while also failing to provide adequate levels of basic social plenty for the masses in the under-developed world. As such, it would appear certain that fundamental revolutionary breeches are presenting themselves. Specifically it is apparent that those revolutionary challenges to the status quo are of a fundamental level and specifically of an anarchistic variety. For anarchism alone represents the directly democratic and equitable process by which a hierarchical ideology is not again forced upon natural lived experience. It is the revolutionary position that, among other things, the social

---

11 Economics still contributes to this revolutionary process, but now alienation becomes a more meaningful force.

aspect of the revolution is viewed as more fundamental than the political. Thus anarchism serves as the living movement towards a redefining of social relations in an unabstracted form. This movement has already begun.

One has to look no further than the development of counter-cultural communities among relatively large sectors of the poor, working classes, and de-classed populations throughout the more developed capitalist world from the post-World War II era to present. It is within these communities that people have been coming together in order to forge a more natural existence which seeks to challenge the historical confines of hierarchical social models while coaxing a more fluid and organically creative means of expression from their own endeavors. Here all historical precepts have come into question in order to uncover the roots of alienation, oppression, and inequity that the affected seeks to dislodge. Sometimes slowly, sometimes meticulously, and sometimes in a moment of brilliance the shackles of nihilism are being rooted out and uncovered. New, or rather more natural processes of social relations are being experimented with within the growing boundaries of this emerging counter-culture. This development is revolutionary by both necessity and nature, and, although at times misguided or ineffectual, represents a path for humanity which is both materially equitable and non-alienating. It is fluid rather than dogmatic and affirming to the actualization of those involved rather than oppressive and hierarchical. It is inherently anarchistic.

This revolutionary path must address the very basic foundations of anti-culture if it is to gain the momentum necessary to topple the walls of social alienation. It cannot become a mockery of itself by advocating quantifiable change at the expense of qualitative revolution. It must demand all in order to gain even an inch regarding those social and psychological factors which presently make people experience themselves and others as cogs rather than the free intricacy that they are, or at least could be. And here the banner has already been raised. And with such, the politics inherent within the counter-culture must remain steadfast in maintaining its natural position as contra anti-culture. It must remain vigilant so as not to become co-opted by its other, thereby becoming itself a closed dogma. It must remain a dynamic interchange of persons and ideas, anti-authoritarian while also unafraid of the unknown. It must know its enemy and boldly seek ways to ruthlessly vanquish it, while itself not becoming a new crutch for the fearful to limp on with. It must exist as a liberator opposed to false precepts; one which functions as the inalienable aspect of a freedom loving-people — not as the coordinating system of blind slaves. It must not rest on its laurels or become content as a closed clique. It must remain open and thereby exert an influence throughout the ranks of the broader under classes while all the while engaging in multiple-level combat with its historic nemesis, the anti-culture. It must unmask the facilitators of oppression and reveal the foundations of alienation. And finally, it must fight against its enemy wherever it is found with the weapons of ideas, living examples, and, when necessary, arms. It is through this struggle that we will reach the higher levels of the social support and growth that we require for our eventual and inevitable victory.

In sum, every moment of unmasking is a moment of culture. But such a moment does not constitute a complete culture insofar as its source is semi-conscious. The rise of capitalism, the rise of radical commodification marks the hour before dawn, and the mind lies somewhere between sleep and dream; between possibility and expectation; servitude and freedom. Culture, in its truest sense, is awake. It is a consciously creative process. But even while the mind sleeps it feels the tension of thousands of years of repression. It twists and turns in its uneasiness and grasps for its lost grounding. Here it formulates rudimentary tools for its struggle. Like the prisoner it constructs a shank, but does not yet realize its true oppressor. Rebellion is this shank. At first the shank is applied to its fellow prisoners; later to the guards; but never to the great warden of all the jails of the world; never to the anti-culture. It is only through bloody trials and tribulations that the warden is finally seen behind the proverbial curtain of poverty and the state. And then, "all that is holy is profaned. All that is solid melts into air, and man is at least forced to face, with somber senses, his true condition in life."[12] And what is revealed "behind the common dark of all our deaths"[13] is the great Dracula figure; the anti-culture. The mind at last is awake, and the rage of centuries flows through its veins. The tyrant is expelled, if not killed, and the pent up creative aspirations of countless lifetimes are unleashed upon the real world. Culture constitutes itself in relation to natural unity, social relations are liberated and the age of anarchism has arrived. The epic comes full circle; wo/man is back home, a little bit older, a little bit sadder, but a whole lot wiser, and free. History does not come to an end but passes into the unknown.

---

12 Karl Marx, *The Economic and Philosophic Manuscripts of 1844.*
13 Jack Kerouac, *Visions of Cody.*

On the Question of Violence & Nonviolence[14]

Left: Peaceful protesters attached by police in Seattle, 1999; Right: Black Bloc marches in Georgetown, Washington DC, 2007

"Let us remember that every great step forward in history has not come into fruition until it has first been baptized in blood." — Mikhail Bakunin

Introduction

Militancy and direct action are not only necessary tactical tools for the anarchist left, but, when correctly implemented, they are also the facilitators of inspiration and motivation for both those involved with the act in question and those who observe the act in question. It is such activity that helps draw numbers into the movement by creating an outlet for the venting of frustration and alienation. In short, militancy and direct action, by challenging the entrenched power of the wealthy ruling class and state, fosters a sense of empowerment upon those who partake, while also furthering creative aspirations by hinting at what a revolution toward a non-oppressive society might feel like.

Militancy and direct action do not carry the inherent qualification of being violent or nonviolent in and of themselves. The slashing of management's car tires during a labor dispute, as well as erecting of barricades and subsequent rioting against the forces of the state during a pro-working class demonstration are both clearly militant actions, but so too is a non-violent workers' factory occupation during a strike as well as occupying major city intersections and shutting down of financial districts during a protest against neoliberalism.

Clearly there are many circumstances in which non-violent tactics are not only advisable, but also the only effective course possible. Furthermore, tactical nonviolence is always the preferred

---

14 2017 note from the author: The essay was written in 2000 and was first published as a pamphlet by Black Clover Press, Montpelier VT, 2001.

course of action when its can bring about the desired objective and subjective results more effectively than, or as effectively as, a violent act. Such practices should be encouraged and taught throughout the anarchist and leftist movement generally in order to maintain a moral superiority over the forces of capital and the state, who of course practice both overt and covert violence with little discrimination on a consistent basis. This commitment to nonviolence is fundamentally based on pragmatism and revolutionary ethics, while finding its material existence through the implementation of tactics. However, nonviolence should, under no circumstances, be understood as a strategy in and of itself. When nonviolence is used as a strategy it transcends its existence as a descriptive term and defines itself as an idea, a noun, as "pacifism"; it becomes an ideology.

When nonviolence is used correctly, as a tactic, it is a most useful tool in the popular struggle. The reason for this is because such a display of resistance is indicative of an underlying threat of violence. For if people are willing to put themselves on the line for the sake of liberty, and if these people are willing to risk bodily harm in such an action, it displays a level of commitment, which, if turned in a violent manner, could manifest itself in the form of a future insurrection; an insurrection where if critical mass is attained could threaten the foundation of state power; that of the ruling class and the underlying anti-culture.

In this case, the southern leadership, embodied in Martin Luther King Jr., expounded upon the need for nonviolence to be utilized as a strategy. However, this movement did not take place in a vacuum. Parallel to the happenings in the South, a movement for black liberation was being launched in the North, and elsewhere, as embodied in the Nation of Islam, later in an autonomous Malcolm X, and then in the Black Panther Party (BPP), and the Student Nonviolent Coordinating Committee (SNCC), a group which formally rejected strategic nonviolence while under the leadership of Stokely Carmichael. This aspect of the movement displayed signs of extreme militancy and was not pacifistic in rhetoric or in character. To the government this represented the logical alternative to which the movement as a whole would turn if certain terms were not ceded to the pacifistic element in the South. The much trumpeted success of the Southern Civil Rights Movement's pacifistic strategy has, despite itself, much to thank to the threat of violence

In the following essay, I will elaborate on the above theme. First, I will discuss situations where political violence in not only necessary, but ethically justifiable. Second, I will discuss the natural disjunction between strategic nonviolence and the poor and working classes, and finally, I will discuss the contemporary bourgeois roots of pacifism as an ideology of the status quo.

When Violence is Necessary

The fact is that there are times when the only way to effectively advance a movement is through the use of violence. Sometimes, this necessity is clearly in reaction to particular act of state violence, other times it is due to more general circumstances. Either way, justifiable acts of leftist/working class violence are always fundamentally an act of self-defense insofar as the very institutions of the capitalist state inherently constitute continuing physical and psychological violence against the great mass of its people.

> "Once the State moves to consolidate its own power, peace has already been broken."
>
> — Che Guevara

More concretely, violence can be understood as absolutely necessary during certain phases of popular struggle. This occurs when:

1. Nonviolent options have been explored yet no ostensible victory has been reached.

In the face of exploitation and oppression, inaction is akin to no action, and hence is tacit acceptance and support of those evils. In addition, the continued implementation of proven ineffectual tactics in the face of these evils must be considered akin to inaction, in that ineffectual tactics translates into the same end result; continued exploitation and oppression of the poor and working class by the hands of the ruling class, bourgeoisie and their lackeys. Thus, it would follow that there may arise circumstances, after the exploration of peaceful options, where the only ethical course available to a movement, or individual, is of a violent kind.

2. Whenever State oppression becomes violent, to the point where the movement itself or large segments of the population or the premises on which the people subsist are threatened with liquidation.

The physical self-defense of a people, a movement, or the premises upon which they subsist, is a self-evident right, obvious in the natural world. To claim otherwise is to deny the bravery, justness and dignity of Sitting Bull and the Lakota of the 1870s, the Jews of Warsaw during the Nazi occupation of the 1940s, the Cuban's defense at the Bay of Pigs in the early 1960s, the man who vanquishes the would-be murderer of his child, and the woman who manages to physically fight off a would-be rapist. To allow for otherwise is nothing but a neurotic self-denying tendency and an unnatural will to suicide.

3. Violence must be understood as a looming fact once the critical mass necessary to seriously challenge a ruling class and state power is domestically reached.

To believe that the state will voluntarily relinquish its power in the face of a moral challenge is as childish and absurd as it is dangerous. History, without exception, has shown that a parent state will react to any legitimate or perceived threat to its domestic power with a ruthless violent suppression of the threat. If that means the murder of large sections of its own population, so be it. Pacifism in the face of such repression translates into no more than the eradication of the insurrectional movement through the means of murder to the sum of absolute death. Once the state finds itself backed into the proverbial corner, it can be expected to act by animalistic instinct; in short, it will fight for its life and will not relinquish until either itself or all of its foes are dead. Let us not forget the 30,000 fallen heroes of the Paris Commune whose blood will forever stain the consciousness of modern France.

Some would argue that the above claim is proven false by the historical fact of Mahatma Gandhi's pacifistic movement; a movement which did succeed in liberating India from direct British imperial rule. However, such a line of argument does not apply in this case, as that particular case did not occur inside a primary capitalist nation. Rather it occurred on the edges of a crumbling empire. The response of the British government would have differed radically if the movement had occurred inside one of its perceived, primary domestic provinces, or if it were a general domestic movement against the state apparatus itself. The former of which is born out in the fact that the present situation in Northern Ireland has its contemporary roots in the 1960s nonviolent Catholic Civil Rights Movement.

Therefore, if the goal of the anarchists and the left generally is not self-eradication through a violent counter reaction and the subsequent consolidation of oppressive forces, it will recognize nonviolence for what it is; a tactic, not a strategy.

Pacifism as Foreign to the Poor and Working Classes

One must also question the ability of a nonviolent movement to generate the critical mass necessary to substantially challenge the entrenched fundamental power structure of the nation/state. Since the death of Martin Luther King Jr. in 1968, pacifism has failed to attract any significant numbers outside of the upper middle and wealthy classes. The reason for such failure is that pacifism does not commonly attract members of the working and sub-working class because it bears no resemblance to their experience of reality or their values and shared history of struggle.

If one's goal is to aid in the building of a serious revolutionary movement, one must be sure that movement is inclusive to those classes that inherently possess revolutionary potential. Thus, it is necessary to construct a movement which is empirically relevant to poor and working class reality. This not only means agitation on their behalf, but also utilizing a strategy which is consistent with the developing/potential class consciousness of such a constituency. If a movement fails to do such, it will fail to draw the necessary critical mass from those classes and in turn will fail to achieve its supposed goals. Furthermore, such failures are probably indicative of the co-option of that movement by ideological prejudices imported from the bourgeoisie; most likely in the form of upper-middle class activists present in the left. Nonviolence, as a strategy is a perfect example of such counterproductive prejudices.

I have often heard discussions among upper-middle class activists about the need to stay away from violent confrontations with the state at demonstrations in order to "not turn people off". The fact is the only people who are likely to be automatically turned off by legitimate acts of self-defense are upper middle class and wealthy types who will most likely never be won over to the side of revolution anyway. On the other hand, it is common that folk from within the poor and working classes are inspired by the direct and unobstructed confrontations with the forces of the status quo. These communities appreciate the honesty, dignity, and bravery that popular self-defense demands. These are the future agents of revolution and they are not as easily turned away by the truth that real struggle entails. Violent self-defense on behalf of, and through a constituency emanating from their class, is a more pure expression of their collective frustrations brought on from alienation and made objective through their continuing poverty or sense of slavery through accumulated debt.

To further illustrate this all one has to do is look at the various strikes, demonstrations, protests, riots, etc., of the past two years to see how those from within the poor and working classes have conducted themselves when confronted with state violence and restraint. Here we can observe the violent uprising of the poor and working class black folk within Cincinnati (April 2001), the anti-capitalist riots of the Quebecois youth A20 (anti-FTAA demo, Quebec City, April 2001), the numerous Black Bloc anti-capitalist actions throughout North America and Europe (Seattle, 1999, through Genoa, 2001) the armed peasant uprisings from Bolivia to Nepal, the massive militant protests of the Argentine working class against the neoliberal policies of the capitalist government (summer, 2001), the violent union strikes within South Korea, as well as countless other examples of poor and working class resistance the world over.

Compare these developing mass movements composed of persons squarely within the more oppressed economic classes to the relatively impotent and groundless protests of strictly nonviolent upper middle class "reformers". Two decades of liberal dominance within the left, from the late 1970s through the later 1990s, resulted in little or no tangible victories, and often resulted in isolating left wing politics from its supposed mass working class base. These liberals, democratic socialists, non-government organizations (NGO's), etc., failed to deliver a mass movement of an oppressed constituency. All they did manage to deliver was countless boring protests, which rarely even received media coverage of any kind, and Walter Mondale, as the losing alternative to Ronald Reagan in the 1984 U.S. Presidential election.

The basic fact is, the strategy of nonviolence is foreign to the poor and working classes, and any grouping which places such an ideology ahead of the real desires and inclinations of the masses of exploited people will inevitably remain marginalized, isolated, and ineffectual. Here they become no more than the would-be mediators of continuing alienation and oppression, if only with a dash more of welfare programs and workplace safety boards.

Pacifism is foreign to the social reality of the workers. For example, few of us who grew up without the privilege of gross excess capital did so without learning the value of knowing how to fight. Unequivocal nonviolence in grade school would have earned us the same thing it does in the political arena; further bullying, further oppression. An early lesson for many of us was the effectiveness of "standing up to the bully." Such an act always carried with it the threat of violence, if not the implementation of violence. To take such a stand without such a commitment would have resulted in nothing more than a black eye. It is from this early age that the more oppressed classes learn the value of violence as a tool of liberation.

Historically violence has proven to be politically relevant through union struggles and neighborhood fights against the exploitation of the poor and working class. The history of the labor struggle is a history of blood, death, and dignity. From the Pinkertons to the scabs, to the police, army, and National Guard; from lynching to fire bombings the U.S. Government, acting as the political ram of the ruling class, more often than not has forced the working class to defend itself through its only proven weapons; class-conscious organization and self-defense, when need be, through violence. This is a historical fact that is apparent in the social underpinnings of working class community, if not always consciously remembered by its inheritors.

In addition, the more advanced elements of the poor and working class has, for 150 years, been exposed to and has autonomously developed ideologies of liberations which not only map the current state of affairs and predict future trends, but also prescribe the justified use of violence as a necessary element of their own liberation. In turn, these ideologies, although often greatly flawed, have been a consistent traveler through the trials and tribulations of these workers since the dawn of the industrial age. When successes were found, these ideologies were also present. Although it is true that much leftist ideology is becoming a dinosaur of the past within primary capitalist nations (i.e. those espousing the various forms of authoritarian communism) it must be recognized that in and of itself it has been responsible for its own transcendence. It is part of the common history of struggle and even with its passing it reserves a place of prestige within the social unconscious of the past and present revolutionary struggle. You tell me how willing the more self-conscious elements of the poor and working classes are to deny this history.

Of course, violence should not be canonized. These same communities implement violence upon themselves in a destructive manner as well. Domestic violence, murder, and armed robbery of members of their own class is a reality in many poor and working class neighborhoods. But, these forms of internal violence can be attributed to alienation as experienced in an oppressive society. Thus, crime rates have historically plummeted in such neighborhoods during times of class autonomy (i.e., Paris 1871, Petrograd 1917–1921, Barcelona 1936–39). Of course, we should condemn such negative forms of violence and work toward their eradication, but we should do so without throwing the baby out with the bath water.

- Violence, both of a positive and negative sort, *is* an element of poor and working class culture. Violence is also a proven tool of liberation in poor and working class ghettos, both in relation to the personal and the political. And finally this reality is further validated by ongoing world events and historical fact.

- Nonviolence as a philosophic universal must be understood as the *negation* of the existence of the poor and working classes. And no, I do not solely mean their existence as an oppressed element; I mean their existence as a class which possesses a self-defined dignity through their ongoing struggle against alienation and exploitation.

Ideological nonviolence is the negation of their shared history of struggle. It denies their dreams of freedom by its sheer absurdity and stifles certain forms of their self-expression through its totalitarian and insanely idealistic demands. In a word, strategic nonviolence is the negation of class consciousness; it is irrelevant at best and slavery at worst. In itself, it represents the conscious and/or unconscious attempt of the more privileged classes to sterilize the revolutionary threat forever posed by a confident, self-conscious, and truly revolutionary working class.

Once again, it is conceivable that some would argue the contrary by pointing to poor and working class involvement in the nonviolent movement in Gandhi's India and/or Martin Luther King Jr.'s Civil Rights Movement. However, the extent to which non-violence was accepted as a strategy by these classes is born out in the events which followed the initial successes of these respective movements. In India the same elements that partook in nonviolent actions quickly, and regrettably, fractioned off into two camps; the Hindu on the one hand and the Muslim on the other. Not long after, these factions had no qualms about mobilizing to fight successive wars against one another. Let us remember that both these factions today possess nuclear weapons, which are aimed at one another. In the southern U.S. many of the same persons who marched with King also adopted a decidedly non-pacifistic strategy in the later days of SNCC, the formation of BPP chapters, and the Black Liberation Army cells throughout the region. In addition, let us not forget the riots which occurred upon the news of King's assassination, turning the black ghettos across the U.S. into a virtual war zone. In the final analysis, both of these pacifistic movements must be recognized as only being such in the minds of their respected leadership. The masses of poor and working class people, which gave these movements their strength, never internalized nonviolence as a strategy; rather nonviolence was no more than a particular tactic to be used as long as its utility bore itself out.

Psychological Roots of Pacifism as a Bourgeois Ideology

So, if pacifism bears no resemblance to poor and working class reality and has no historical or sound philosophical base, what can its existence, as a strategy, be attributed to? The answer is: the deformed ideology of the progressive element of the bourgeoisie and petty bourgeoisie — in other words that of the classes composing the higher and lower levels of the wealthy privileged classes.

It is true that many individuals from these classes have become legitimate and outstanding revolutionaries through the process of becoming radicalized and declassed; Mikhail Bakunin, Karl Marx and Che Guevara to name but a few. And of course, there are many such individuals in our movement today. But, it is also true that many bourgeois elements present in the left still cling to their class privileges and prejudices as if a gilded crutch. They are oddballs in that they are bourgeois yet are driven by a self-loathing as facilitated by class guilt. On the one hand they wish to rectify the ills they feel responsible for, and on the other they are too unimaginative and weak of constitution to cleave themselves from their class privileges and the relative security that entails. Hence, they cling to the only political strategy which can, in their minds, both absolve them from their materials sins and maintain the status quo of their class security; in a word, they become pacifists. In this move they reject the dialectical materialism of both anarchism and communism by subjecting themselves to an idea at the expense of concrete experience.

Pacifism lacks any sound material bases. A quick observation of nature will tell you that the natural world is not without violence and human beings are not outside the natural world. Life is violent. Everything from the eruption of a volcano, to the lion's killing of her prey, to human ingestion of a vegan meal, possesses a degree of violence. Think of all the weeds that were killed in the production of that tomato, or of all the living microorganisms that our body necessarily destroys through ingestion, or through the very act of breathing; that is violence.

Like the eighteenth century French philosopher Rene Descartes, these charlatans reject the fact of the body for the phantom of the mind. They create the idea of unconditional nonviolence and enslave themselves to it; instinct, lived experience, historical fact, be damned. Through their ideology they become the same beasts of dualism that have tethered the human race from Plato to Catholicism.

Pacifism is fundamentally at odds with anarchism in its view of the state. Pacifism functions by the maxim that the tacit and active perpetrators of oppression (i.e. the state through the ruling class) possess an inherent ability to rectify themselves if the true appalling nature of that oppression is unmasked to them. Hence, it is also assumed that the ruling class possesses the ability to make such an observation and that it will display the desire to make such change. Anarchism contends that the very existence of a state apparatus insures the continuing oppression of the exploited classes. This is due to the inherent tendency of power to corrupt those who possess it; and those who possess power seek to consolidate that power. The state apparatus tends to safeguard itself from such possibilities through the creation of bureaucratic institutions which entail a codified dogma specifically designed to maintain the status quo. With this development class oppression becomes an irreversible fact, within the statist paradigm, even in the unthinkable unlikelihood that large elements of the ruling class were to desire its radical reforming. In this sense the state is a self-propelling evil that is no more capable of eradicating class oppression than it is of eradicating itself; Frankenstein's monster resurrected. Therefore, pacifism is fundamentally at odds with anarchism. Either the state is potentially a vehicle for liberation, or it is an institution of slavery. Plain and simple.

Bourgeois pacifists become modern ideologues of a confused status quo. They adhere to pseudo-rebellion, and in doing so they serve the function of bolstering the state through the implementation of a strategy that acts as an abstracted semblance of insurrection; a false, non-threatening insurrection squarely within the parameters of the predominant anti-culture. And here they defuse the revolutionary potential of any movement they touch by acting as the unconscious arm of the expanding anti-culture apparatus of false appearances and mundane stability. For as long as their strategy lacks any real potential to fundamentally challenge class bias and status quo; as long as such a strategy is devoid of the true ability to deconstruct the economic and cultural system that allows for the establishment of the bourgeoisie and petty bourgeoisie; as long as this strategy takes on a language of righteous and pious revolution, these self-loathing activities of a physical comfort can go to sleep at night both feeling redeemed through their rebellion and secure in knowing their tacitly oppressive luxury will be there for them again, tomorrow.

What further makes these pacifists oddballs, is the fact that through their pseudo-revolutionary activity they incur an alienated relationship with the less analytical elements of their own class, who in their ignorance constitute the class majority. These elements mistakenly view them as class traitors. This is ironic because nothing could be further from the truth. These people stand fundamentally in solidarity with their roots. And, if their activity has any ostensible effect on the larger movement, it is to prolong the day of insurrection, not to expedite it.

If left to their own delusions they would not deserve such discussion, but they, like Christian missionaries, seek to spread their neurotic illusion to new populations; in this case the poor and working classes. And in doing so they have infiltrated the leftists and anarchist movements and even now threaten to rob it of its pressing relevance by divorcing it from its learned experience.

The poor and working classes are naturally not drawn to pacifism. If pacifism becomes the prime mode of operation for leftists and anarchists organizations, these organizations will cease to have any legitimate tie to their natural constituents. Although it would be ignorant to contend that such an ideology will fail to gain a certain degree of reluctant converts among naturally opposing classes. If such irrationalities never occurred in society, Italian and German fascism would never have manifested themselves with the power that they did.

In short, aspects of the poor and working classes can be expected to adopt a self-denying ideology if that ideology claims to offer liberation and if that movement in which it is contained appears to be the most prominent in the field. This is not to say that the true movement will be abolished through such a scenario, any more so than it denies the ultimate historical relevance of dialectical materialism, it is only to say that it will prolong the day of reckoning by robbing the oppressed classes of their truly revolutionary organizations.

Conclusion

Perhaps the best way to have repelled Franco's fascist invasion of Spain in 1936 would have been for the C.N.T. and F.A.I. to hold a peaceful sit-in? Maybe Adolph Hitler would have reversed his genocidal policies and instead made strides towards a free society if enough Jews and gentiles would have peacefully marched in Berlin. If non-violence was the strategy of the Devil, he'd probably be ruling heaven right now... no.

In the end analysis, just as there is a place for tactical nonviolence, there is also a place for violence during certain phases of a popular movement. This can manifest as a tool of self-defense or as the midwife of state disembodiment. On the other hand, pacifism, as an ethical system of action, is nothing but an absurd dilution born out of resentment and fear and projected upon the struggles of the poor and working classes by oddball elements of the bourgeoisie. As long as such a strategy is allowed to occupy a prominent role among the ranks of the left, the left will equal the total sum of the socially inept ruling class.

In summation, nonviolence can be used in many circumstances as an effective tactic, but it is irrelevant, irresponsible, and utterly ridiculous to even consider it as a strategy. So yes, nonviolence should be utilized as a tactic where pertinent, and in turn pacifism, as an ideology and a strategy, must be purged from our movement.

NEITHER WASHINGTON NOR STOWE
— COMMON SENSE FOR THE WORKING VERMONTER:
A LIBERTARIAN-SOCIALIST MANIFESTO[15] (Third Revised Ed. 2014)

Artwork by Xavier Massot

Note: The original document was printed in 2004; it was greatly expanded and revised in 2007 and updated again in 2014. Since the document was first drafted, the Montpelier Downtown Workers Union has folded, and other political realities have emerged. With this in mind, the authors updated the document where they could or at least inserted dates as reference points for events or organizations. Even so, the sections on the MDWU were retained as they map out a realistic model for future organizing.

The Peoples' Republic of Vermont, 2004 (and Revised 2014) —As Vermonters we are perhaps the most weather conscious people in North America. We feel the winter winds through the drafts of old farm houses, smell the melting snow when collecting our sap buckets, hear the birds of summer while tending our farms and gardens, and see the beauty of fall written across the hills in oranges, reds, and yellows. Many of us still work with our hands, be it as loggers, farmers, carpenters, midwives, or crafts-people. When the leaves fall we still hunt deer, and many of us still cut our own firewood a year in advance. Even the many of us who live in town still grapple with the

---

15 2017 note from the author: This essay was penned by myself with the exception of 'The Yoke Within' which was penned by Sean West. The entire work was reviewed in great detail by the Green Mountain Anarchist Collective and modified in order to represent the consensus view of the Collective. The Green Mountain Anarchist Collective (especially Sean West, Lady, Will Dunbar, and JM) as a whole greatly contributed to the content. The essay was first published in Catamount Tavern News, 2004.

dirt roads during mud season, and swim in country lakes during the warm months. We know our neighbors, drink cider and beer around campfires, and during the first Tuesday in March, we still debate and vote at Town Meeting. We, for the most part, have maintained this way of life despite the over development, consumerism, and government centralization that has plagued much of the continent. We maintain this, in part, for reasons beyond ourselves. The rugged terrain of the Green Mountains and near arctic winters limits our potential for certain forms of development, while also shielding us from less hardy outsiders. Because of this remoteness our Green Mountains often feel a century away from Boston, and a million miles from New York. Yet we are still tangled in the treacherous web of Washington politicians and the wealthy elite from Wall Street, to Texas, to Stowe. We are our own people, yet we are compelled to mimic the same bureaucratic structures in our government and economic dead ends in our communities that strangle the common working person from California to Maine.

A Peoples' History

> "The gods of the valleys are not the gods of the hills."
>
> — Ethan Allen

The history of Vermont is one of independence, democracy, and justice. In the 1700s, we, as common farmers, successfully fought our own war of independence against New York, and then later, the British Empire. In our early years we achieved sovereignty based on a directly democratic, more empowered, Town Meeting system and continued as an independent republic for 14 formative years. We were the first state to guarantee its citizens the right to vote, even when they were not landowners, and we never allowed slavery. From the Green Mountain Boys, to the underground railroad, to those who volunteered to fight against slavery in the Civil War, to those who battled against Fascism during and before World War II, we have never shirked our responsibility in fighting the good fight, when we have deemed it such, and when the call has come. In a word, we are a people who dare to lead both by example and struggle.

More recently, we have lead the nation on such basic issues as providing healthcare for children, raising the minimum wage, civil unions, legalization of medical marijuana, mandatory labeling of genetically modified seeds and food, and we are the first State in the

Nation (2006) to elect a Socialist, Bernie Sanders to the U.S. Senate.[16] Vermont is also the only U.S. State with a strong and viable Third Parties (as of 2014, the Social-Democratic VT Progressive Party has 10 persons elected to the VT House & VT Senate, as well as one person elected to Statewide office: Doug Hoffer as State Auditor). In addition, the far left VT Liberty Union Party is also considered a Major Party. Being in front of other regions, demanding more for the common good than the poverty of global capitalism normally allows for is both our birthright and historical calling. But being a pace in front of a slow runner is not good enough to guarantee the maintenance of our way of life nor the emergence of a freer, equitable society beyond the shackles of international corporations and their two national political parties.

In a word, while the goddess of agriculture still looms above the State House, our farms are quickly disappearing. From 10,000 family operated dairy farms a generation ago to only 1,200 today (2004), "free trade" and the corporate takeover of agriculture have driven us to fight for the very survival of this dignified way of life. Our once powerful manufacturing base, which formally included highly productive machine shops from Brattleboro to Springfield to Newport has faded, moving to the super exploited markets of China and Mexico. To fill the void, the tourist industry (ski resorts, hotels, retail shops, restaurants, etc.) has emerged as a major employer. Unfortunately, this shift has emerged as the mass substitution of dignified, good paying jobs with benefits (the type that you can raise a family on) for those that pay close to the minimum wage, carry few if any benefits, and demand that us working Vermonters smile, dance, and entertain those upper middle class and wealthy out of state tourists who view Vermont as little more than their quaint New England theme park.

So the question becomes, where are we now? If we retain our current trajectory will the Vermont we leave to our grandchildren resemble that which we were raised in? Will farms still dot our hills, or will our red barns be replaced with more ski resorts, chain stores, and inns for the rich? If the latter becomes true, we must recognize the fact that future Vermonters will be compelled to get by on no more than minimum wage, little or no healthcare, and the confines placed on our tradition of democracy by corporate control and federal dictates. The bottom line is that we, as the majority, are standing at a crossroads at which we can choose the path of capitalist homogenization, or, rather, lead the way back towards direct democracy, local control, and the social advancement of the common good.

---

16 Bernie Sanders also launched his candidacy for U.S. President openly as a Socialist in 2015.

The Yoke of Washington and Wall Street

> "For Vermont, of all people, would be the most miserable, were she obliged to defend the independence of the United Claiming States, and they at the same time at full liberty to overturn and ruin the independence of Vermont."

— Ethan Allen

The United States of America, and much of the remaining world, operates above all else according to the rules of capitalism. Under capitalism, the basic goal of society becomes the private accumulation of wealth for the elite few. In other words, the major institutions of society value the production of goods and services that are capable of generating a maximum amount of profit. What is best for the common good is often obscured by what is considered best for economic consumption. With such, working people (who are by far the vast majority of the population) are seen simply as a necessary resource for corporations and private owners. Instead of viewing workers and small farmers as equal members of the broader society, the owners and bosses see us as no more than a necessary resource in the field of production. In a word, we've become akin to the machines — we've become objects of exploitation.

Our labor is used not as a means to uplift society as a whole, but as a tool to make a select few very rich. On the job, we are often compelled to work under the near dictatorship of the boss. Even when we work for ourselves, we are still dictated to by the wealthy that hire us, the corporations who subcontract us, as well as the ebb and flow of the capitalist economy. In short, we are compelled to engage in work in order to create a massive overall profit that we will never see, and if we don't like it, and we speak up, we face the likelihood of being fired. The schools teach us that this is democracy. For forty to sixty hours a week we live under a dictatorship in our workplaces, and this is acceptable?

Insofar as social and economic policy is concerned, the federal politicians, who are usually bought and paid for by the rich, don't ask what we think or what we want. Instead they take into account the "needs" of the owners. They pass legislation that makes the rich richer and the poor poorer, and adopt trade agreements that translate into the foreclosure of family farms and the relocation of factories to countries and states where workers have even less rights, and where wages are even lower than they are here. And again, these politicians write laws that allow the rich to skip out on paying their share of taxes, and instead rely on us working class folk to foot the federal bill. And what do we receive in exchange for such taxes? Healthcare? Affordable housing? Free higher education? No. Our money is used, by and large, to subsidize the corporations, and to build bombs and tanks that are deployed at the whim of the President and in the interests of the elite.[17]

Even in the larger picture we are being screwed by the out of state corporations and the feds. While we struggle to get by on the sweat of our labor, our raw materials (milk, timber, granite, produce, tourist monies, etc.) are, on the one hand, shipped out of state for refinement and then shipped back to be sold to us at a profit that we will never see. On the other hand, much of the accumulated capital, from among other things, the tourist industry is carpeted off to banks and rich people who have never even stepped foot in the Green Mountains. In this way, Vermont has the same economic relation with the U.S. as that of a colonial possession. Just as the American Colonies (and much of the world) came to understand such a colonial relationship to be detrimental to the social, economic, and political well-being of their citizens, so too do increasing numbers of conscientious Vermonters.

In essence, the federal government demands that we provide them with money, send our children to die in their wars, sacrifice our rights for the profit of the few, and to do so without complaining. This is the directive of Washington DC and Wall Street, and this is the yoke which is placed over the neck of the working people of both Vermont, the rest of the nation, and much of the world. So do we learn to live with this yoke, or should we seek to break it — once and for all?

The Yoke Within

> "It overwhelms the individual from birth. It permeates every facet of life, so that each individual is, often unknowingly, in a sort of conspiracy against himself. It follows from this that to revolt against this influence that society naturally exercises over him, he must at least to some extent revolt against himself."
>
> — Mikhail Bakunin

As if it wasn't enough to have the federal government and big business on our back, we also have foes closer to home. The greedy capitalists that own the resorts, the yuppies that we have to wait on, managers that run the factories; these are the daily reminders that we're forced to work within the confines of the U.S. economic machine.

---

17 As of spring 2007, Vermonters stationed in occupied Iraq are being killed at a rate of six times the national State by State per capita average.

For example, let us take a look at the case of Stowe. Nestled on the busy thoroughfare of Rt. 100 and in the shadow of Mount Mansfield, this quaint village represents, to many of us working Vermonters, what is wrong with the current set up. Million dollar second homes for the wealthy of Toronto, Connecticut and beyond dot the hills. Workers from Morrisville, Hardwick and Elmore make the daily trudge to labor in the tourist shops that line Main Street, to staff the ski resorts, to manicure the lawns of the rich, and wait on them hand and foot at their catered parties. This Vermont theme park for mostly rich out-of-staters has grown so large in its scale of operation that hard working people of the surrounding towns cannot perform all of the necessary labor to keep the lazy rich people content. Hard working folk from Jamaica and other countries are recruited to staff the tourist industry. Young working people, who travel around the country working at resorts just so they can afford to ski or snowboard, sell themselves into a glorified form of indentured servitude for a season. Working people from around the country who immigrate to our Green Mountains for their beauty and quiet end up facing the ugly crowds of the tourist buses and their shrill chatter while ringing them up at the register.

In this poker game we see the workers whose cards leave them with only their wits to play the game, and the wealthy flatlanders always with a royal flush in hand; but there is another character whose hand is at play and who shuffles the cards to keep the deck stacked against the common Vermonter. That is to say, there is the local elite who own the hotels, the restaurants, the big landscaping companies, the real estate firms, the car dealerships. There is a local status quo in power in Stowe and Montpelier, in Brattleboro and Killington, and throughout Vermont who profit off the maintenance of this system of exploitation and inequity. While they play real hard at trying to maintain the image of regular good ol' Vermonters just like everyone else, their interests (and profit margins) lie more in tune with the wealthy, both here and out-of-state, than with us workers, be we Vermont born and raised, or recent arrivals to the Green Mountains.

Here is the picture: A small dairy farmer signs off on the foreclosure of a family farm as old as the independent Republic of Vermont while an entrepreneur in Stowe celebrates the acquisition of a new shop at which common Vermonters will labor for poor wages to make him richer. A Vermont National Guardsman in Iraq gets blown up by a bomb while a member of The Cody family (owner of several Washington County car dealerships among other businesses) sits comfortably and safely behind a desk as a Four Star General in the US army. A carpenter hitchhikes to the jobsite because he can't afford to get his car fixed until next week, let alone pay for the skyrocketing gas prices, while "caring" capitalists Ben and Jerry make a shitload selling their company to the multi-national corporation Unilever. Our good ol' boy Governor Jim Douglas gives $350,000 of our tax dollars to the ski industry to subsidize their advertising costs while he scolds dairy farmers asking for a $500,000 investment to buy their own dairy processing plant (*circa 2004). The liberal led government of Burlington does some remodeling to bring in department stores and fancy boutiques while a family in the old North End has to sell off their home because yuppies have driven up the property taxes.

There are, in fact, two Vermonts: one of wealth and privilege and one of hard work and sweat. If Vermonters have any chance of success against the forces of Washington and Wall Street, the battle must start in our own backyard against the business and political elite of Montpelier and Stowe. We must guard against the sly maneuvers of both the conservative and the liberal status quo in Vermont, and fight to win more power for ourselves in our towns and workplaces. Could our efforts ever cultivate a harvest hardy enough to withstand the strong, cold winds of Washington and Wall Street if we do not till our fields first? Can you start a good sugaring season without first cleaning out your sap buckets? The answer is no. There will be no victory over the enemy without before there is victory over the enemy within. For it is the privileged and powerful locally and their dupes who will stand as the first serious line of defense for the privileged and powerful classes in general. So do we bow our heads, mutter curses under our breath, and continue to subsist on the scraps they throw to us or do we dare to struggle and dare to win against the local elite?

A Second Vermont Revolution

> "Go your way now and complain to that damned scoundrel your governor. God damn your governor, your laws, your king, council and assembly."
>
> — Ethan Allen

So, what is to be done? We can choose a different way; a way that will allow our grandchildren to experience the independence, democracy, self-sufficiency, and natural beauty that are the gifts handed down from our common ancestors. If we choose this path to freedom, we can set our course in such a manner that our future will not be simply a still life of the past, but one that reflects new possibilities for equality, direct democracy, and social stability. There is no reason in the world that we cannot both honor the past, while paying homage to a future wherein all Vermonters are allowed, among other things, free access to healthcare, higher education, housing, childcare, and decent jobs. This is the trick; remaining true to our roots while capturing the spoils of technology and the potential of social cooperation. So what would such a Vermont look like, and how do we get there? Well, the seed of such a place is already in our hearts, and through such, has already begun to show signs of germination.

Back in the 1700s, before Vermont was a state, we practiced a form of direct democracy through an empowered Town Meeting system. Imagine for a moment that the legislature didn't meet in Montpelier. Imagine, in fact, that there is no legislature at all. Instead envision a system working throughout all the Green Mountains whereby all major decisions are made through local Town Meetings. Now of course one, or two, or even 30 Town Meetings don't have, nor should they have, the power to impose their views on all of us. However, would it not be more representational of our collective general will if a majority of towns voted to pass a certain regulation, law, or resolution? Well, that is how the early years of Vermont were defined and that is how the great American revolutionary Thomas Paine believed it should be. In other words, we used to all get together in our different communities in order to discuss, debate, and publicly vote on all the big issues that affected Vermont as a whole. And if a majority of towns passed something, it was considered a done deal. And again, the way in which they tallied votes was to have representatives of every town meet in order to report what the majority of their community felt was best.

Of course, Vermont is a different place than it was back in 1776. No longer are the majority of us small farmers, and therefore our own bosses. Today, Vermont is a place where most of us work for someone else, and where the remaining farms have to struggle to remain viable in the larger capitalist world. In short, Vermont, like nearly everywhere else in the modern world, is a society divided by economic classes, and again by the interests of the large population centers, like Burlington, as opposed to the small rural communities. Therefore, the rebirth of our tradition of direct democracy would have to take these factors into account.

Town Meeting

> "The basic unit of all political organization in each country must be the completely autonomous [town], constituted by the majority vote of all adults of both sexes."

— Mikhail Bakunin

We have witnessed the reinvigoration of our Town Meeting system since the 1980s. What began as towns passing resolutions against the perceived dangers of nuclear weapons has grown into a widespread movement of communities taking stands on any number of issues. Now a days it is common for us to pass resolutions for or against any number of issues; be it against GMO foods, for or against Vermont Yankee Nuclear Power Plant (closed down in 2014), in support of the Bill of Rights (and against the USA PATRIOT Act), in favor of wind power and other renewable energy sources, in favor of universal health care, for the impeachment of the US president, in favor of pulling the VT National Guard out of Iraq, etc. These resolutions have been declared "non-binding" by the state government and are viewed by some simply as a way for common people to make their views known to the General Assembly. On the other hand, the statewide debate over Act 60 (the law which is intended to provide poorer children as good an education as rich children) witnessed a remarkable chain of events. During the height of the debate, a small number of wealthy towns (West Dover, Stowe, etc.) voted to withhold their property tax money from Montpelier while they were fighting to restore the old system. These rich towns were generally motivated by self-interest and greed (not wanting "their" money to be spent on text books for lower income children in Hardwick, etc.), but at the same time, their actions demonstrated a new emerging resolve among towns to reassert their own sovereignty over that of the Capital.

The future re-establishment of direct democracy in the Green Mountains will, in a large part, rely on the extension of the power of Town Meeting, though be it a power aimed at utilitarian ends — not economic chauvinism. But how will this be achieved? One thing is clear, the politicians in Montpelier will not simply hand it to us. Our only chance at winning will be through the coordination of a statewide movement, based in the towns, which seeks to extend our local authority with or without the approval of Montpelier. Imagine if you will a statewide effort to place a resolution on the majority of Town Meeting agendas which declared that:

> When and if fifty percent, plus one, towns/cities representing a majority of Vermonters pass any given resolution, all local revenue and cooperation will be withheld from the State government until such time as that resolution becomes the common practice of the land.

It will be through such an effort that we will begin to reclaim our democratic traditions that have been obscured through 200 years of capitalist centralization and upper class domination of the political system. In order for us to do this, we must begin to bring such self-empowering resolutions to our various Town Meetings. We can do this individually, town by town, or through the formation of a large non-sectarian coalition of those networks of Vermonters, Rural Vermont, the anti and even pro Vermont Yankee groups, the anti-Patriot Act organizations, the anti-war coalition, which are already mobilized and capable of getting resolutions placed on a good many Town Meeting agendas. Would such an empowered Town Meeting system translate into a direct democracy in and of itself? Given the modern basis of our economy, as well as the diverging interests of the remaining farmers, and other working class people, it would seem reasonable that such an empowered town meeting system would only be one part of the equation. If we are to truly and honestly help build a freer and democratic Vermont, we would do well to find ways to extend this direct democracy to the farm and the workplace.

The Farmers

> "My farming business goes on very brisk but I tremble for bread and corn... it is a pinch with us and will be so till harvest, prey help us."
> — Ethan Allen

Farming has always been a part of our culture. Let us remember that the legendary Green Mountain Boys, who were the scourge of New York authority and the British at Ticonderoga, were no more than small farmers themselves. In our past it was these homesteaders who, when needed, banded together to fight the good fight for the common cause. Today their struggles tend to be against the large capitalist agribusiness. Where they once fought Red Coats and Sheriffs, they now fight against the unfair trade policies of NAFTA, the FTAA, and federal and state politicians who time and again sell them out to their capitalist underwriters. Only one thing remains the same...they are still fighting for their free existence.

While we have lost many farms throughout this long fight, those that remain have begun to organize. To date, over 300 farms have come together to create the Dairy Farmers of Vermont (DFV). This group represents a staggering eight hundred and fifty million pounds of raw Vermont milk (or one third of all that is produced in the state). DFV, which was formed in an old barn in the Northeast Kingdom, is presently fighting for the rights of Vermont farmers generally, for higher wholesale prices (with the aid o f organized labor), and as of the fall of 2006 has opened a farmer owned dairy processing plant in Hardwick called the Vermont Milk Company. In line with our traditions, DFV operate according to directly democratic principles. In other words, no decisions are final until they are brought before a vote of all the members. And here the rule is one farmer, one vote. Likewise, their processing plant, which pays farms several dollars more per hundred weight for raw milk than their corporate counterparts, is run democratically by farmers themselves through a farmer board of directors.

Whereas it is way too early to know the full extent of what victories DFV will ultimately win, and although we cannot say for certain how this organization will grow in the coming years, we can say this: the more farmers are organized, the more power they will have when confronting corporate America. In the past, when most Vermonters grew crops and kept livestock, we could count on Town Meeting to voice their unique concerns and interests. However, because of the changing economic landscape, we cannot do so now. Today, many farms are isolated in communities that increasingly rely on tourism and other industries for jobs and revenue. Therefore, farmers' voices are often drowned out in the multitude of other perspectives. For this reason we need to support such democratic farmers' groups as DFV. As long as we value this important link to our past, and as long as self-reliance remains a Vermont ideal and goal, we must support those emerging institutions that fight for the preservation of local, small, agriculture. And besides, if one of our goals to provide healthy food for ourselves and our children, should that food not, when possible, be cultivated right here where we can both watch it grow and take pride in knowing those who produce it?

We may agree that all this is desirable, how does it relate to the broader picture of a more free and democratic Vermont? Well, the present course of the DFV, and other like-minded farmer groups, is similar to what we see happening in the Town Meeting movement. These groups are the nucleus of democratic change, and, by virtue of their existence, demonstrate the potential for expansion. It is conceivable that the DFV or a future organization will extend their membership to other farmers (not just those in dairy). And imagine, if you will, that after winning more concrete gains they were to reorganize themselves into local, countywide sections. Each one meeting several times a year and operating, like Town Meeting, according to directly democratic principles. Let us imagine that such an organization began to develop strong means of communication with the Town Meeting movement. Could we not expect such an organization to eventually run and regulate agriculture on a local and statewide basis the same way that an empowered Town Meeting system would give voice to the concerns of the residents of local communities? From our standpoint, the answer must be a hardy yes!

Of course, such a direct democracy of agriculture would have to be solidly based on a just foundation. Therefore the individual farms would do well to be managed democratically with all those who work the land and machines being themselves empowered to articulate the relations in which they labor. And here let it be clear that we do not call for something that is very different from our current practices. Is it not true that most our farms are worked by a single family? Don't the adult members of those families already operate according to the natural give and take of family decision making? Would not these small farms who currently hire a few field hands be stronger by incorporating their ideas, perspectives, and energy more thoroughly into the operation? The answer to these questions are again yes. If we achieve such democracy, both directly on the farm and in the countywide organizations, we will be well down the road of achieving real democracy across Vermont. However, for this saga to begin to reach completion we would have to first also address the concerns of those who labor off the farms, in the factories, in the shops, and on construction sites. For if the democracy we envision ends in the Town Halls, and on the farms, many of us would still be left in the shadow of alienation of servitude during the near daily nine to five.

The Workplace

> "Federalist organization from the bottom upward, of workers' associations, groups, communes, counties, regions, and finally whole peoples, is the sole condition for true, nonfictitious freedom."
>
> — Mikhail Bakunin

When most Vermonters were farmers, many of us belonged to the local Grange. Today, most Vermonters work in other industries, and many of us belong to unions. Right now tens of thousands of us are union members. Of Vermont's total population of just over 600,000 it is estimated that 100,000 people are either union members, retired union members, or immediate family members of the two. More than 10,000 state workers and retirees belong to the VSEA. 10,000 more belong to AFL-CIO, including many ironworkers, plumbers, writers, factory workers, communication workers, carpenters, and nurses. The independent United Electrical, Radio and Machine Workers (UE) claims hundreds of members across these mountains, and the National Educators Association (NEA) claims thousands more. In a word, large sections of working Vermonters are organized across the region in numerous sectors. And again, over the last decade many of these unions have come together in the spirit of mutual aid by becoming members of the Vermont Workers' Center coalition.

The Worker's Center, like the Dairy Farmers of Vermont, and in the tradition of Town Meeting, operates as a democratic organization. Affiliated members (unions, some social justice groups, and individual working class people) have a vote on a steering committee that sets the priorities and political positions of the center.[18] Here, under one big tent, working people are able to come together in common cause in order to fight for that which the capitalist economy is loath to grant them: better pay, more democracy at work, and social justice has become not just the struggle of isolated people or separate unions, but the common fight of an increasingly united working class. And as this spirit of solidarity has been kindled among worker organizations, it has had a reverberating effect upon the elected union leadership. In 2003 the Vermont AFL-CIO elected a reform, pro-democracy, candidate to serve as State President.[19]

However, as Vermont's manufacturing base has eroded due to corporate greed and the federal policies of so called free trade, this sector has been increasingly replaced by low paying service and retail jobs. And here, union concentration (and decent wages and benefits) has been seriously challenged. This shift in the economy of course presents a unique set of challenges to the Vermont working class movement.

In response to this the Vermont Workers' Center in cooperation with the UE helped to launch a historic citywide union drive aimed at the 800 service and retail workers of the capital city. In 2003 the

---

18 In 2003, the major Vermont unions, through the Workers' Center, passed a resolution condemning the invasion of Iraq.

19 In 2006 this President, Dan Brush, was compelled to step down after his union, the Teamsters, decided to break with the AFL-CIO at the national level. However, the VT AFL-CIO remains a strong affiliate of the Workers' Center, and continues to play a leading role in such progressive causes 'ending the war in Iraq' and 'the establishment of a universal single payer healthcare system in Vermont.

Montpelier Downtown Workers Union (UE Amalgamated Local 221) was formed, and today the union has won contracts in two shops, is promising two more by the fall, has members in more than a dozen other shops, prints a monthly newspaper for area workers, and has established a citywide steward system and grievance procedure.[20]

Like Town Meetings and DFV, this young and innovative union has organized itself as a truly democratic voice in the community. Instead of taking the dictums of the bosses at face value, they have begun to create a directly democratic space through which workers are free to hold meetings of their own, and therefore begin to decide how they think things should be run. The days of politicians, the rich, and the Chamber of Commerce calling all the shots may be numbered after all.

In April 2004, the union held a Workers' Town Meeting at which union members from more than a dozen different city shops participated. At the meeting, the working conditions of the area service and retail sector were discussed, as were various strategies for how they could advance their social visions and economic demands. It was there that members debated and then democratically voted to establish the citywide grievance procedure, and to form a Workers' Defense Squad. These facets of the union are now beginning to be utilized by workers across Montpelier as a means of building further democracy, fighting the bosses, and gaining social respect. Tellingly, the Defense Squad, which in principle is the direct action wing of the union dedicated to supporting the grievance procedure, is made up of not only members of the Downtown Workers' Union, but allied members of other area unions such as the Carpenters, the Teamsters, the Nurses, the NEA, and the Printers (all of which are members of the Workers' Center coalition).

While this new union still has far to go on the road to the empowerment of the Montpelier working class, it cannot be stressed enough that their initial successes carry positive ramifications for workers across Vermont. As word of their victories spread throughout the hills, it is possible that workers in other cities and towns will follow suit. And as they begin to build such democratic unions across the state, there can be no doubt that the voice of the common woman

---

20 In 2005 the union changed its affiliation to the Industrial Workers of the World, renaming itself the Montpelier Workers' Union, and becoming open to members outside the capital city.

and man will begin to eclipse that of the politicians, landlords, and wealthy.[21]

Okay, so the question again becomes, exactly how does the building of new democratic worker organizations, and development of inter-union solidarity, relate to the overall task of transforming Vermont for the better? Aside from the fact that unionized workers have job security, better pay (on average), and more democracy on the job than their nonunion counterparts, the above discussed developments in the labor movement seem to point to a broader trend. First of all, the more established unions are becoming open to more internal democracy. Second, the example of the Montpelier Downtown Workers' Union shows the potential for building new, directly democratic unions among the ranks of low paid workers. And third, the emerging sense of organized class solidarity would seem to allow for a more dynamic labor movement then could previously be expected. These three developments point to new possibilities. Case in point is the recent rise of worker cooperatives across the state, of which there are currently 10 intermittently located between Brattleboro in the south, and Burlington to the North. (circa 2006). Could this not be a sign of a future that is yet to take full form?[22]

Even so, could it not be argued that when and if the Town Meeting system is further empowered that us workers will no longer need the protection of labor unions? This, in that they as the majority class will be fairly represented through their communities. While it is true that workers are the majority, it is also true that many towns, like Stowe, entail hundreds of workers who do not, and/or cannot, live where they work. Therefore, in order to give a voice to those, who by their labor,

---

21 As of 2006, the union has gone dormant. However, the fact that the union was able to exert real power during two years of activity has demonstrated the basic effectiveness of this innovative model. Tellingly, while affiliated with the UE the union won a staggering 70% of its grievances despite not having the benefit of a legal contract in most of the shops where the grievances were fought. And again, in many cases the union was, among other things, able to win unjustly fired workers their jobs back. Politically, the union also helped to successfully defeat a town vote aimed at raising the local sales tax; a tax which the union viewed as being fundamentally regressive and representing a kind of pay cut for local employees who are compelled to purchase basic goods in town. While this particular union has gone dormant, it will live on as a model to be learned from and built on in future organizing campaigns.

22 These cooperatives are workplaces that are owned and directly controlled by those that labor within them. In themselves they represent increasing instances of working class people coming together to exert direct democratic control over their occupational life and offer a limited glimpse as to what a freer system of labor would look like. As of July 2006, these cooperatives include Red House construction in Burlington, the Langdon Street Café in Montpelier, the Brattleboro Tech Collective, and the Common Ground restaurant both in Brattleboro.

make the functioning of that community possible, we must recognize the absolute need for the integration of worker organizations with the Town Meeting system. Union plus Town Meeting equals Democracy! In addition, it is hard to imagine a situation where the power of Town Meeting and farmer organizations are effectively expanded without the further maturity of the Vermont labor movement. In a sense, for any one of these interests to have a chance at superseding the power of the rich and that of the General Assembly, they must all develop together, as supporting beams of a united and popular movement. While the towns have the power to withhold cooperation with the centralized government, and the farmers the strategic ability to control local food production, we workers, through our organizations, have the all-important ability to withhold our labor. Without our participation, NOTHING in Vermont, or the world for that matter, other than the rising and setting of the sun, could continue to function. Without our participation capitalism and the system of government that has come to underwrite it, would crumble.

With this being said, after the Downtown Workers' Union or future like organizations reach an advanced level of maturity, they should seek to develop further ties with the rank and file of other unions also located in the same city or town. In the case of the Montpelier Downtown Workers' Union, maybe this will be partially achieved through the ongoing inter-union work of the Defense Squad. Maybe this squad will eventually develop into an action committee that does not confine itself to the struggles of local 221. It is possible that it will emerge as a committee that is prepared to take direct action in defense of all Montpelier workers, those from different unions, and those that are yet to belong to a union.[23] And again, as such relations of mutual aid develop, however they come about, is it not possible that some crucial worker related issue will come to the surface which compels all the unions of Montpelier to come together in one great workers' council?[24] For the moment, the eyes of Vermont are on these

---

23 In the fall of 2004, the Defense Squad voted to establish itself as an independent working class organization willing to come to the aid of any and all area workers/ unions that requested such assistance. However, as of 2006 the Defense Squad in effect has been disbanded. Even so, its existence during the formative years of the Montpelier Downtown Workers' Union helped prove that such an organization is possible. And again, the impressive 70% grievance victory rate of the union had a lot to do with the implicit threat that the Defense Squad represented to the elite business owners. Most Defense Squad members remain active within their unions and the Vermont Workers' Center.

24 It is also possible that this coming together of local unions will come about through participation in local AFL-CIO Central Labor Councils. Already the Washington-Lamoille-Orange County Central Labor Council, headed by Traven Leyshon, has a policy whereby any local union can affiliate into the group, even if

workers, and it is up to them to set the example for struggles that have not yet risen to the surface.

As the fight goes on, we shall see what happens. But one way or another workers all across the Green Mountains would do well to come together in such organizations. In a word, if you work in a nonunion shop, talk with your coworkers and form a union. If you are already in a union, get involved with it, fight to make it more democratic, and if it hasn't already become a member of the Workers' Center, propose to your membership that you join today. And of course, while we struggle to win mid-term bread and butter victories for our class, we must seek to integrate unions into local and statewide networks of mutual aid capable of making political decisions, engaging in effective strategies, and nurturing internal practices consistent with direct democracy. If we achieve all this, could we not assume that it will be us workers who one day will be in a position to self-manage the sectors of the economy we already know so well? Just as we must struggle to create farmer organizations that are capable of coordinating Vermont's basic food production, we must do what we can to bring more of our fellow workers into the organized fold, while transforming our existing unions from within, into bodies that are capable of holding production together without the exploitive presence of corporate owners and thick headed bosses.

In summation, a good union is no different than Town Meeting; it is a form of Town Meeting that is daily reinforced through activities on the shop floor and finds its larger expression through the integrated efforts of workers across industrial lines. When we were all farmers we met in Town Hall to decide our own fate. Today, all that has changed is that we now work in hundreds of different jobs, often in towns where we do not live, and the communal place where we go to make decisions has come to include our Union Halls. As the fight to regain our democratic freedom comes full circle, we must recognize that it is impossible to recreate the past; one cannot step in the same river twice. Our world has changed, and with it the directly democratic process of Town Meeting must come to include countywide farmer organizations, and integrated worker councils. It will be through these three pillars of democracy that we will again come to know the dignity, responsibility and privilege that come with a truly free and empowered people.

---

they are not members of the AFL-CIO. Today [2007] this CLC not only includes AFL-CIO unions but also the Teamsters.

Freedom and Unity

> "The solidarity which is sought, far from being the product of any artificial authoritarian organization whatsoever, can only be the spontaneous product of social life, economic as well as moral; the result of the free federation of common interests, aspirations, and tendencies."

— Mikhail Bakunin

Town Meeting, democratic farmer organizations, and worker councils; these are the three building blocks of a free and prosperous Vermont. Each of these organizations, both at a local and regional level, would stand for the organized interests of the people. But in and of themselves these organizations do not necessarily translate into a functional direct democracy. If we cannot find a way to tie them all together, we will be left in the quagmire of having three separate, though popular, institutions. If this were the case it can be assumed that they would inevitably compete with each other for overall sovereignty, and in the process they could fail to surmount the powers of Washington, Wall Street, and the State. Let us recall that in a divided house, the tyrant remains king.

Therefore, we must find ways through which all three are integrated into one functioning system. Ideally, each body would represent one vote. For any decision to be made, we could require that two out of three of the bodies vote in its favor. In other words, if a single town, or a small number of adjacent towns sought to pass a resolution that would only affect those communities, we could require that both the farmer organization(s), and the worker councils that exist in those communities also debate and vote on the issue. If two out of three vote in favor, then it should be done. Conversely, the farmer organizations or worker councils could also bring issues to the fore, which the related Town Meetings would have to vote on. And again, when decisions have to be made on a broader level, we can require that all three bodies vote on the question at hand during something akin to a greatly empowered Vermont wide Town Meeting Day. Of course, most members of society will have two votes; one through the town where they live, and the other either in their local worker council or county farmer organization. Therefore, in order for such big decisions to be democratically made, the general meetings of these bodies would have to be staggered. For example, on the first Tuesday of every March, all the towns would hold their meetings. A week later the farmers would hold their county meetings. A week after that, the worker councils would hold their meetings. If a majority of towns, which represent a majority of Vermonters, passed a given resolution then it would register that the towns, collectively, voted yes. If a majority of the county based farmer organizations, representing a majority of farmers, passed a resolution, then it too would be considered a yes vote. And again, if a majority of worker councils, representing a majority of workers, passed a resolution, then it would be counted as a yes vote. There are several options for how resolutions would become law. A Vermont-wide resolution could be considered law if a majority in two out of the three bodies voted in its favor or, perhaps, a free Vermont would require a majority in all three bodies for a resolution to pass.

So how would resolutions be placed on all these agendas? After all, if we are to coordinate all the functioning of Vermont ourselves (without the centralization of the General Assembly), we will have to see to it that certain basic issues are addressed, in every local body all at once, and in a timely manner. With well over 200 Town Meetings, an equal amount of worker councils, and 14 farmer organizations, it is not practical to think that a few committed individuals will be capable of getting enough signatures in each locality to get any single issue on all the local agendas. Furthermore, such a task would have to be performed once, twice, or even four times a year! Assuming that such dedicated individuals did mobilize, is it not likely that dozens of similar, yet competing resolutions would also be placed on the agendas, piecemeal, across the Green Mountains? How could Vermont smoothly function given these inherent difficulties?

First of all, we have to remain vigilant that we do not begin to dismantle the democratic rights of individuals and groups in the name of efficiency. Therefore, as is the case now with towns, people should always be allowed the option of privately getting signatures in their communities in order to get things placed on their local agenda. And if other organizations wish to have specific issues addressed in multiple towns (or for that matter in the farmer groups or worker councils), they should have the right to attempt to do so. However, these means of expression are not enough to guarantee the practical operation of running all of Vermont. For this reason, we should seek to build a system through which any one Town, worker council, or farmer group has the right to ask that a proposal that they, on the local level, endorse, be placed on all the agendas across Vermont. And in order to synthesize redundant proposals, the Vermont wide bodies of the three organizations should annually elect a coordinating committee, who would all work together and whose job it would be to make it so. Such a committee would not have any legislative powers. All they would be empowered to do is rationalize the various proposals that are presented for debate across these hills. In order to discourage the concentration of duties, and partisanship of interests, such persons should not be allowed to be elected onto multiple seats. In other words, a person should not be allowed to run as both a Town Meeting and farmer or labor coordinator at the same time. While such a system seems to solve many problems inherent in directly democratic systems, one operational question remains. As has been alluded to above, under this system free market capitalism would be replaced with a more socially responsible and equitable self-management system. Food production will be rationalized and coordinated through the united efforts of the farmer organizations, and production and services will be carried out through the directly democratic labor unions. One may ask, exactly who within these groups would be responsible for coming up with such a complex and integrated plan? With the farmers, considering that their overall numbers and local bodies will be relatively few, the solution is comparatively easy. During their regular Vermont-wide meeting days, the general membership would be free to set the general goals and direction of such production. After this, an elected, statewide farmer select board will be responsible for the formation of specific plans on how such membership directives will be carried out.

In relation to industrial production, transportation, services, and all else in between, the answer is a bit more complex. While the workers, as a whole, through the local worker councils, should be democratically allowed to express their general vision, specific issues within specific industries will have to be addressed by those who labor in those capacities alone. For example, while the general membership of the combined worker councils (in collaboration with Town Meeting and the Farmer organizations) may vote to increase Vermont's reliance on renewable energy sources,[25] it will be up to

---

25 Establishing in-state electricity, and then energy self-sufficiency through community-owned and worker-run renewable energy projects, needs to be a top priority for a free Vermont. Our goal is not the socialism of darkness but rather the equitable and democratic reconstruction of the best aspects of the modern era. Already, as of 2012, the State of Vermont, through Democratic/Working Families Party Governor Peter Shumlin, had declared the goal of serving 90% of our energy needs from renewables by 2050. This move towards renewables is further demonstrated in the successful mass movement to shutdown Vermont's

all relevant workers who will be carrying out the project (utility, construction, etc.) to come up with the exact plan on how this will be done. While workers will be brought together in geographically organized councils, it will also be necessary to retain a parallel trade union structure in order for specifics to be worked out. In essence, this reality is akin to a group of people deciding that they want to have a house built. While the decision to build and the general features of such a house would be left to them, the actual blue prints would have to be drawn up by an architect. In a word, the people as a whole will give direction, and the expertise of the related workers will find a way to make it happen. And again, as with the other popular bodies, these parallel trade based bodies must operate according to directly democratic principles. Finally, as is the case with the farmers, the workers will have to elect Vermont wide worker select boards both at the council level and the individual trade level in order for the general directives of the combined membership to be carried out according to a detailed and coordinated plan. The last problem that such a directly democratic system would have to solve is how disagreements are resolved between these bodies, and how voting deadlocks could be overcome. Imagine a situation where an important decision has to be made. Let us assume that the nature of the decision does not allow us to simply vote no, but rather that one way or another we have to take some kind of action. Say that the proposal that is intended to address the issue is voted down by both the majority of Town Meetings, and the farmer organizations. If this were to occur, we should require that elected delegates from all the towns, farmer organizations, and worker councils meet in order to discuss the positions of their communities. Such a body would encompass roughly 500 total delegates. While these delegates would not be empowered to make any decisions, they should be expected to discuss, debate, and propose compromises to the issue. In turn, they should seek to come to a commonly accepted position, which they could bring back to their local bodies where it could be again voted on. (*Note: This power dynamic would be the exact opposite as it is today, where the decisions of Town Meeting are considered non-binding and the decisions of the General Assembly

---

sole nuclear power plant (and Vermont has no coal plants). As nuclear goes, wind farms and solar installations are already being built. A freer Vermont would be wise to make sure that any utility scale renewable plants are owned by the people, run rationally by the workers, and supported by the town(s) they are located in. And of course family and community scale renewables should also contribute to our overall energy needs as much as possible.

are considered law.) Of course, such a system does not guarantee perfection. There should be little doubt that heated arguments and impasses will arise. However, we are not trying to put pen to a utopian kingdom. Rather, the system that we are sketching is simply a real democracy. And with democracy, despite all its potential flaws, the maxim that more than half the people will make the right decision more than half the time is a great improvement from the money driven bureaucracy that we currently struggle with.

A Peoples' Bill of Rights

> "Equality and justice demand only a society so organized that every single human being will-from birth through adolescents and maturity-find therein equal means, first for maintenance and education, and later, for the exercise of all his natural capacities and aptitudes."

— Mikhail Bakunin

The achievement of the above directly democratic system would, in and of itself, shine like a light for all the farmers and workers of the world. But does it guarantee that which capitalism presently denies us? With democracy would we all have healthcare, housing, jobs, higher education, etc.? Not necessarily. Such a democracy only guarantees an equal vote and equal voice. It does not mandate equal treatment outside the Town Hall, Union Hall, or Farmers' Hall. For this reason, such a society would have to include a basic bill of rights that sees to it that the wealth and opportunities created by the combined efforts of the workers and farmers, as well as one's individual liberties, could not become monopolized by any one group of citizens. Just as we must all put into society, we must all have equal access to the fruits of that society and all the while we cannot forsake our natural freedom. Therefore, such a peoples' bill of rights must guarantee, among other things, the following: 1.) ample food, 2.) decent housing, 3.) jobs, 4.) free healthcare, 5.) free higher education, 6.) equal and integrated rights and treatment for all persons regardless of profession, gender, race, disability, religion, or sexual orientation, 7.) the maintenance of all individual liberties to the effect that they do not curtail the liberties of one's neighbor or society as a whole, or 8.) the right to defend these principles by all relevant means. These eight points must serve as the basic unalienable rights of the entire society. If we are to truly deliver a free Vermont to our grandchildren, these rights must remain non-negotiable, and the basic guiding principles of all our collective endeavors.

The Worth of Labor and Exchange

> "I am a convinced advocate of economic and social equality because I know that, without it, liberty, justice, human dignity, morality, and the well-being of individuals, as well as the prosperity of nations, will never amount to more than a pack of lies."

— Mikhail Bakunin

Unlike under our current economic system, there can be no artificial debate about whether or not a free society can afford these guarantees. Once we liberate ourselves from the exploitative relations of capitalism, and once our productive forces are self-managed through collectively controlled means, we will be able to reap the benefits of a rationalized economy; one that is geared towards the betterment of the people as opposed to the accumulation of private wealth for the elite few. And again, when our economy is self-managed, our collective resources will no longer be siphoned off by the bosses. There will be no more over paid CEOs, no more union busting lawyers, and no more flatlander corporations with their hands in our pockets. Together we will create a more socially productive economy; one that serves the needs of the people, and not the irrational desires of the wealthy.

Let it also be known that the ultimate victory of working Vermonters over the abstract forces of capitalism will be reached through a new, equitable, form of exchange. No longer will such a system make a daycare provider work 40 hours in order to get one hour worth of medical care. No longer will a farmer have to bust their ass the entire year just to be able to keep the electricity on. No longer will corporations and owners force us into creating products for the wealthy that we, ourselves, could never afford. When the yoke of Washington, Wall Street, and the rich is broken, the rule will be that an hour of labor will be worth an hour of labor. When we achieve real democracy we will have the power to extend our social equity not only into politics and the workplace, but also to the economy itself. Therefore the abstract monetary system that we currently toil under must be replaced with a more sustainable "labor hour" model.[26]

Within a labor hour model, one hour of work would be worth exactly that. Here a teacher would receive the same base pay as a farmer, as would a carpenter and a logger. And again, when said logger required the services of an auto mechanic, a labor hour note would be used as a symbol of that equal exchange for every hour that the mechanic worked on the logger's behalf.

---

26 In some very small and/or cosmetic ways the recent establishment of local/ community currencies such as 'Burlington Bread' can be seen as a nod in the direction of the labor hour model — circa 2006.

Wouldn't such a system take away the incentive to do a good job insofar as the hardworking would receive the same pay as the slackers? No. A worker, laboring within a social context that gave that person effective say in the direction and conditions of said labor would in all likelihood take on a new sense of pride in her or his job performance. This would seem reasonable in the same sense that folks who work in cooperatives can be observed to increase production and improve the quality of their work when they are made to feel directly part of it in a meaningful and creative way. Besides, common sense tells us that when we are evaluated by our friends and peers we are often more motivated to live up to our potential than when spied on by our boss. Even so, such a system, in addition to paying each person a labor hour for every hour worked, would, up until a point, also pay certain other notes depending upon expertise and performance. In other words, a worker in any given field should be paid an additional 'journeyman hour' for every hour worked once they show a general competence in the craft. And again, some workers should even be paid an additional 'master hour' on top of their labor and journeyman hour if and when they demonstrate true mastery of their occupation. In certain professions, this three tiered system would also require that the worker in question pass certain written and practical tests before a review committee of elected masters in the given field. Such testing, for example, would make sense in the medical field. Of course each industry would have to make these decisions and define the various parameters as best suits the trade or skill. Such a tiered system could be fair and equitable as long as opportunities for gaining knowledge and advancement in the field are made equally available as a free social service and right.

But would such a system be fair to those who labor at jobs which entail an elevated level of physical danger such as iron work or underwater welding? Acknowledging the social utility and inherent danger of many jobs, it would make sense to recognize such workers with an additional hourly payment of a 'danger hour' on top of their labor hour and any further journeyman or master hours. The designation of certain jobs as 'dangerous' would be made democratically through the workers council system.

Finally, each of these individual notes of exchange (labor hour, journeyman hour, master hour, and danger hour) would retain the same exchange power of the other. Therefore, no person would receive an income more than four times above that of the lowest paid worker. For example, a master iron worker would receive four distinct bills of equal exchange value for every hour of labor. On the other hand, a novice general store clerk would receive only one bill for every hour of labor. In this case the master iron worker would be making four times the exchange value an hour as compared to the novice clerk. This tiered system would be economically rational insofar as the labor of journeymen would qualitatively and/or quantitatively surpass the labor of novices in the same field. The same would hold true in relation to the labor of the journeyman and the master worker. Here, folks would be held to this standard by their peers and their trade councils.[27]

The payments of labor hours (as well as additional notes) would be issued either directly by those requesting the service or by a democratically accountable body of the related worker/trade/farmer council(s). In instances where the exchange of labor between Vermonters is direct and/or potentially arbitrary in its timing (i.e. payment for the tasks of a chimney sweep) the former would likely be mode of exchange. In instances where the exchange of labor falls under the category of a necessary social service (i.e. a visit to the doctor regarding illness or accident) the mode of exchange would likely be that of the later. This should be the case insofar as the exchange of labor should never act as a psychological and/or physical barrier to receiving basic human services least we not remain true to the social principles underlying the broader community. As for where the payment notes would come from, they should be recouped, in part, from retail centers and other facets of the community that in themselves do not directly produce a unique and tangible product. Therefore, if one was to buy a pound of butter, one would be paying (in labor hours) for both the effort that went into the production of that butter, as well as a small percentage towards the overall upkeep of social services. In addition to this, workers should have a percentage of their labor hours go directly back into the system in order to guarantee the overall social sustainability of economy.

---

27 The relative difference of pay regarding novices, journeymen, master, and workers whose jobs entail serious danger (potentially making four times more than the lowest paid worker) may sound like a big difference, but when one considers the massive disparity of earnings and wealth that exists currently under the capitalist model (a model through which 10% of the population control 90% of the wealth, and where one man, Bill Gates, has sixty billion dollars while ten thousand men and women — the approximate total population of Barre! — are homeless and penniless in Los Angeles, CA), one begins to see how a four tiered labor hour system would result in relative economic parity. Here such a system of parity would also guarantee the ability of society to provide all its residents with a dignified set of social services and human benefits. To put it simply, the fruit of our labor would no longer get lost in the bank accounts of the elite.

This system differs from our current model in several important ways. First and foremost, all products and services are made available at cost. In other words, there is no corporation or insurance company jacking up prices to make their major stock holders or private owners richer. Second, every resident is provided direct and unfettered access to all forms of social service, utilities, housing, etc. The economic price for these benefits is directly figured into the labor hour system, and is evenly dispersed throughout society in a fair and equitable manner.

As for exchange value, it will be important that prices of goods be fixed at a rational rate. If we are not to reinvent the inequities of free market capitalism, we should seek to abolish the notion of 'surplus value.' Why? The notion of surplus value is the corner stone of profit, which in turn is the granddaddy of worker exploitation, corruption, and greed. Under capitalism the idea is that those on the top of the economic food chain can generate more capital for themselves by squeezing more production out of those who work under them. If folks are compelled to work for wages and benefits that do not accurately reflect the amount of capital that their actions generate (but rather degrade that value), then that surplus, or stolen value can be concentrated at the top. It's the basic way in which the rich manage to screw us while we work our ass off and they get richer. As things stand under capitalism the deck is always stacked against the worker and small farmer.

In place of capitalism our economy should instead function according to an equal exchange system. As alluded to above, the price of a gallon of milk, for example, should be directly linked to the amount of hours that go into producing, transporting, packaging, and distributing that product. If it turns out that it takes an average of a half hour of labor to get a gallon of milk into the hands of a factory worker, then that worker should be compelled to use half a labor hour (plus the adjusted amount towards overall social services) as a means of fair exchange for that product. Likewise that same factory worker should, for example, pay one labor hour (or journey-master-danger hour) for one hour of plumbing work.

What about those who run general stores and the like? Would they not be in a position to accumulate quantities of labor hours that are not proportional to the amount of hours they actually work? Would this not throw the whole system off balance and possibly give rise to class divisions? If looking at such shops through the lenses of our current system, the answer would be yes. But instead, as touched on previously, we should understand retail shops essentially as exchange centers where one's previous labor can be traded in for an item which was produced through another's effort. In this capacity the items themselves will have a fixed value, adjusted to include social services, which will not only equal the amount of hours they entail in production and transportation, but also the amount of labor hours it requires to reasonably staff and physically maintain the shop in question. Therefore, such an equitable system would allow for the shop workers to be paid, per hour of labor, according to their tier, as well for the general upkeep of the facility, and no more. Such prices and payouts would be set democratically by related worker councils. Any additional labor hours which the shop generated would be put back into the system as a means to maintain the closed, yet flexible and sustainable nature of the model.

As for artists, musicians, writers, and the like, these valued folk would also be organized into workers' councils and their own trade council, through which their economic stability would be organized, more or less as a social service. Art must be considered a necessary element of a free society and therefore artists must also be allowed to earn a living. After all, is Vermont not in part defined by our folk arts? Do not the old poems of Robert Frost and the continuing performances of the Bread and Puppet Theater define in part who we are? Should not the development of our culture be supported to the best of our abilities? As long as we understand the politics that we hold dear to be a reflection of the directly democratic and laboratory culture that underlines whatever political structures we willingly construct, the answer must be yes. Therefore, if this free politic is to maintain itself and in fact grow over years and generations, we must continue to find ways to encourage and support those means of cultural expression that reinforce our identity as a free and independent people.

As for those who are unable to work outside the home, be it because they are compelled to care for a new child, be they elderly, or be they disabled, basic labor hours and/or service/exchange stamps should be issued to them by a related elected body within their local Town Meeting. If Vermont is to be equitable and fair we owe it to all our neighbors to provide those basic necessities that are made possible by our collective effort.

In principle a labor hour model should be understood as a very sustainable, closed, yet flexible system. While the above gives the basic parameters of how such a system would function, the details, especially the particularities within each profession and the necessary interplay between them all, will ultimately have to be mapped out by those future workers' councils, trade union councils, and farmer councils that are directly involved.

But would not this labor hour model result in a State bureaucracy of a massive proportion? Isn't it a bad idea to allow the government to set prices and pay? Well if we were talking about the government in the form that we currently experience it, then maybe. But within a directly democratic Vermont there would be no central government in any contemporary sense. Instead of agents of the State dictating prices and procedures, it would be working people and small farmers just like you and me. It would be through our democratic organizations that we would discuss these issues and seek solutions to problems and rational means to common goals. If we didn't like the form the regulations took, all we would have to do would be change them. When Vermont's economy is self-managed at all levels through Town Meeting like bodies, it will be us, the common folks who will be in charge, not appointed or elected representatives who retain power over the will of their alleged constituents. What this system seeks to achieve is the antithesis of capitalism; instead we call for an economy of the people, for the people, and by the people. This is our right, and this is our future.

As for property tax, this facet of the modern capitalist economy will cease to exist. Property, or rather a home and a family hunting/ fishing camp, will be considered a right of adulthood. Apartment buildings in the towns and cities will become cooperatively run, rent free, by the residents. Second homes will likewise be considered an impossible luxury until all people have a first home.

Such a system will support itself through a rationally implemented balance of labor as articulated through the three branches of democratic society (the town, farm, and workplace organizations). Where a void is found in certain segments of the social wellbeing, the democratic will of the people can, instead of asking for tax dollars, call for the special labor of those in the related field(s). As for trade with regions beyond Vermont, such practices of equal exchange can be extended to such parties if they too come to live within such a liberated system. If, however, they still toil under the yoke of the oppression, and if the item in question is deemed necessary by the democratic voice of Vermonters, then related worker/trade councils can be charged with negotiating the terms of such an exchange with the external party. If an acceptable deal can be struck, fine. If not, simply put we would have to 'make do, make without, and git 'er done,' or so the old Vermont saying goes. All told, the labor hour system will put more meaningful equity and social security into the hands of us common Vermonters than, after accounting for bills, taxes, and necessary living expenses, they do today under the confines of the federal government and capitalism.

So how could such an economic system be implemented across the Green Mountains? Just as the empowered Town Meeting structure, the farmer organizations, and the worker councils all would have to form, then democratically vote to empower themselves, so too will these bodies have to vote on and pass the basic principles set forth above. One thing is sure; it will only be through us farmers and workers ourselves taking our democratic destiny in our own hands that we will be able to accomplish this libertory task. Washington, Wall Street, and even the politicians in Montpelier will never do this for us. In fact their very existence depends on maintaining the status quo at the expense of our dreams, desires, and even basic needs. Hence it will only be through our collective action, through our self-empowering decisions that such a Vermont will be born.

Self Determination for the Abenaki

> "We the Missisquoi Ind's of Abinaquis or S' Johns Tribe have inhabited that part of Lake Champlain time unknown to any of Us."
>
> — Abenaki Statement to British Concerning Territorial Rights, 1766

The Abenaki, The Original Vermonters, constitute one issue which is yet to be addressed. What will be the future status of the Abenaki? Despite winning official recognition from the General Assembly in 2006, and specific recognition of four tribal governments by 2012 these Native Americans are yet to achieve true self-rule or tribal lands on a sustainable scale.[28] Instead of self-determination and

---

28   Like the Town Meeting movement towards more local democracy, the modern struggle for Abenaki rights is also a relatively new development. Following hundreds of years of extreme oppression, including a forced sterilization program in the twentieth century, the Abenaki sparked the current drive towards justice as recent as the 1970s, on the heels of the continent wide

solidarity, the Abenaki have faced down four centuries of attempted genocide. From brutal military attacks directed against entire villages in the 1600 and early 1700s to the forced sterilization programs of the early 1900s, the Abenaki have had to fight for their very survival. In a free Vermont this historical travesty would morally have to be set right. Currently (2014) the Abenaki number approximately 2000 citizens in four tribes. The Missisquoi Tribe occupies the Champlain Valley, Northwest Vermont, and has a strong population cluster in and around the town of Swanton. The Nulhegan Tribe occupies the Northeast Kingdom. The Koasek Tribe is located along the mid-Connecticut River Valley. The Elnu Tribe calls Southern Vermont its home. Although these tribes have State recognition, they do not have reservation land, or a meaningful political role within our current social constructs. In fact, these combined 2000 tribal citizens, who are some of the lowest income people in Vermont, hold only two modest tracts of land as their own (in the current legal sense). The Missisquoi Tribe collectively owns land around a sacred Abenaki spring (Town of Brunswick). The Nulhegan Tribe established collective ownership over a forest and working sugarbush (with hunting camp) outside the Village of Barton in 2012. While the latter sugar bush is capable of generating $40,000 of annual income from sugaring (at capacity), and while the establishment of this tribal forest is truly a historic achievement, considering that there are 2000 Abenaki Tribal citizens throughout Vermont, its economic and social impact is limited. Bottom line, just as other Vermonters should be free to define their own future, so should they; such desirable future must include political power, basic sovereignty, and the ability to meet the needs of its citizens.

Therefore, the Abenaki, as a free nation, should have the right to decide whether or not to establish politically independent regions, proportionate to their numbers and sustainability needs, in their core historic regions. As such, the Abenaki must be free to run these regions in any democratic way they themselves choose as is best able to meet the needs and wishes of its tribal members.

If the Tribes choose to remain an integral part of Vermont, they must be embraced in such a way as to respect and preserve their distinct cultural heritage, and guarantee their political self-determination. A way to achieve this would be to recognize the non-concentration of

American Indian Movement. This epic fight for survival is still some time off in reaching its full maturity — and thus victory!

their numbers (as Abenaki reach a majority in few if any towns), and to grant them an at-large town charter. Doing so would recognize their rights to meet independently as a cultural based municipal body, with defined rights and responsibilities. Under such a premise, each Tribe would be granted such a charter, and when the town met on Town Meeting Day, the tribes could meet in a parallel Tribal Council. Such Tribal Councils would then elect the same (or similar) persons to serve in the same or similar capacities as their kin the towns. Instead of a Town Select Board, one would elect a Tribal Council, and the Chair of the Select board would here be understood as the Chief. Instead of a Town Constable, one would elect a Tribal Constable, etc. Not being strictly geographically based (rather based on Tribal citizenship), some of the body's functions would have to be modified or creatively envisioned in order for them to serve their internal needs best. But in a free Vermont these details would be discussed and agreed to by the Tribes, and the broader Vermont community, then memorialized in the tribal charters (i.e. at-large town charters). But regardless of how such details sugar out, these Tribal Councils need to be fully integrated into the broad Town Meeting system. There votes, resolutions, and proposals, would be treated with equal rights and recourse as would those of the towns.

Through such a system, tribal citizen who choose to take part in a Tribal Council would forgo their right to take part in the Town Meeting in the community they live in. This, insofar as to allow otherwise would be both physically impossible (as these district bodies would be meeting at the same time and in different locations) and unfair as it would provide the partaking person to cast two votes in what is essentially one grand decision making body. But on the other hand, Abenaki citizens would retain their second vote in their workers' or farmers' council (which would not be distinctly Abenaki), as they would remain within the broad social and economic boundaries of a free Vermont.

When we achieve this level of meaningful Abenaki recognition (be that the integrated Tribal Councils or full political independence), we will have gone a long way in righting the historic wrongs perpetuated upon a people who have contributed so much in the creation of what we now call Vermont. This is only right, and this is what we much achieve.

In Defense of Freedom

> "I am a hardy mountaineer and scorn to be intimidated by threats. If they freight me, they must absolutely produce some of their tremendous fire, and give me a sensitive scorching."
>
> — Ethan Allen

If we achieved all this, would not the forces in Washington act to support those among the elite who stand to lose out due to our freedom? Would not the American Empire refuse to let us traverse paths that diverge from their own? This would be a decision that Washington would make on its own. But let Vermonters recall that it was under just such duress that the old Republic of Vermont was first formed. Back then it was the Royal New York Colony that sought to corral our communities by force. This challenge was met and bested by the Green Mountain Boys. Later, during the American War of Independence, it was the British Empire that sought to put a lid on our growing democracy. And again, even though Vermont contained only 30,000 residents, and even though the English were considered the most powerful and populace empire of its day, common woodsmen and farmers rose up, electing their own officers, to deliver the Brits two major blows; the first being the taking of Fort Ticonderoga, the second being the English defeat at the Battle of Bennington. In other words, Vermont is not new to resisting the advances empires and states. And as in the past, Vermonters, if united, will inevitably rise, as will our allies among the working people and small farmers of the world, to whatever occasion our destiny demands.

Vermont as a Northern Star

> "I wish all the worms which were ever permitted to torment an innocent being were in my body all at once... I'd take a dose of hellfire and destroy them all."
>
> — Ethan Allen

While we struggle for freedom right here among our Green Mountains, we must understand that we are not alone. Millions of others, throughout the continent and beyond, are fighting for similar aims. Commonly such aims, direct democracy, farmer and worker self-management, and the guarantee that all people have access to the basic necessities and social services, is referred to as a libertarian form of socialism; namely that of anarchism. In an anarchist system, there is no longer a ruling class. Instead all people have an equal say in the direction of society. And again, this system differs from capitalism in that the products of labor are not geared to the interests of an elite few, but rather the common good of the whole.

As Vermonters, we must also recognize that the fight to win such freedom does not start and stop at our frontiers. As we write this document, millions of workers and farmers, in every corner of the continent and the world beyond, are struggling to achieve similar victories in their distinct regions. We would do well to support their efforts, as our fight is linked to theirs as long as we are engaged against the common enemy of greed, bureaucracy, centralization, capitalism, and the rich. The final defeat of capitalism will only come when its chain of oppression is broken at many links.

And again, when we achieve our victory, we must be prepared to extend our hand in friendship and cooperation with those farmers and workers beyond our mountains. We must do so in order that we, together, forge a new means of cooperation that seeks to achieve a broader society in which all people are free to experience the world without the deadening weights of poverty and alienation.

The Vermont Spring

> "Crowd your settlements, add to your numbers and strength; procure firearms and ammunition, be united amongst yourselves. I hope to see you face to face, next spring."
>
> — Ethan Allen

As working class and farming Vermonters, we owe it to our cultural past, the future of our grandchildren, and ourselves to seek the fulfillment of our common dreams and aspirations. We can no more accept a future where our mountains are further masked by the two dimensional trappings of capitalism, then we could a world without seasons. Before consumerism, bureaucracy, and centralization obscure our culture of independence and equality, we must come together in order to reassert that which is just. For this we must continue to build the popular organizations that will inherit our hills, and we must build them so as they face the proverbial south. And for us, that is toward direct democracy, socialism, and creativity. In a word, we are a people who continually look toward the end of winter, and friends, with a little hard work, the spring will find us.

Page 98: Top left, Van Deusen marching in first Black Bloc against DNC, Chicago, 1996; top right, Van Deusen circa 1993 at age 20; second row, left, Van Deusen 1999; right, Van Deusen crouching, with members of the Green Mountain Anarchist Collective and ARA in Vermont 2002; Van Deusen holding banner on left with members of the Green Mountain Anarchist Collective leading Black Bloc against fascism, Lewiston Maine 2003; Van Deusen at Labor Day march in Burlington, 2003; bottom row, left: Xavier Massot (L), Hefty (M), Van Deusen (R), Brattleboro 2003; right, Van Deusen's Catamount Tavern News Press Pass 2007.

Page 99: Top left: Van Deusen on Verizon picket line, Montpelier VT 2015; top right (and second row, left), Van Deusen at Union Motorcycle Run with AOT-Vermont State Employees' Association members and supporters, Montpelier VT 2016; second row, right, Van Deusen while on cross country motorcycle trip 2017; bottom left, daughter Freya Van Deusen at Woman's March honoring her great-great grandmother, suffragette & poet Abby Crawford Milton, Montpelier VT 2017; bottom middle, wife Angela Ogle & Van Deusen 2016; bottom right, son William Walram Van Deusen on bike, 2016.

BLACK BLOC TACTICS COMMUNIQUÉ[29]

Members of the Green Mountain Anarchist Collective and Anti-Racist Action in Vermont, circa 2002

Introductory Notes from the First Edition

The following document is presented with the intention of furthering the basic effectiveness of our movement by advocating various tactical practices that we hope will be adopted by the Black Bloc as a whole. The inspiration for this work comes from our complete love for the creative ability/potential of humankind and our uncompromising dedication to social revolution. Portions of this work tend to take on a

29 2017 note from the author: The first edition of this essay was written exclusively by myself and was adopted by the Green Mountain Anarchist Collective. This second edition which appears here includes changes made by the Green Mountain Anarchist Collective and Columbus ARA (Ohio). These changes were penned primarily by myself and Lady at the direction of GMAC and ARA. The essay was first published in Barricada Magazine, 2000. The work was first published as a pamphlet by Kersplebedeb Publishers, Montreal, Quebec, 2001.

militaristic tone. This tone should not be misconstrued as a back door justification for arbitrary hierarchical models of organizing. Rather, the reality of our militant struggle necessitates the language used in order to most accurately depict our objective circumstances and the methods we must employ in order to come closer to victory. Here it should be pointed out that under no circumstances do we advocate any organizational model that in essence is not compatible with those utilized democratically by Anarchists and revolutionary workers as practiced during the Paris Commune (1871) and the Spanish Civil War (1936–39). In order to put this work together, we reflected on our own collective experiences as well as looked to history to learn what works within an anarchistic framework and what does not.

It is our intention here to present an accurate, yet brief, analysis of the present state of the movement generally, as well as the steps we (the Black Bloc) must take in order to further the cause. Also, the below proposals are directly intended for Black Bloc incorporation only. For any across the board Anarchist adaptation of the more militant proposals (such as found in the section Preparations For Increased State Repression) would lead to the weakening of the all-important above ground community organizing efforts. We view these efforts as primary to the general cause in that it is through them that the wider populace is brought over consciously to the Anarchist Left. Our struggle must be conducted at all levels. Lastly, we encourage you to read this work and discuss it within your collective and/or with other folk within the Black Bloc anarchist community. It is our hope that such collectives and interested people connected with the Black Bloc will sign their names (not necessarily their given names) to this and implement the tactical proposals suggested below. In the likely case that the below document is partially unacceptable to our community of struggle, it is our hope that such points of contention be discussed, debated and amended as necessary in order to reach Black Bloc consensus. We here ask that the various Anarchist newspapers and periodicals open up their letter sections for this purpose.

Our Movement Grows

During the course of the past year and a half (since the Battle of Seattle) we have been witnessing/participating in a maturity of the larger social protest movement as well as the smaller (yet growing) revolutionary Anarchist movement.

This is a result of eight basic reasons:

1. The experiential emptiness of intensified neo-capitalist

commodification of pseudo-reality and its necessary results of mass alienation, anxiety and Boredom.

2. The continuing failure of the present system to alleviate material deprivation (poverty) amongst certain sectors of working class and poor.

3. Overt attempts by leading neo-capitalist powers to homogenize world economy/ culture through elitist centralized organizations such as the World Bank, International Monetary Fund and World Trade Organization has triggered a populist backlash and motivated the usually dormant trade unions.

4. The reconciliation of previously splintered counterculture (urban "punk," rural "hippy," etc.) has allowed for a wider base from which shifts in popular social consciousness are disseminating.

5. Increased communications abilities throughout the populace have resulted in organizational/mobilization advances amongst the social protest and revolutionary Anarchist movements.

6. Experience gained by organizations throughout the last decade has vastly increased the practical ability of the movement as a whole.

7. The generational maturity of the children of the 60s and 70s has now come to full fruition. This is a fact that should not be overlooked as we intend to build on and further destroy where our mothers and fathers left off. And finally,

8. Police repression as experienced throughout the United States and Canada during the course of this last year and a half has had the result of radicalizing 10,000s of previously Liberal demonstrators from one coast to the other and back.

Anarchism and the Broader Movement

While the broader movement has affected some important practical and consciousness building victories, it is still too malleable and indecisive to put an uncritical trust in its visual organizations (as encapsulated in the Direct Action Network).

As revolutionary Anarchists we must continue to support and encourage its participatory and directly democratic currents while steering it away from its unconscious tendencies towards spectacular abstraction and Liberal capitulation. We must continue to do this through the dissemination of revolutionary Anarchist theory as well as by DIRECT example, both of the kind on the streets, in community organizing efforts and in regards to our lifestyles. This must continue to be a priority both at demonstrations as well as within the particularities of our local communities.

In this capacity we must be vigilant not to limit our dialectical interactions with the movement itself. In a word, we must continue to reach out to the yet included masses. For it is only through their direct participation that the present system of oppression will be forever disintegrated and thrown into the wastebasket of history.

The Development of the Movement

For all of the above reasons, this past year and a half has been marked as a progressive stepping-stone towards the continuing resurgence of the revolutionary Anarchist movement. This in spite of certain painful setbacks such as the demise of the Love and Rage organization. The objective historical situation, as well as our newfound practical abilities, has resulted in us moving two steps forward for every step back. However, before we become full of conceit, let it be said that we have many, many dangerous steps to traverse before we reach the end of this epic.

Our Local Communities

It is in our specific communities that we (Black Bloc and Anarchists generally) are able to push the evolutionary Anarchist movement forward through diligent and relevant community organizing throughout the ranks of the disenfranchised. Here we must continue to do this by forming workers' cooperatives, community centers, newspapers, the creation of Anarchist art as well as by direct political action whenever possible. At the large demonstrations we are able to push our movement forward by the organizing and subsequent action of our Black Bloc.

At Demonstrations

It is by virtue of the uncompromising militancy of this (our) Bloc that Liberal demonstrations are transformed into insurrectionary happenings. By physically defending ourselves against State (police) attacks, we add a serious dimension to an otherwise timid movement. By effectively defending non-violent protesters against the assaults of the police (such as at the A16 action in DC) we demonstrate the extra-symbolic power of the people while increasing the relative effectiveness of the overall action. By attacking and destroying Capitalist private property (such as in the Battle of Seattle) we go beyond rhetoric and actually inflict real material damage upon the urban out-posts of the oppressive and totally uninteresting commodified empire of the new Capitalists. By our method we transform indecisiveness and restraint into REAL action.

Those upper middle class Pacifists who clamor that we are wrong by virtue of our demonstrated principles should be reminded that the only legitimate goal of mass demonstrations is to effect relevant social and revolutionary change for the benefit of the working class, poor, and declassed peoples. It is not, nor never should ever be, to be arrested and brutally beaten for the sake of some vain association with Gandhi or Martin Luther King Jr. Furthermore, let us all reflect upon the fact that India today is presently in shambles due to continued Capitalist exploitation, and the American blacks are still treated as second-class citizens by the State apparatus and plutocracy alike. These are travesties that only a genuine and victorious international revolutionary Anarchist movement, utilizing both violent and non-violent methods, will be able to fully rectify.

 It is in this very real context that we fight. We will not, nor should we, compromise our hatred or love any more than we will compromise our goal of complete social revolution, Anarchy, and the dream of all of humanity unshackled from the chains which are both seen and unseen.

We make no apologies.

The Necessity of Increasing Our Tactical Abilities

However, the forces of the State (specifically the FBI and police) have been studying us for some time. Hence it is absolutely necessary that we further develop our tactical understanding and practical street abilities if we are to maintain, in fact increase, our militant capabilities.

In this regard there are some basic steps that we must take in order to meet this challenge:

1. Increased organization of street fighting force;
2. Regular physical training in between actions;
3. Facilitation of pre-emptive strikes;
4. Preparation for eventuality of intensified State oppression and the shifting of the movement of social protest into that of direct social revolution;
5. Increased internal social and political education between actions and development of theory.

At the present time, the mobilization of our forces is done in such haphazard manner that our ability to combat well-trained and disciplined State forces is limited. In fact it is only by virtue of our revolutionary dedication and iron constitutions that we have been able to combat these forces with the level of relative success that we thus far have. They (the forces of the State) fight out of hatred of diversity and free expression and for a paycheck. We fight out of hatred of oppression and love, and simply because it is the just thing to do.

However, as the agents of the State modify their present tactics, based on their direct experiences and vast intelligence reports from Seattle to Quebec City, they can be expected to achieve a further level of effective superiority over us in the near future. Therefore, it is absolutely necessary that we begin to reorganize ourselves in such a way as to again bring certain advantages to our side.

Increased Organization of Street Fighting Force: The Formation of an Elected Tactical Facilitation Core

Our experiences over the course of the last year and a half have taught us a lot regarding the actual and potential effectiveness of Black Blocs during large demonstrations.[30] A16 demonstrated the effectiveness of a large Bloc when used in tight conjunction with non-violent, direct action oriented contingents. It showed us how the combined tactics of physical self-defense (from the Bloc) and non-violent lockdowns can, at this historical juncture, result in effective occupation of large sections of the city-scape. J20 showed how a tightly knit Bloc, lined with defensive banners around its perimeters, can help foster confidence and act as a more substantial deterrent to targeted police arrests. A20 showed how even a relatively small Bloc (as on Saturday, the 21st) can become a substantial fighting force when the physical and mental commitment is there. However, our experiences have also illustrated certain shortcomings that we thus far are yet to overcome. Specifically our lack of a democratic tactical command structure has hindered our abilities to act with more punctuating speed and tactical ferociousness. In certain circumstances this failure has resulted in us becoming bogged down in indecisiveness (specifically regarding movement), and hence has put us in danger as well as led to arrests (i.e. on the Monday of the A16 action) . Therefore, we contend that

---

30 2017 note from the author: I marched in my first Black Bloc in Chicago during the demonstrations against Bill Clinton and the Democratic National Convention. With me was my cousin Chris P. who is now an IBEW Union Steward, and comrade AM.

we need to develop a democratic tactical command structure that heightens our mobility while simultaneously not compromising our Anarchist principles.

In regard to this, we propose that the present use of elected affinity group spokespeople be expanded to that of acute tactical facilitator (a-tacs). The role of this person should be to help facilitate the organized movement of their immediate section as recommended by the general tactical facilitation core (*to be discussed below). In addition, each affinity group should also elect an alternate in case the first is incapacitated due to injury or arrest.

Following the general meeting of the Black Bloc, at which the broad plans for the day's action should have already been discussed debated and then decided upon based on consensus, all such elected a-tacs should meet in private (such privacy here is recommended as a security precaution) . At this meeting a general tactical facilitation core (g-tacs) should be elected, again by consensus. These g-tacs should act as the facilitators of Bloc movement in such a way as it complies with the general plan of action as defined at the prior open meeting. The identity of the g-tacs will be made discreetly known to all trusted affinity group members through their elected spokes/a-tacs as befitting following the conclusion of the closed spokespeople's meeting. Any affinity group which has had their a-tac elected to the tactical facilitation core should elect a new a-tac.

In cases in which the Bloc is expected to be large and to march en masse, affinity groups should be made responsible for specific positions within the Bloc; specifically the front, right side, left side and rear (this should be done at the general open meeting). This would essentially create four main perimeter clusters within the Bloc. (Note: the use of clusters is further discussed below.) In turn the elected g-tacs should number 12 persons. These persons should emanate out of the perimeter clusters, which they will be responsible for (this will be further discussed below). These twelve should be further divided into four groups of three. In turn these three should be positioned as such:

1. A person at the specific perimeter cluster, which they will be directly responsible for (front, rear, left or right);

2. A person near the middle of the Bloc where they will be together with the representatives of the other perimeter clusters;

3. A person to act as a runner between their perimeter cluster g-tac and the g-tac group in the middle.

In general, all time-sensitive decisions specifically regarding movement should be recommended by the consensus of the central g-tac core based on information emanating from the specific perimeter tacs, and reliable reconnaissance information.

In addition, these g-tacs should also entail certain role-specific support persons in order that they are able to function efficiently and safely. Hence, all g-tacs stationed at the perimeters should be equipped with two persons from their affinity group or otherwise, one of which should be responsible for maintaining radio communication with reconnaissance teams and/or other important constituents. The other should be present in order to watch the tac's back. We must be aware of the fact that these folk will quickly be identified by the forces of the State, and therefore will likely be singled out for arrest. Likewise, the central g-tac core should also be equipped with a few persons on radio, and a few persons concerning themselves with security.

Also, the specific roles of the various g-tacs, be it runner, perimeter person or core group, should be rotated as the day's action ensues. Again, such a rotation is to limit any developing trend aimed at a psychological tendency towards authoritarianism amongst the central g-tac core. And again, it should be reminded that the function of these folk would primarily have to do with Bloc movement (i.e. which road to take, which way to go at an intersection). They will not be playing the role of generals or abstract leaders in any way.

Here it is important to stress several things. First, we do not advocate the creating of a permanent officer clique. These elected positions should only last as long as the action at hand. If the action lasts more than a single day, then it would be good to elect new tacs for the different days. Also, their positions should be revocable by the general whole at any time.

Lastly, the influence which they shall wield will not be beyond the role of facilitators of a general plan adopted to the general meeting of the Black Bloc. Any steps they may attempt to take beyond these perimeters would be grounds for dismissal. And of course, we are not advocating the formalization of any authoritarian army structure. It must be made clear that all participants in the Bloc innately reserve the right to disobey tac suggestions as well as to desert. In this the adoption of such a structure would be consistent with Anarchist principles of organization. The Anarchist militias recognized the need for such structure during the Spanish Civil War and so should we.

Individual Affinity Groups

Affinity groups, generally numbering between 3 and 10 persons, should organize themselves in ways in which they see fit to reach their goals in the specific action at hand. Determining the focus of your affinity group in relevance to the specific action allows for the creation of a specialized affinity group.

Within these affinity groups, it is suggested that there be one person who carries a skeletal assortment of first aid equipment (saline solution, vinegar, lemon peels, water in a squirt bottle, rescue remedy). Furthermore, it would seem a very sound suggestion that every person involved in the Black Bloc take a basic first aid course, or have general knowledge of protest-related first aid practices. Like physical training, being trained in first aid would heighten our overall combat abilities.

It should be decided if the affinity group must use a radio/cell during the action. Radio/cell use may be needed in certain affinity groups, but by no means is it necessary to overflow the streets with unneeded communication devices. Communication can in turn be lost by the trampling of channels and untrained use. More radios will never be the answer to organization and information, but the strategic placing and use of these devices will forever enable our effectiveness. Roles of the other persons in the affinity group, in addition to the aforementioned role of the medic and possible use of a radio/cell operator, depend upon the type of affinity group (function) . The affinity group should solely decide this themselves.

Types of specialized affinity groups include, but are not limited to, a front line (defensive), offensive, reconnaissance, property related, medic, support, noise, and pre-emptive.

A front line affinity group would contain shields and/or heavy body armor. This type of affinity group would potentially oversee the formation of the front line. They would motivate and call for other shields from within the Bloc, in aiding the formation of a solid line. This affinity group would provide a rally point to help provide the Bloc position. They would not be a part of a charge line, but instead hold as a point to retreat back to if the charge proves faulty. In addition, this affinity group is at the correct position to oversee the building of barricades.

An offensive affinity group should be highly mobile and enthusiastic. These affinity groups should be prepared for confrontation. The offensive affinity group can also come prepared to fill specialized tactical needs. Creativity is encouraged. The definition of this group will be left at this.

A reconnaissance affinity group operates outside of the Bloc, gathering information. Communication is held closely with the larger Bloc, keeping them informed of police movements and numbers. When State weaknesses are detected, this affinity group should inform the Bloc of opportunities for advancement.

The Bloc should have their own medic affinity group. For optimal coverage, medic groups could split to cover all sides of the Bloc as a whole. Having our own medics does not mean that they help only Black Bloc members, but ensures their movement with the Bloc.

Property-related affinity groups also exist in our movement. The roles of these people should not be known to anyone who is not in that specific affinity group. In relation, information on affinity groups who form for pre-emptive strikes against the State should also be held from the Bloc. Any information on the plans or existence of these two groups will only weaken their security.

There are also support affinity group roles. One idea is an affinity group dedicated to dealing with panic situations. This group would number no more than a few groups per cluster/side (the use of clusters is explained below).

There could also be a supply and networking affinity group responsible for carrying food, water, and handing out communiques to neighborhood people and non-Black Bloc protesters. The carrying of water also has a dual purpose of use for eye washing if necessary.

A noise affinity group is useful in keeping enthusiasm and drive in tiring situations. The sound of music can create sudden drives of energy and joy within the Bloc where none exists, and can send a contradicting message of power to the enemy in battle. Creativity is also encouraged in this area; i.e., Black Bloc bagpipe players would bring immense courage and enthusiasm to many, as radical cheerleading does to others. We should continue to embrace, and forever elaborate, on this humanistic approach to battle through music and cheer. For this is in our favor, and the State is forever unlikely to employ such an emotional tactic.

Clusters

An affinity group should strive to be a part of a cluster of 5–10 diverse affinity groups. Each cluster should have its own flag to serve as a rally point. These flags, distinguishable by different patterns or colors, would be used as markers. The purpose of these markers is to serve as a point of retreat, or simply as a visual aid if a person(s) is severed from an affinity group. Each cluster should be able to function as its own entity. To facilitate this, affinity groups should strive towards communication prior to attendance at the action.

Clusters naturally form based on trust relationships between diverse individuals and collectives, and should continue by these means. This being said, the general meeting of the Black Bloc should still be used as an opportunity for practical networking; such as what specialized affinity groups are needed to complete the offense, defense, and support of a cluster, enabling the cluster a fully functioning body. When a pre-organized cluster decides that it is lacking in certain of these categories, and when that cluster feels comfortable incorporating a relevant at-large affinity group into their fold, then by all means they should do so. Here, the more balanced and self-contained we can make the various clusters the better. And, the more affinity groups are connected with larger functioning clusters, the more effective and secure the overall action will be.

Each cluster should take responsibility for certain aspects of the Black Bloc as an entity. The basic options for a cluster to choose from should be 1.) perimeter clusters, 2.) at-large clusters and 3) reserve clusters (*reserve clusters are discussed below in the section titled 'reserves'). The organization of the clusters into the above roles should be done at the general meeting of the Black Bloc, before the spokes/a-tac meeting.

The Black Bloc as a physical entity in motion should be defined by the formations of four perimeter clusters. One taking its position at the front, another at the rear, and the other two on the right and left. As mentioned above, each of these four perimeter clusters should be equipped with a distinct flag, so as to provide an obvious rallying point.

These perimeter clusters must take responsibility for maintaining a tight line of security around all edges of the Bloc as a whole. Specifically, they should concern themselves with the section which they are directly situated (front, rear, left, right).

It is also desirable that the various defensive and offensive affinity groups and persons of each perimeter cluster work in organized conjunction with each other during times of need. For example, if the Bloc finds it necessary to retreat from a given position, all persons from within the effected perimeter cluster and all noncluster/at-large cluster folks carrying defensive equipment such as shields should maintain a position in the rear, facing the enemy, in order to cover the retreat from rubber bullets, bean bags, etc. Likewise, during offensive maneuvers, all persons equipped with the relevant offensive gear should place themselves in the front, as should a limited number of shield bearers in order to limit the effectiveness of the enemy baton. When necessary, relevant reinforcements from the other perimeter clusters should be prepared to move into the fray. However, this should only be done when absolutely necessary in that it is always desirable to maintain a strong defensive perimeter around the Bloc as a whole. This is all common sense of course.

At-large clusters should maintain positions within the space created by the formations of the four perimeter clusters. They should act according to their own direction, yet be prepared to reinforce the perimeter clusters, if attacked. Also, a major task for the at-large clusters should be the organization of charging lines prepared to go over and through police/military defensive positions when and if desirable and/or necessary.

Towards this goal, it may prove desirable to utilize tactics previously practiced by (among others) German black blocs. Namely that the interior of the Bloc be organized by straight lines (from right to left), each line being one or two affinity groups. In turn, affinity groups forming an at-large cluster should consciously position themselves in successive lines. Such lines make for tighter internal security, while clearly allowing for the Bloc to conduct sustained and successive charges against the enemy if and when such an action becomes necessary.

Property related affinity groups, be they connected with an at-large cluster, or independent, should be allowed free access in and out of the body of the Bloc by the relevant perimeter clusters as necessary.

The organization, or rather ability to call for the practice of such above discussed maneuvers, should often be expected to emanate from the g-tacs as manifest through the cooperation of affinity groups. For it will be the g-tacs who are generally most informed about the overall combat situation, and positioning of the Bloc. This is a tactical practice that the g-tacs should be prepared to responsibly facilitate.

All and all, the further incorporation of the above cluster model can be expected to result in ourselves achieving a higher level of immediate situational tactical ability than we currently possess. In addition, the demonstration of such abilities can be expected to frighten and demoralize the enemy.

Reconnaissance and Communication

It is necessary that the Bloc contains a sophisticated system of combat reconnaissance and communications. Reconnaissance should be conducted by pairs and/or affinity groups on bicycles equipped with radios and/or cell phones. In turn, the general tactical facilitation core should also be in possession of radios and/or cell phones. Throughout the action, reconnaissance teams should be scouting out all possible avenues of Bloc travel and consistently be reporting back to the g-tacs. This way, the mobilization of the Bloc will be able to be conducted with a reasonable level of educated decisiveness.

Other elements of the reconnaissance folk should be operating in action zones not immediately in the vicinity of the Bloc. The purpose of these is to keep the Bloc informed on the general situation of the broader action, and in turn, be able to notify the g-tacs of potential hot spots where Bloc presence is required.

Individual affinity groups who are in possession of radios should be informed as to the channels on which such communications will occur. This way the Bloc as a whole will be generally informed in regards to the broader situation.

Also, non-Black Bloc affinity groups involved in acts of civil disobedience should also be informed as to the channels of radio operation as well as the numbers of the relevant cell phones, so as to allow them the ability to call in for assistance when and where necessary.

Finally, as alluded to above, persons directly involved in reconnaissance should be expected to emanate out of the various clusters. However, a more desirable method would be for a whole affinity group to converge on the action prepared to act as a specialized cell in and of itself. Preferably this group would reside in the city in which the action is taking place, in that such persons would be in a better position to scout such already known urban terrain. In addition, those who choose to act in a communications role need to have radio skills. Various codes and channels to use should be discussed only with other Bloc members who hold radios. There are several tactics which can be used when doing communications. Each cluster should arrive to the action with methods for communicating internally.

Reserves

Historically many battles have been won by the situational deployment of reserves as a tactical force. This tactic has traditionally been practiced and proven successful by the United States military and police departments. The use of a reserve force is not currently a tactic adopted by the North American Black Bloc. It is important that we consider this tactic as one that could potentially enable us to better combat the brawn of the State.

The State has always had the advantage over us when it comes to brute force. Their ability to use reserves, bringing in busses full of fresh, new, geared up soldiers, will always be a threat to us. We, on the other hand, spend hours/days fighting with the same gear and little, if any, relief from our strains. In all fairness, we must study the military tactics employed by State forces and adopt those elements which are relevant, effective, and consistent with our beliefs as Anarchists.

The potential use of Black Bloc reserves could prove empowering for several reasons. One being that the use of reserves has historically proven to be successful. Second, imagine the psychological effects this somewhat sophisticated tactic would hold over minds of the State. Both these points being said, this does not mean that reserves should always be used when a Black Bloc has presence at an action, it is only to say that such possibilities can be discussed during the general meetings of the Bloc. Deciding whether reserves will be used should occur in planning, before the acute manifestation of the action at hand.

When a reserve force is organized at an action, they can be used when the larger Bloc is surrounded by police. In this circumstance, the reserves are called in to fight a police line from the other side, resulting in the police being surrounded by the Bloc as a whole. In addition, reserves can be used to hold a location for the larger Bloc to later use as a destination for retreat. Sending in a smaller number of reserves could also be ideal for added force to push through a police line or barricade.

The U.S. Army holds one third of their people back as use for reserves. This is an ideal number for a fighting force that can make a strong push when an optimal battle point is reached. With this in mind, when the Black Bloc reaches over one thousand, it would be desirable to hold 300 or so in reserve. This number should change with proportion. If the Bloc reaches two thousand, numbers held in reserve should reach about 600. If the Bloc is less than one thousand, no reserve should be posted. With such small numbers, a reserve force would only result in the general weakening of the Bloc when we need all able bodies for immediate release on the streets.

There are pros and cons for our Bloc to discover when and if there is a decision to use a reserve force. These must be recognized, and therefore it is important that options be discussed. City-scape (i.e. are the roads narrow or wide?), Bloc/police size, and the situation of the action on hand (are large portions of the city occupied by non-violent lockdowns or are police/national guard free to roam the urban terrain?) must be weighed. This should all occur at the general meetings of the Bloc. The details of forming a reserve, if any, and means of communication should be discussed after the election of the g-tacs at the spokes/a-tac meeting. Following the election, such sensitive information can be worked out at a g-tac meeting where only those with an immediate interest are present.

This meeting should establish the location of the inactive reserves, as well as radio/cell communication procedures. This reserve force should maintain radio/cell communication with the body of the Bloc by communicating with the g-tacs. Decision to mobilize should be placed in the hands of the g-tacs. Note that the g-tacs receive their information on the seriousness of combat and the need for reserves from cells of the larger Bloc. The g-tac's decision to mobilize a number of inactive reserves is given when groups within the larger Bloc call for backup. Relying on this is important in order to consider the many needs of the active members of the Black Bloc.

Deployment (where and how many) of the reserves should be left to the g-tacs. Specifics of how to meet this deployment through which streets to take, etc., should be left to the affected affinity groups. When speed becomes an issue, the elected a-tacs within the effected affinity groups should be prepared to make educated suggestions (which those affected are free to adopt or not) . The exact location of the reserve forces should not be revealed to the Bloc as a whole. The only people who should be informed of their exact location should be the g-tacs. It is also suggested that location of the reserves are formally decided upon at the last moments, when the position is soon to be held. This is necessary in that the common knowledge of their location would expected to result in this information leaking into police hands through common infiltration techniques. In turn, this knowledge would almost certainly result in the State (police) attacking our isolated forces.

All reserve forces should be divided into reserve clusters of roughly fifty persons each and be strategically placed around the action zone. Reserve clusters of fifty would be desirable in that such a number is small enough to maintain optimal mobility and non-visibility (to the searching eyes of the State), while being large enough to maintain a minimum of self-contained fighting ability. Such a reserve cluster would be large enough to fight their way through a regular police line if necessary (one row deep 24 across or two rows deep/12 across each), to reunite, when called for, with the larger Bloc. Dividing these forces into such smaller, more manageable reserve clusters, allows for them to be called in as needed. It essentially skips the step taken to divide numbers of the reserved Bloc, and allows for greater security in the event that reserve locations are discovered by the State (where it is possible that one cluster is uncovered by the State, it is unlikely that all will be).

As alluded to above, it is not always necessary when reserves are needed, to call all of their existing numbers. The further division of these reserves into smaller clusters allows them to be called in based on geographic proximity and/or required force, and will result in optimal mobility.

When a relatively large number of reserves are called in, say three clusters of fifty, they could converge on the acute scene of battle from several directions. When properly utilized, such tactics could be expected to confuse and stifle the State's comprehension of the developing combat situation. It is also conceivable that such tactics could be coordinated so as such enemy forces are effectively flanked, thereby forcing the enemy into retreat, or routing them entirely.

When the reserve force is inactive, a low profile must be maintained. They should keep a distance that places them away from acute attack, while being close enough so that the police cannot easily break their reemerging with the rest of the Bloc. The distance the reserve clusters fall back from the larger Bloc could be just a few city blocks, but nonetheless should be decided by the reserves clusters themselves, with g-tac input.

Lettering of the reserve clusters would be beneficial for g-tacs to better manage the location of these reserves. For example, reserve cluster B resides on the East side of the larger Black Bloc, and the g-tacs know this. The g-tacs are then able to call for reserve cluster B, (simply by referring to 'cluster B') without giving an extraneous amount of directions and information over the radio/cell, therefore resulting in less information for the State to get their hands on. We should assume always that there are infiltrators leeching around us, and the word 'reserves' should never be used when communicating in public.

Prior to the reemerging with the Black Bloc, combat with the State should be avoided by these reserves, unless in self-defense, or unavoidable. Maintaining a low profile is vital. It is desirable that the reserves de-Bloc and become 'regular.' Black Bloc clothing should be worn underneath 'regular' clothing. This enables the reserves to blend in better and become less distinguishable as members of the Black Bloc to police helicopters and informants of the State. When they are called for by the g-tacs, the reserve cluster(s) should remove their 'regular' clothing to reveal their true colors underneath. The 'regular' clothing could be discarded and thrown away. Keeping a change of clothing on your person for later use is, of course, a personal decision. However, anything which is not of absolute necessity, should not be carried.

The absolute condition necessary for reserve effectiveness is deployment speed. Without this, they may be prevented from reemerging with the larger Bloc and/or fail to reach the scene of acute action at a time when their force can swing the immediate struggle in our favor. For this purpose the reserves should be organized as a sort of light infantry. They should possess only the minimum of riot gear to refrain from their being weighted down. This means that they should eliminate gear which would obstruct quick lightweight movement, such as helmets, shields, heavy body armor, or large backpacks. They should be equipped only with gas masks or vinegar-soaked bandannas, and a minimum of offensive gear (as individuals and affinity groups see necessary). The only exception to this should be the medics, who should carry a skeleton assortment of related equipment. It would be ideal if all reserves were equipped with bicycles so that the greatest level of mobility could be reached. Such bicycles can be used for offense and defense, and must be discardable. However, in the absence of such bikes, reserve clusters should be composed of affinity groups/individuals who are in good cardiovascular shape. These forces must be prepared to run up to a mile at full speed, and then immediately engage in battle. This is something to keep in mind when such forces are being initially organized.

When and where this reserve is utilized correctly with speed and strength, it can be expected to cause surprise and demoralization among the ranks of the enemy. The very fact that we demonstrate these fairly sophisticated maneuvers can be expected to result in the enemy questioning their personal security and apparent tactical superiority. It is just such objective and subjective shifts and developments at the acute scene of conflict that can and will lend itself to the swinging of fighting momentum to our side. Of course, this positive development can and will only be sustained if the Bloc holds fast in the face of the increased police ferociousness and brutality in the conflict at hand. This situation should be expected to occur in direct relation to police feeling that they are in real danger due to our utilization of serious tactics. Here, one should recall that all animals are most dangerous when they are backed in a corner and sense their own demise.

Additional Security Precautions: Maps, Radios, IDs, Names, Etc.

While it is sensible that all affinity groups (all persons for that matter) have a detailed map of the area of operation, it has been proven that such maps must absolutely be marked only in code. During the R2k action in Philly, at least two Black Bloc individuals were arrested in a pre-emptive strike approximately forty-five minutes after a Black Bloc meeting (at which they were in attendance) and an hour and a half prior to the demonstration proper. On their persons were maps of the downtown equipped with penned-in locations of the various Black Bloc emergency convergence sites as well as areas where the Bloc intended to focus their activity as well as locations where they planned on marching in order to accumulate material for barricade construction when and if the day's developments demanded.

These maps were not encrypted, and therefore, by detaining, searching and subsequently recovering these maps from these individuals the police achieved the advantage of knowing the intended movement of the Bloc before it happened. It is impossible to know exactly what effect this intelligence had on the day's events (as it is also difficult to surmise whether or not the police had informants at the prior meeting as some have maintained), but regardless, this mishap represented a major slip in security. Therefore, it is absolutely necessary that from now on all such maps be encrypted so as to avoid this slip up.

In addition, all radio communication should be conducted with the use of preplanned codes and frequencies where and whenever possible. All such codes and frequencies should be made known to all parties who have a legitimate interest in maintaining radio communication with us.

Also, it should go without saying that nobody, under any circumstances, should carry any form of ID or personal contact information. If you get arrested with this information it will only be used to [mess with] you.

Lastly, do not refer to yourself or others you know by your real full name while in the vicinity of the action. The less we make public our actual identities the better off we are regarding possible legal action and State harassment.

Communiques

It is important that all Black Bloc actions be followed with a comprehensive communique, which is whenever possible composed by a large representative volunteer committee from the various affinity groups. This communique should discuss the action in terms of why it occurred, why specific conflicts/tactics developed and how this immediate struggle is connected with the broader Anarchist movement towards a liberated and creative world.

To achieve this, a post action meeting should be arranged at a secure location. The details of when and where it will be held should be decided upon at the pre-action meeting of elected a-tacs/spokespeople (after all other issues are resolved) or at the general pre-action meeting of the entire Black Bloc (also after all other issues are resolved.

Such communiques are important in regards to reaching out to the broader populace, as well as in debunking the demonization of our activities as can be expected to emanate out of the corporate press (and also often from the Liberal Left and orthodox/conservative Communist press).

In addition to a post-action communique, it is also important that separate communiques be composed prior to the action and distributed during the action. These should also discuss the reasons why we take to the (our) streets the way we do as well as address the broader social issues which brought us to the action at hand. The individual affinity groups should facilitate these. In turn the affinity groups and/or relevant support persons/support affinity groups should take the responsibility of distributing them during the action to the public and the Left-independent media as they see fit. All such communiques should be signed with the name of the responsible affinity group or individual as to maintain accountability. All anonymous statements must be assumed to emanate out of the bowels of State, with the purpose of discrediting us.

Anarchist Principles of Tactical Leadership

The idea of setting up such a democratic chain of command is not to diminish the free spontaneity of the Bloc, but is simply to increase the general mobility and fighting ability of the Black Bloc during time of need.

The primary functions of the above discussed general tactical facilitation core (g-tacs) will simply be to guide the direction of Bloc movement and the ability to call for the deployment of reserve clusters. In regards to the former, this would minimize regrettable time consuming debates as to "which way to go at various intersections." The more we can avoid such time-consuming indecisiveness the better, as such slowdowns carry with them the potential to put the whole Bloc in danger of police surrounding and subsequent immobilization. And given the forces of the State's advantage in weaponry, immobilization is akin to defeat. Such was the case during the A16 action on Monday, where shortly thereafter the tail end of the Bloc (who was then immersed with non-Bloc elements) was cordoned off by police and subsequently arrested.

In regards to the latter, such ability to call in reserves at relevant times could be the difference between immediate victory or defeat. And in this case it is necessary to place this ability in the hands of the elected g-tacs in order to guard against any misuse brought on by agent provocateurs, and/or to prevent general time-consuming tactical debates which the heat of direct conflict does not allow for.

With this proposed organizational model, a relatively small Black Bloc (containing no reserves) numbering roughly 200 would have the effectiveness of twice that number in regards to our present abilities. And likewise, a larger Bloc numbering 700, with a reserve force of 300, would dramatically gain in tactical ability.

Physical Training In Between Actions

In between actions it is of vast importance that we increase our physical abilities through the practice of regular exercise, muscle building and self-defense training. At present, the Black Bloc is considerably lacking in certain of these compartments. This is true to the point where individuals who possess muscle tone are sometimes distrusted as potential police agents.

The fact is, if we are going to defend ourselves against the forces of the State, we should take our physical conditioning at least as seriously as our enemy does, and preferably more seriously. The reactionary police and military are aware of the importance of this in regards to their own effectiveness, and so should we.

Pre-emptive Actions

The forces of the State are regularly known to take pre-emptive measures against demonstrators prior to their actions. They regularly infiltrate us and make arrests before any general demonstration or acts of civil disobedience begin. They also start their tactical mobilization long before the sun comes up prior to the demonstrations on any particular day. In order to neutralize this advantage, limited elements presently engaged in Black Bloc actions should independently take countermeasures. Here sabotage of police (and when necessary, National Guard) equipment is our best bet.

If one of the primary advantages of the forces of the State is their mechanized mobility, then we should strike out against these repressive tools by effective, clandestine means.

Separate affinity groups under their own direction should voluntarily coordinate such actions. These groups should number very few in relation to the broader Bloc, and should not take part in any subsequent above ground actions thereafter during the day's events. In addition, the intent and identity of these groups should obviously remain absolutely secret to the Bloc as a whole.

There can be no chain of command between them and the rest. They must operate completely on their own, voluntarily, and by structural models of their choosing (as long as they are consistent with Anarchist principles of organization). Such clandestine activity, if performed effectively, holds the possibility of considerably disrupting the abilities of the enemy, and therefore can substantially place new advantages with the Black Bloc.

Preparations For Increased State Repression

The stronger our movement becomes, the more likely it will be that the State will more thoroughly criminalize Anarchism, specifically of the Black Bloc variety.[31] As we speak, we must assume that the FBI has

---

31 2017 note from the author: I was arrested in 2000 while seeking to protest the Republic National Convention with the Black Bloc. However, comrade AM and I were picked up about an hour *before* the planned action (shortly after attending a planning meeting of the Black Bloc). I was charged with 'possession of instruments of crime' and 'possession if instruments of crime, conspiracy.' After three days I was released on a $10,000 SOB which would be owed if I failed to appear in court. I never did appear in court and a warrant was issued for my arrest (which stands to this day). In 2001 I was also arrested in Columbus Ohio at a demonstration against the prison system. There I was charged with a class

already compiled a dossier on many of us. We must also assume that many of our local Anarchist organizations and collectives are already being watched and that infiltrators are working on penetrating our ranks; in certain cases we have no doubt that they already have.

In addition, as our movement progresses into more serious phases, we must anticipate a much more violent State reaction against us. This clearly occurred in the late 60s and we must fully understand that it will happen again. This tendency is already developing a clear trajectory. The shooting of three demonstrators at the Gothenburg protests, and the killing of Carlo in Genoa illustrates this as an undeniable fact.

As committed revolutionaries of practical mind, we must prepare for eventualities. This is no game. In such we must form clandestine networks wherein we can maintain the ability to exist as an underground fighting force if and when the circumstances demand. Such an underground force must entail, among other things, access to alternative identification, known and trusted safe houses, friends in strategic positions, access to materials of necessary subsistence (i.e. food, medicine, etc.), an underground means of communication, ways to pass unseen through international borders and the know-how to continue our militant activities underground.

The fact of the matter is, when our above-ground activities draw the response of police shotgun blasts, the mass long term incarceration of our militants, or when it all becomes a socially acceptable farce within the blanket of the spectacle, then we must be prepared to meet the challenges of the State by other means; still militant and concrete, yet underground.

Furthermore, it must be understood that when extreme crisis situations occur, the kind which would force us underground, there will not be the time to organize the basic means of such an existence. Likewise, when the greater social breakdown of the presently dominant system occurs, there will not be time to organize a solid popular fighting force. Therefore, we must prepare now for that which we recognize as an inevitable outcome of our revolutionary activities.

IV felony, destruction of government property. After a week in jail and posting $1200 cash I was released. While those charges were reduced to misdemeanor levels, I ended up vacating the resulting probation requirements and therefore am also wanted in the State of Ohio. If apprehended in this state, I would owe them three months in prison. Therefore Ohio and PA are states I seek to avoid, or stay under the radar in if and when I am compelled to step foot in it.

We must and will attack the leviathan head on, then from the shadows, and then again face-to-face. The only result can be social revolution.

Here we would like to remind you that firearms are still legal, as of print, and easily attainable in the United States.

Development of Our Social and Political Understandings

Lastly, we must practice self-discipline in regards to our continuing practical and theoretical studies of social and political ideas during the times in between actions. For the Anarchist movement, as stated by Bakunin, is driven by "the instinct to rebel," but it is also done so by the conscious emergence of a revolutionary people. The folk who make up the Black Bloc should be examples not just of Anarchist fighting courage, but also of Anarchist awareness. We should study the histories of the Paris Commune, Revolutionary Ukraine, Kronstadt, Spain, as well as the Paris revolt of '68. In addition we should read the writings of Bakunin, Kropotkin, Makhno, Emma Goldman, Meltzer, Guy Debord, and Bookchin to name but a few.

In a word, we must expand our relevant understandings in order to completely transcend the oppressive indoctrination that the State has perpetuated on us since the time of our birth. We must exercise our capacity for understanding in order to realize our creative consciousness. And finally, we must strive to further develop Anarchist theory in directions directly relevant to the contemporary modes of neo-Capitalism; namely that of radical commodification and consumerism.

Conclusion

In conclusion, this communique is put forward with the intent to spark the constructive development of our revolutionary abilities. It is not meant to be authoritative as much as it is intended to facilitate a positive internal dialogue. However, it is our hope that at least some of the above suggestions are seriously debated and then adopted by our fellow Black Bloc Anarchists.

We encourage you to replicate and distribute this communique however you choose (as long as it is not done for Capitalist profit).

In Solidarity,

—The Green Mountain Anarchist Collective
& Anti-Racist Action

Anti-WTO Protests & The Battle of Seattle[32]

Black Bloc, Seattle Washington, 1999

Seattle is the action which has put the present (2002) social protest movement on the map of North American mass consciousness. It did not mark the beginning (or end) of a movement. Rather it represented the first significant expression of social unrest against the capitalist slave system in the U.S.A. in a generation. With the joining in of the North American population, the movement against the contemporary modes of capitalism has truly become international, and everywhere.[33]

Seattle was a glorious rebirth of a demand for an end to the insulting and deadly march of corporate power. The world is in the hands of irresponsible, money starved vampire organizations who feed themselves by the selling and trade of increasingly trivial and noxious products. The most powerful of these organizations are the World Trade Organization (WTO), the International Monetary Fund (IMF)

---

32 2017 note from the author: This essay was written in 2001 and was first printed in The Black Bloc Papers, Insubordinate Editions, Baltimore MD, 2002.

33 2017 note from the author: I was not in Seattle or even North America when it hit. At the moment I was living in Seville, Spain. By the fall of 1999 I was vaguely aware of the planned protest (a flyer made its way to the farm I was working on in the Northeast Kingdom of Vermont), but I saw no reason to ascribe historic dimensions to this looming protest. When the demonstrations did hit, I was as surprised as the rest of the world when in was front page news in the Spanish newspapers. In my neighborhood in Spain (Alameda de Hercules) the local branch of the Socialist Party organized discussions about the actions (which I attended). I also took it upon myself to spray-paint a large statement of solidarity with the protesters on our local government building.

and the World Bank (WB). The functioning fact of these intensely authoritarian, abstract and elitist organizations unquestionably warrants a protest, if not a global civil war.

To begin to completely understand the significance of Seattle, one must first understand the international movement against neo-Liberalism in which it is situated. America is, in fact, a rather late bloomer within the scope of protests pertaining to the global problems endorsed and pursued by world Capitalist organizations. Protests against the WTO and the IMF and other like organizations ran rampant throughout the world long before Seattle. In 1998, over 28 countries held anti-Capitalist protests on June 18th (J18), timed to coincide with a meeting of the Group of Eight (G8). The most notable among these were in India and Brazil where in the former, hundreds of thousands took to the streets. During that same year the United States itself began to rumble with protests, small riots, capitalist property-related arsons and bombings (most of these were claimed by the underground Earth Liberation Front).[34]

In addition, large sectors of the world were and continue to be in a process of de-stabilization due to popular uprisings against a forced capitalist program (i.e. the continuing Zapatista revolution in southern Mexico, the popular uprisings in Bolivia and Ecuador, the increasing riots in Europe, and serious workers' strikes in Russia).

At N30 (November 30, 1999 in Seattle) up to 100,000 people from within organized labor and the Left took to the streets in order to put forth their opposition to the World Trade Organization. Within this vast array of demonstrators, an Anarchist Black Bloc took to the streets in order to inflict material damage upon corporate banks/businesses, correctly viewed by them as real incarnations of the economically and culturally homogenizing Capitalist force we are beholden to. The Bloc, following police attacks on non-violent protesters, proceeded to move through the streets of Seattle smashing bank and corporate windows. In some cases the contents of the business in question were expropriated from the building and subsequently left in the streets. State officials contend that the Bloc inflicted $10,000,000 in

---

34 2017 note from the author: The Statute of Limitations having past, I will say here that I took part in an Earth Liberation Front action in 1998 in West Nyack NY (which is the home town of my mother, Cheryl "Partridge" Van Deusen, and the entire maternal side of my family). The action, which included CP, targeted a developer who was clearing woods in order to construct expensive upper middle class homes. The woods in question were located in the edge of a working class neighborhood and were used by locals (including my personal friends and family) for outdoor recreation. The action included the pulling up of survey flags, spray-painting ELF graffiti, and the sabotaging of heavy equipment. An ELF communique (which I no longer possess) was sent to the local daily newspaper, but as far as I know was never published.

damage. This is most likely an overestimation designed to blame the Anarchists for damage caused directly by the police force, and at any rate is most likely just misinformation.

The main thing to remember when thinking of N30 is that it was an action of such scope and power that it caught the American public by surprise, thereby giving birth to a momentum which has continued to provide a positive revolutionary impetus within the confines of American society.

That being said, it did not materialize out of nowhere. Rather it was the flower of a decade of domestic organizing and hard won movement and growth. But still, Seattle marked the time when it all came together. We had our own sophisticated Independent Media Center (IMC). We had training and years of proven tactics at our disposal. We had dedicated radical legal teams. We had an intended program of 'jail solidarity.' We had the rank and file union workers turning out in common cause. We had the radical environmentalists. We had a diversity of tactics ranging from legal rallies to port side strikes/shutdowns, from non-violent sit-ins/blockades to physical self-defense and corporate property destruction.

A significant part of this mass mobilization was organized through directly democratic and participatory means via open spokes-councils (these pre-planning meetings were open to all protesters and functioned through the vocal participation of spokespeople from the numerous affinity groups involved). In short, we finally had the functioning mass coalition that has been lacking in the United States since the Great Depression of the 1930s. We finally had a chance; and for that we could not be ignored.

In all, the protests consisted of four main days which coincided with the scheduled 'behind closed doors' meetings of the WTO delegates. The delegates' stated task was to map out an economic strategy for the new century/millennium. The direct action oriented protesters' stated task was to shut down the undemocratic and anti-worker proceedings. Given the mutually exclusive goals of these factions, it was clear that only one or the other would succeed. And in this case, we, the people, won.

The opening day of the WTO meetings (Tuesday, November 30th) were met with thousands of direct action protesters occupying all key access routes to the planned site of the meeting. Police responded with violence (tear gas, rubber, wooden and plastic bullets, batons, etc.) but the protesters would not relinquish control of the streets. Elements of the Black Bloc met police assaults with acts of physical self-defense and counter-aggression. Bottles, rocks, etc. were hurled at advancing police lines. Dumpsters were dragged out onto the street and lit on fire. Also, a highly mobile Black Bloc roved the downtown smashing corporate property and demolishing all police vehicles and limousines that they came upon. In addition a 50,000 strong Trade Union march slowly made its way through the city. Of those, a smaller number of the rank and file (primarily from the Longshoremen, Sheet Metal Workers, Steelworkers and, of course, the Industrial Workers of the World—the IWW Wobblies) diverged from the sanctioned parade course and made their way to the front lines of confrontation.

The result of these large numbers and demonstrated diverse actions was that only 350 of the expected 3,000 WTO delegates were able to attend the opening session. Subsequently the opening session was cancelled. The price? Several hundred injuries and 68 arrests.

The following two days were also filled with thousands of protesters engaging in acts of civil disobedience, this despite a government declaration of the downtown as a "no protest zone." In response to the continuing militancy of the demonstrators, additional police authorities were brought into the fray including hundreds of National Guard troops. This time was marked by severe police brutality more than often directed against nonviolent protesters. Subsequently the reports of injuries skyrocketed as did the numbers arrested. On December first alone more than 500 were incarcerated.

By day four — Friday, December 3rd — the city and the WTO meetings were in disarray. While city officials and Capitalist delegates seemed to be disheartened, the demonstrators remained committed. On that day a labor march of more than 10,000 defiantly paraded through downtown in protest of the "emergency" ordinances banning free speech and free assembly. This was done in conjunction with other direct actions which targeted WTO delegates. At the end of the day (actually sometime into the night) it was publicly announced that the meetings had utterly broken down due to internal rifts (and external pressure) and that no 'progress' was made concerning the economic agenda of the coming year... The meeting was shut down.

The aftermath? Again the poor and working class the world over were reminded that the ruling class is not omnipotent, not even in their primary home nation. They can be defeated when we stand united. As a final thought let it be said that the United States is the home of Capitalism, and to have gained a serious foothold against this beast in its own lair is a victory, a clear signal to history that the time for change is coming.

A:16 — A March On The Capitol: April 2000[35]

Black Bloc,

Washington DC, 2000

Between April 15th and April 17th (2000) over 40,000 people converged on Washington DC to protest against global Capitalism and specifically against the continuing practices and policies of the International Monetary Fund/World Bank (IMF/WB) which are consistently devoid of any substantive environmental concerns and are clearly in contrast to the interests of the world's poor and working classes. The protests were called by various elements of the Left in response to meetings being held by these organizations which were to take place during this time at the World Bank building.[36]

As with most recent (2002) large demonstrations, the protest constituency was composed of three elements:

1. A large number of Liberal/Reformists from within Nongovernmental Organizations (NGOs) and organized

35 2017 note from the author: This essay was written in 2001 and was first printed in The Black Bloc Papers, Insubordinate Editions, Baltimore MD, 2002.
36 2017 note from the author: I attended these rallies. On April 15 I was caught up in a mass arrest of hundreds of protesters (there being no Black Bloc that day). I managed to escape, along with fellow anarchist Carlos Pecciotto of Chicago, by opening a manhole cover and descending into the city's sewer system. On the 16th I marched with the Black Bloc for the day where we clashed with police on a number of occasions. On the 17th, while fighting as part of the Black Bloc, I was arrested. Having ditched my ID, I took part in jail solidarity actions from inside the DC Jail. These actions included a hunger strike and non-cooperation with prison authorities. After five days we won; all being released without having to provide proof of identity and only being subject to a minor fine (which was either waived or paid by outside supporters).

labor (i.e. AFL/CIO). This contingent was present in mass on April 16th, and primarily concerned itself with a legal rally at the Washington Monument. Their number can be estimated at 30,000.

2. A significant number of Left Liberals, Greens, Socialists, Communists, environmentalists and Anarchists. This contingent, organized in part through the Direct Action Network, utilized a participatory consensus based means of democratic organization and was committed to following through with acts of non-violent civil disobedience. This group's stated goal was prevent the meetings from taking place. Their number, as of April 16th, can be estimated at between 10,000–15,000.

3. A tightly-knit grouping of militant Anarchists known commonly as the Black Bloc. This contingent was organized internally through the various revolutionary Anarchist federations and informal networks. As a group it also utilized directly democratic, consensus based organizational means, while maintaining a fluid yet distinct identity/relationship with the larger protest contingents. Tactically, they hoped to maintain themselves as a highly mobile regiment capable of absorbing and reversing police and/or National Guard assaults if deemed necessary. Disrupting the status quo of Capitalism was definitely a conscious goal. Their numbers on April 16th can be estimated somewhere slightly over 1000 and somewhat less on April 17th.

The combined tactics of these three groupings culminated on Sunday, April 16th with large parts of the city being effectively occupied by demonstrators. All the obvious above ground access routes to the site of the meetings were cut off. Police were prevented from moving freely throughout these areas. Additionally police assaults on non-violent blockaders from the second contingent were, on several occasions, beaten back by physical means by the Black Bloc. By nightfall, 40 were arrested. However, the protests failed to shut down the meetings. This can partially be attributed to the government's likely use of restricted underground access ways into the convention center as a means of transporting IMF/WB delegates.

While April 16th was the most effective day and involved the most people, actions were also conducted by small affinity groups during the week prior to the main event. Also, on April 15th a large march against the prison industrial complex involving a couple thousand people took place. This march lacked a formal Black Bloc. Subsequently, while in a state of peaceful disbursement, the police blockaded approximately 600 people from the rear of the march with relative ease. At that point the police proceeded to arrest (nearly) all of these protesters. To our knowledge, only two of these individuals escaped incarceration by descending into the sewer system through a manhole (they were both Black Bloc anarchists, one being this writer).

In addition, April 17th saw more mass protests. However, this day was marked by relatively heavy police repression (supported by the presence of the National Guard) and bloody street fighting between the Black Bloc and the State. By the end of the day, over 700 more people ended up in jail (bringing the several day total to 1350), including approximately 20 from within the Black Bloc. A total of three federal felony charges were filed, including at least one directed against a Black Bloc anarchist. What ensued was a 5 day period of jail resistance from within the penal system under the banner of 'Jail Solidarity.'

This strategy called for collective bargaining of release conditions, non-violent resistance/non-cooperation, a building of respect and solidarity with the general prison population and functioned according to consensus. Of those arrested, 155 persons took part, including a small number (including myself) from the Black Bloc. The presence of the Bloc in jail proved important in that it curtailed what would have otherwise been a Liberal, Pacifist tone of the prisoner communiques. In the men's wing of the prison, such Anarchists helped (not without non-Bloc support) push the social/political analysis of the jailed activists in a more thorough/radical direction. This was achieved through the democratic consensus process by which the prisoners made all collective decisions including the official endorsements of composed messages to the outside. In this way the few individuals attached to the Bloc were able to block any motions which publicly endorsed simple reformism and/or ideological Pacifism.

Overall, the strategy of Jail Solidarity meet with relative success which included a lessening of charges and fines of $5 and the release of prisoners without having to present identification. The prisoners were released on April 21st and April 22nd. The A16 action is considered a success as it proved beyond a shadow of a doubt that Seattle was not a fluke. Once again, thousands mobilized and confronted the Capitalist State while risking both physical harm and jail. In short, even though the IMF/WB was still able to meet, the demonstrations proved that such an arbitrary organization of the world economy towards the elitist ends of the ruling class cannot freely occur without popular resistance.

In addition, the activity of the Black Bloc proved effective in conjunction with other means of direct action. Importantly, the Bloc managed to make inroads into the consciousness of the larger social protest movement by providing non-violent activists physical protection from State brutality and by fighting fire with fire. The combined tactics of April 16th utterly demoralized the police, causing them relative confusion and immobilization.

THE BATTLE OF QUEBEC CITY[37]

Black Bloc, Quebec City Quebec, 2001

The April 2001 protests in Quebec City against the Free Trade Agreement of the Americas (FTAA) were the most serious and militant in North America in recent memory. Certain moments began to take on the air of civil war. Scenes from Palestine emerged and faded in the course of two days and nights in the northern spring. At least one protester was critically injured after receiving a rubber bullet to the throat. One unconfirmed report has come to this writer's attention that an elderly woman, who was a resident of the city, died of causes related to ingestion of massive amounts of police tear gas and/or other

---

37 2017 note from the author: This essay was written in 2001 and was first printed in The Black Bloc Papers, Insubordinate Editions, Baltimore MD, 2002.

chemical weapons. A multitude of others were hospitalized. I saw one person carried off with two broken legs. Also many cops were injured, at least one seriously. The police fired thousands of cans of tear gas and other like agents at us (often directly into the crowd). They utilized water cannons, liberally fired beanbags and rubber bullets at us. They attacked us with batons and made use of attack dogs. Anarchists and militants generally protected themselves with homemade shields and responded with bottles, clubs, rocks and Molotov cocktails. In the days leading up the clash prospective anti-Capitalist militants were arrested with small explosives in Quebec. Some others were nabbed with dynamite while attempting to cross the border. Things have changed. The movement is becoming more serious; more complete. And it will only get heavier as we begin to win.[38]

The A20 actions were geared against a meeting of North, South and Central American heads of State (4/20–23) assembled to discuss the proposed expansion of the North American Free Trade Agreement (NAFTA) to include all American States with the exception of Communist Cuba. Such a functioning agreement would utterly [stiff] the North American industrial working class as well as the indigenous and working people of all Latin American Nations. In contrast to this convergence of heavyweight puppets, 75,000 people made their way to the streets of Quebec City in order to unmistakably make their opposition known. This on top of a large positive turnout from the local city population may have brought the numbers up to closer to 100,000.

The two primary days of mass organized resistance took place on Friday, April 20th and Saturday April 21st, with smaller actions occurring on the 22nd. The first day, primarily organized by CLAC and CASA, both being more or less Anarchist influenced organs, were the smaller of the two, numbering well over 20,000. Here the barricades erected around the older part of the city, where the conference was being held, were challenged by thousands of militants. At one point protesters, the majority of which can be considered Black Bloc Anarchists, managed to topple 150-300 feet of the chain link security fence. However, the police were able to maintain their lines, not without some intense struggle, and hence the meeting was not stormed. However, the meeting was delayed. Word on the street is

---

38 2017 note from the author: I took part in these actions along with members of Anti-Racist Action-Columbus Ohio. Prior to action the Green Mountain Anarchist Collective smuggled these ARA members into Quebec, crossing a border mountain on foot under the cover of night.

that this was due to President Bush's concerns regarding the security of the perimeter. I suppose he remembers us from Inauguration day?

Street battles continued all afternoon and into the evening, and were complemented by sophisticated cyber-attacks targeting corporate and State interests via the internet. An extended siege took place in front of a theater where Black Bloc Anarchists battled police with projectiles. Here protesters suffered some injuries due to rubber bullets and tear gas canisters fired directly at them, but fortunately many potential casualties were averted due to the heroic defensive action of a group of maybe 10 Black Bloc Anarchists armed with shields. These brave folk faced down countless volleys, putting themselves between the police and the protesters. It goes without saying that they absorbed many rounds of police projectiles that would have otherwise connected with the crowd. They did this and suffered their own related injuries in the process. I witnessed one Quebecois give them a twenty spot in order that they get a beer on him later in the night. If you ever meet any of them, I suggest you buy them a pint for their efforts as well. They deserve it.

Eventually the crowd was forced back by riot police. The protesters' numbers began to diminish as the day began to wane, and at some undefined point all dispersed, and retreated to wherever it was that they slept, or drank, and began to contemplate the clashes guaranteed for the following day.

The next morning brought tens of thousands more into the fray. Thousands of Quebecois Left-Nationalists emerged poised against the Capitalist status quo. Tens of thousands turned out for a rally called by organized labor. Thousands more, made up of Greens, Socialists, Liberals, Anarchists and Communists, students and workers, fanned out across the city creating a virtual carnival of resistance; loud and unmistakable if not sometimes obscured by thick clouds of tear gas and the 'BANG! BANG!' of police weapons. And yes... A Black Bloc emerged from this. I say emerged because its initial organization for the day seemed to be lacking. Instead of all meeting in a defined spot and moving as a large group, black clad Anarchists and affinity groups simply began to find each other and in such several smaller Blocs eventually surfaced. Some smashed bank windows (one bank was lit on fire), others went to the front and engaged riot police with rocks and bottles. Some from the Bloc also helped facilitate the toppling of the security fence at several junctures throughout the day.

The total number is hard to estimate. Possibly there were several hundred from the Bloc present at the day's action. One of the largest cohesive sections numbered around 75. This contingent launched several attacks on sections of the perimeter fence, and unloaded a number of petrol bombs at the police in the process. These attacks were more charges, brief clashes and tactical withdrawals than sustained battles. However, wherever they marched in the residential working class neighborhoods, they received healthy cheers from residents and other protesters alike; the only noticeable exception emanating from a contingent known as SalAmi (French for 'bad' or 'dirty friend'). This group booed the actions of the Bloc. It has been reported that in at least one instance individuals connected with this group went so far as to attempt to physically restrain persons engaged in militant direct action. While this contingent of self-proclaimed "non-violent" activists marked the exception to the general rule, their demonstrated hypocrisy in engaging in violent acts against the Bloc, justified in the name of ideological non-violence, deserves mention as a sickening example of non-solidarity and counter productivity. For the most part the Bloc ignored them to the best of their abilities, deciding that any internal conflict would be better dealt with after the demonstration at hand. Eventually, the above mentioned section of the Bloc made its way to a portion of the city which the highway entered upon. There, a long battle was sustained by themselves and more than 1,000 additional protesters in the rear. It was there that protesters fought with police for a matter of hours. At that juncture a police line stood exposed. This seemed a tempting target as most police enjoyed the relative security of a chain link fence separating them from demonstrators. However, this line was covered by sharp shooters armed with "non-lethal" fire arms and tear gas grenades. Despite this advantage in armament, Black Bloc Anarchists consistently hurled gas canisters back at these cops and on occasion made attempts at charging the line. Unfortunately all such attempts were driven back by force of police projectile weapons. After several hours a phalanx of riot police swooped down on the protesters from the rear and after another extended battle forced them from the scene. The Black Bloc Anarchists and protesters generally fell back to positions directly under the highway ramps. There they lit barricades on fire and held the police at bay for long hours into the night.

That day of protest, like the day before, failed to halt the FTAA meetings. But it did cause an early adjournment most likely due to tear gas filtering into the air ducts at the convention center.

All and all Quebec marked a turning point. Although it did not have the immediate psychological impact on the general North

American population as did Seattle, it did result in the further militant radicalization of the actively involved social protest population. It showed how much street power we can wield even when greatly under-supplied in relative riot gear.

This action lacked the acute psychological weight of Seattle for two reasons. 1. Seattle took the world by surprise. In Quebec, anything short of a complete shutdown of the FTAA meetings was to be expected. 2. Quebec was marked by a virtual media blackout in the United States. When protest reports did surface, numbers were put at the low thousands as opposed to the tens-of-thousands that were present in actuality. Also, to my knowledge, all reports of injuries (both serious and otherwise) were completely ignored by U.S. corporate media. As far as the mainstream media was concerned the meeting took place without a hitch or a significant display of popular opposition. This media blackout was supported by an FBI raid and subsequent functional disruption of the Seattle Independent Media Center as well as a similar attack, by Canadian officials, on the Quebec equivalent. These raids were officially justified by the surfacing of an anonymous email posting on the organization's open access website, which reportedly made threats against President George W Bush's life. The end result was that the flow of accurate independent news reporting from the scene was greatly stifled, while the corporate propaganda of CNN, NBC, The New York Times, etc., flowed more or less unhindered. However, the effectiveness of this initial campaign of reactionary propaganda can be expected to recede as protesters begin to tell the real story of events in their hometowns across the continent. The truth will spread by word of mouth alone in due course.

As far as the action itself is concerned, the events of Saturday the 21st once again demonstrated the ability of even a small, yet dedicated Black Bloc. However, one has to pause and wonder whether or not the police barricades could have been surmounted if only the Bloc was formulated in a more cohesive, organized form. Also, it demands mention that while many who took part in the Bloc(s) that did emerge were prepared with body armor, gas masks, clubs, etc., many more were equipped with no more than a black bandanna, and whatever rock or stick they happened upon. And even so, they managed to fight heavily armed forces of the State with ferocity for hours. Again one has to wonder what way the tide would have ultimately turned if a substantially larger percentage of militants were properly equipped. Of course this relative unpreparedness had a lot to do with the fact that many chose to attend with only a skeleton kit of required gear for fear that Canadian officials would conduct searches at the border crossings and at random highway check points (as was rumored) en route, and that such equipment would be used as grounds for non-entrance, detainment and/or leveling of political conspiracy charges.

To round out this report let me reiterate the numbers. In the days of protests more than 450 were arrested. A good percentage of them taking place on the night of the 21st. All told, there were 75–100,000 social protesters pitted against approximately 10,000 well equipped and highly trained Provincial and Federal police, primarily stationed behind a protective barrier. In the clashes at least one cop was seriously injured with another 71 treated in hospitals. On our side at least 100 required medical attention. In all the State fired 5000 tear gas canisters in order to repress the voice of the people.

DC AND THE TWIN TOWERS: A BATTLE POSTPONED[39]

The World Trade Center, September 11, 2001

The demonstrations planned for the capital during late September of 2001 (timed to coincide with the meetings of the IMF-WB) were anticipated to be the largest and most militant yet in the growing U.S. anti-globalization movement. Coming on the heels of mass anti-capitalism actions in Europe (Gothenburg, Sweden and Genoa, Italy), many believed that these actions would mark a new phase in the domestic class struggle. Upwards of 200,000 people were expected in the streets, and the Black Bloc was expected to reach sizes at least double that of the previous year. Some law enforcement officials

---

39 2017 note from the author: This essay written in 2005 and was first printed in the second edition of *The Black Bloc Papers*, Breaking Glass Press, Shawnee Mission, KS, 2010.

were publicly stating that they expected the Bloc to be 10,000 strong. While this should be considered an overstatement, it is possible that it could have reached numbers closer to 3000.

Key anarchist collectives across the continent were formulating plans which would have brought Black Bloc tactics to a new level sophistication. The two most prominent possibilities (which were not necessarily considered to be mutually exclusive) were to 1. occupy a recently closed down hospital, and 2. Organize a highly mobile street fighting brigade utilizing a more comprehensive internal structure.

In the first case, it was believed that by taking over, and holding this hospital, the Bloc would be able to focus attention upon the failure of the social system under capitalism, and the growing demand to prioritize human needs over corporate profit margins. In the second case, it was hoped that the Bloc would be able to reach a new level of effectiveness without falling into the pattern of disarray and confusion in the face of police attacks. These bold plans were not without risk. The police shooting of Black Bloc protesters at recent demonstrations in Europe added to the already intense atmosphere. With the death of anarchist Carlo Giuliani, who was shot in the head during the G-8 protests in Genoa, nobody was taking the encroaching demonstrations lightly. However, as events unfolded, these experiments in Black Bloc tactics would have to wait.

The tragedy of the September 11th attacks would not only compel the main event organizers, the Mobilization for Global Justice coalition, to pull out of the protests, but also tens of thousands of previously committed union members, and leftists.[40] The IMF and World Bank, for their part, eventually moved to cancel their meetings. As the World Trade Center fell, taking with it thousands of innocent lives, the Left paused. For a moment confusion and fear swept the nation. In the immediate aftermath of the attacks, troops surrounded the White House, parts of the capital were evacuated, the borders were shut, all commercial aircraft were grounded. Rumors ran wild about other terrorist attacks. Much of the government went into

---

40 2017 note from the author: On 9/11/01 Lady and I were in western Canada driving a 1978 Ford van (with Vermont plates) across the continent. That morning we intended to cross the border into Montana, however the border was shut down. We then decided to drive to Quebec where we would more easily be able to slip back into Vermont at a remote rural crossing. I remember driving east all that night while Lady slept in the back. Listening to the unfolding news on an old Walkman (the van radio did not work), smoking the last of our BC dope, and always aware of the northern lights to my left. When the news became too much I turned the dial and the first music that came in clear enough was the Rolling Stones' Sympathy for the Devil. The apocalypse felt at hand... 'and the last man blinked.'

secured hiding. For many Americans, the situation was beyond their comprehension. One must keep in mind that the U.S., unlike Europe and much of the world, has not suffered a modern war on its own soil. Americans are not accustomed to living like folks are compelled to in places like Palestine, Syria and Baghdad. The U.S. government came crashing into this void like gang busters.

First they told us the attacks were launched by foreign Islamist extremists. Then they told us this enemy would have to be hunted down and killed in order to preserve freedom. What they didn't tell us was that many of these terrorists where trained and supplied by the CIA during the Cold War. A generation ago the Federal Government bet on these people as a secret weapon, wound them up, then pointed them at the Soviet Union and her allies. In addition to directly challenging the security of the Soviet Union's southern borders, they hoped to limit communist influence in the Arab and broader Islamic world. One should recall that at in the 1970s the predominant armed, underground organizations (and popular movements) were left wing and secular by nature. Groups like the Palestinian Liberation Army were found working with left wing European guerrillas like the Red Army Faction and the Provisional Irish Republican Army. And again, Arab states, who often claimed a degree of socialism, displayed strong sympathies for the Eastern Bloc. These were trends that the Western capitalists sought to overturn through the covert support of Islamist extremism. The maxim, 'the enemy of my enemy is my friend' may, at times, be true. But what happens when your primary enemy disappears? So yes, on September 11, 2001, just over ten years after the collapse of the Warsaw Pact, the U.S. experienced a horrendous act of terrorism on its own soil. But this was a tragedy of our own creation.

As the smoke was still rising, the government moved fast to use this attack not as a moment for self-reflection—not as a chance to reevaluate past foreign policies that may have backfired, but (suspiciously) as a tool to attempt militaristic homogenization abroad, and pacification of dissent within. President Bush immediately announced the intension to go to war with Afghanistan, who he claimed were shielding those responsible for the attacks. Congress pushed through the now infamous USA PATRIOT Act (rumored to have been largely written following Seattle) which essentially stripped the protections guaranteed to civilians under the Bill of Rights. Police and military spending grew exponentially. And by 2003 it became clear that 9/11 would also be used as a pretext to invade and occupy oil rich Iraq. However, let's not get ahead of ourselves.

In the days immediately following 9/11 it became clear that the U.S. would invade Afghanistan. In response the planned IMF–WB protests evolved into not only an action against globalization, but also against the impending war. The Anti-Capitalist Convergence and a new anti-war coalition (ANSWER) called for a demonstration on September 28th. Religious and pacifists organizations such as The American Friends Service Committee called for a rally on the 29th. On the 28th, an estimated 10,000 people took to the streets voicing their opposition to war. Of these nearly 2,000 were represented in the explicitly anti-capitalist contingent, including a Black Bloc several hundred strong. Simultaneously, more the 80 solidarity demonstrations were organized in dozens of other U.S. cities and across the globe. Some of the larger of these were in San Francisco (10,000), Los Angeles (2,000), and Athens Greece (10,000). In D.C. events got underway around 9:00 a.m. with the anti-capitalist contingent, behind a banner that read "No War But Class War", and the Black Bloc marching from Union Station. As this group approached the IMF building riot police encircled them. After an hour long stand-off, the pigs relinquished, and the march moved to link up with the larger protest organized by ANSWER. Along the way they passed a construction site where workers cheered their support.

After linking up with the other demonstrators, the combined forces of thousands of people headed towards the Capital building. Both phases of the march included a limited number of confrontations between the Bloc and the police. Even so, the day was largely peaceful, and only a handful of protesters were arrested.

The following day a rally was held by overt pacifist elements drew an estimated 3,000 people.

While 10,000 anti-war demonstrators is a far cry from the 100,000 previously expected at the IMF-WB actions, the demonstration should be understood as a powerful statement against the path that the powers that be were about to traverse. Given the level apprehension and fear cultivated by the government and corporate media following 9/11, it is a testament to human fortitude and willingness to stand on common principle that anyone, let alone 10,000 were willing to make their opposition known in the streets of Washington, D.C.

Concerning The Long Term Viability of Forming Workers' Councils[41]

NEFAC

Proposal To:
The Northeastern Federation of Anarcho-Communists

Submitted By:
The Green Mountain Anarchist Collective (NEFAC-VT)

The Old Socialist Labor Hall, Barre, Vermont 2004 — The current social and political dynamic within North America, and much of the western industrialized world, is one of both growing hope and an escalation of capitalist oppression.

41 2017 note from the author: This document was written by myself, with the exception of the first 13 paragraphs that appear in the subsection *Origins of the Vermont Workers Center and Internal Structure* (these 13 paragraphs were taken from the essay *Class Struggle In The Green Mountains: Vermont Workers' Center*, which was written by Lady of the Green Mountain Anarchist Collective, and was published in the Northeastern Anarchist, 2003). The entirety of this document was adopted as an official proposal to NEFAC by the Green Mountain Anarchist Collective. The proposal was presented at the spring 2004 NEFAC conference held at the Old Socialist Labor Hall in Barre Vermont in 2004. The proposal was discussed and debated at length by the assembled member collectives, and although not being without vocal supporters, NEFAC declined to adopt this strategy and (even though NEFAC did much solid organizing during its time as a federation) largely failed to articulate any unified strategy during the years of its existence.

While workers are being attacked by the forces of capital, and while the U.S. ruling class embarks upon imperialist campaigns of war, conquest, and cultural-political-economic homogenization, a mass movement is building within the very walls of the empire. The 1999 Battle of Seattle witnessed the coming together of a great and diverse new American left. As the anti-globalization movement matured, culminating in the 70,000–100,000 strong Battle of Quebec City in 2001, a mass anti-capitalist, pro-democracy movement was in full swing. This momentum was effectively stalled due to the hesitation demonstrated on the part of the left immediately following the tragic September 11th terrorist attacks on the Twin Towers, and the four civilian jetliners. However, momentum against the empire not only became reinvigorated, but grew to massive proportions with the people's movement against the imperialist invasion of Iraq. Let us not forget the more than half-a-million people who marched in opposition through New York City on February 15th. Nor should we forget the tens-of-thousands of others who marched in hundreds of other North American cities and small towns.[42] Let us also remember the 13 million people who took part in sister demonstrations across the world, making February 15th, 2003, the largest day of global protest in the history of humankind. While we did not succeed in stopping the war, we did, temporarily, make the neo-conservative's scale back their rhetoric about invading other nations such as socialist Cuba, communist Korea, Ba'ath controlled Syria, and Islamic Iran. And like in the streets of Seattle, DC, and Quebec, this opposition included millions of union workers (i.e. U.S. Labor Against The War), socialists, anarchists, students, environmentalists, and many others. In short, while the audacity of the ruling class grows, so too does our movement towards socialism and direct democracy. It is with this in mind that NEFAC must begin to up the ante, and develop a coordinated strategy with the end goal of popular victory.

---

42 2017 note from the author: In Vermont, just before the start of the invasion, 3000 rallied in the capital of Montpelier, making this the largest political protest up until that time in the capital. When the war began, 5000-6000 marched in opposition in Burlington; this equaled the largest political protest ever seen in the state also up until that time (a march also in Burlington against the Vietnam War in the early 1970s). Together with members of the Green Mountain Anarchist Collective, I was at both rallies. At the Burlington rally the Green Mountain Anarchist Collective helped direct a break-away march that left the permitted route and held up traffic for some time. Fourteen years later both these rallies were dwarfed by the 2017 Montpelier Woman's March (against President Trump) which drew a record shattering 20,000 protesters (in a city with a population of 7800). I was pleased to have attended this rally too along with my wife Angela, our daughter Freya, and our son William.

What is this popular victory? While it would be arrogant to state exactly what a post-capitalist, democratic, socialist world would look like (as this will be defined by the people themselves), we can, at minimum, say that it will be one where communities are organized by directly democratic assemblies, industry and agriculture will be coordinated by directly democratic unions, and all people will have (among other things) access to food, housing, healthcare, higher education, childcare, jobs, and social security.

While it is always possible that some unforeseen crisis in western capitalism will spur the spontaneous creation of such a society in the northeastern part of North America, it presently appears unlikely in the near future. Therefore, the task of NEFAC should be that of building the subjective and objectives conditions necessary for such an unfolding of social liberation. And here, such focused activity will entail the building of democratic mass organizations that reflect the free society that we intend to achieve. In other words, we must prioritize the building of directly democratic peoples' assemblies in our communities, the building of integrated workers' councils in industry, and building of democratic farmers' organizations where we can. In the initial phases of such a project it will be likely that these organizations will not present themselves as complete, mature bodies focused on social revolution. Rather they will be initially focused on concrete issues that people have a direct and obvious personal/class stake in. For example, instead of calling for a general peoples' assembly, in many cases it will make more sense to build tenants' unions in sections of a city, or for us to call for a peoples' assembly in response to a specific issue (as was the case in Vermont after the imperialist invasion of Iraq). Our experience in the Green Mountain State has been that farmers are not presently inclined to come together except for immediately practical reasons, such as to fight against the drastically low price paid by larger capitalists for raw milk. And finally, it is unlikely that workers' councils will come into being devoid of years of prior groundwork and a spark issue that mobilizes people into avenues already created for their participation. It will be through these concrete issues that people will become more open to the full critique of capitalism. For every step of the way we can begin to demonstrate how each of the issues that directly affect them is tied to other issues and how they are all wrapped up in the false totality of capitalism. But first things first.[43]

43 While such an analysis will likely be attacked by fringe elements of the American anarchist community, we must remain steadfast in our recognition that North America, and more specifically the northeast, is a very different

Currently NEFAC is not strategically focused or coordinated on a broader federation level. Beyond the vague strategic commitment to: 1.) direct intervention in the class struggle; 2.) work on housing/poverty issues; 3.) anti-fascism; and 4.) fighting for immigrants' rights, we do not coordinate our activities in an effective way. One collective will prioritize free speech struggles, while another does solidarity work on a local labor strike, while another may be involved in any number of different local campaigns. While all these activities are good, they do not lead to a measurable advance in the revolutionary workers' movement in the northeast as a whole. By enlarge many of these activities are reactive, as opposed to proactive. While they do result in small victories against specific capitalist attacks, the culmination of these distinct campaigns do not necessarily lead to the overall weakening of the capitalist system or the strengthening of the workers' movement. We need to formulate a coordinated plan, to be implemented across the northeast that can begin to demonstrate real measurable success over a period of years. Our times require that we find a way to move ahead in a concerted effort towards the ends of weakening capitalism and building a directly democratic socialist system that can take its place. If we do not do this, it is likely that the objective historical opportunities that the present holds will be lost, and serious moves towards socialist victory will not be possible for at least another generation.

In the following sections of this document we will propose one such strategy for the raising of class consciousness, working class empowerment, the creation of duel power, and the general advance of the revolutionary left — that strategy will aim for the creation of workers' councils in all areas where NEFAC is active. We recognize that any strategy that solely seeks such formations is inherently incomplete as workers' councils are only one element of what rightly

place than Italy was in the 1970s, or Germany was in the 1980s, for that matter, Europe today [2004] (which is by enlarge composed of social democratic nation-states). Europe, for several generations, has been marked by a more advanced socialist movement, and within such a reality armed struggle, as well as the militant rejection of moderate trade unionism may make perfect strategic and tactical sense. However, where we live, write, and organize today (that being the northeast of North America) is a place where the trade unions only represent a minority of the workers and their numbers are declining, and other than in Vermont & Quebec, democratic socialists are not represented in government. While Italy in the 70s was a place where workers were militantly rejecting that state's transformation into a social democracy (instead in favor of a workers revolution), the USA and Canada are currently in a process of rolling back the modest class gains made by earlier generations. In the USA the incomplete victories of the New Deal are quickly disintegrating under the constant attacks of neo-conservative elements of the ruling class which presently is in control of the federal government.

should be a three prong strategy. Ideally NEFAC should be seeking to build workers' councils, peoples' assemblies, and democratic farmers' organizations. For it will be three these three bodies (all working together) that true democracy and socialism will be both functional and possible. However, proposal will only seek to deal with one of these aspects of the social revolution. While reading and considering what follows, one should bear in mind that that GMAC does not propose that the below strategy by superimposed upon collectives and individuals who are currently doing work that relates to the building of either peoples' assemblies or democratic farmers' organizations. This includes collectives and individuals that are engaged in the building of tenants' unions; of which we understand as a potential building block for the eventual formation of directly democratic neighborhood organizations (i.e. people's assemblies). The below proposal is only intended for those collectives and individuals who are not presently engaged in these other two activities, or those which do not plan on becoming engaged in such activities in the near future.

The proposal will be broken down into a number of sections. We recognize that any proposal that calls for the formation of workers' councils, without giving adequate context, is both hollow, meaningless, and utopian. Therefore, we will begin this document with a detailed discussion of the class struggle in Vermont over the course of the last ten years. We have included such sections in order to give context to how and why we think NEFAC is and/or could be capable of bringing together such workers' formations. It is our contention that the lessons of the Vermont working class have a direct relevance upon the class struggle throughout the northeast. However, for sake of clarity, this document will first give a definition of workers' councils, followed by a brief framing of the question as to how they can be achieved. It is to this task that we now turn.

Workers' Councils As Real Democracy & Revolutionary Power

The concept and practice of workers' councils (also called soviets) has long been recognized by the revolutionary left as a powerful means to fight the forces of capital when and if they begin to take shape. Historically workers' councils are directly democratic bodies of workers who come together at the shop level. When shops are too large to feasibly hold meaningful participatory decision-making meetings, delegates are elected by each section of the shop representing all aspects of labor. In turn, these shop-level councils seek to federate with other councils in order to coordinate activity on a wider more socially comprehensive basis. In principle, these councils are capable of taking over, democratizing, and coordinating industrial production without the exploitive presence of an authoritarian ruling class. In real practice, such formations have often acted as a defensive force against a still present capitalist class. Such councils often came together during times of great national or class crisis and have achieved differing degrees of organizational success. We saw Russian workers' councils form in response to the intense social-political conditions brought about by World War I in 1917 (resulting in the October Revolution and the fall of the Provisional Government). We saw them form in Germany in 1919 (resulting in an unsuccessful workers' revolt), and again in Spain in 1936 (in some regions resulting in two years of workers' self-management). More recently, the financial crash of the neo-liberal Argentine economy (2002-present) again witnessed the mass creation of such councils (resulting in the ouster of several pro-capitalist presidents and the seizure of numerous factories which continue to operate under worker self-management).

Where such councils form it is often only a matter of time before the capitalist state becomes extremely vulnerable to left-wing insurgencies. Here in the U.S. despite an increasing economic hardship, imperialist wars, and the rise of the domestic police state, workers are yet to take such an action in any large scale way. But what if it was possible to build the conditions necessary for such organizations to form? What if we could find a way to create these conditions that would lead to such formations, even if a single catastrophic event did not show up on cue? If we could build networks of such councils, all directly democratic and controlled by the workers alone, we would be in a better position to see workers call for organized general strikes, direct actions, and an upping of their confidence as witnessed through their demands and expectations. Through the existence of such bodies we would be in a better position to seize and manage the means of production and commerce when conditions allow. We, in a word, would be in a much more advanced phase of our epic struggle to democratize and socialize our world.

If such a movement is again to be built, it must allow for certain variations that account for what is possible, and, given certain conditions, probable. A modern resurgence of these councils would more likely be based on a larger geographic proximity, rather than on a small shop level. In other words, given the daunting task of forming hundreds of small councils in a single section of a city, while simultaneously fighting for more local democracy in already established unions, it may make more sense to create larger councils where workers from numerous shops come together into great directly democratic bodies. In the event that such bodies prove too large for meaningful debate, discussion, and general participation, it may be possible for each separate shop to elect delegates (in proportion to the size of the particular workforce) to carry the sentiments of the particular shop to the larger body. However, these are details that will have to be worked out through the democratic decision making of those directly affected.

An additional benefit of forming workers' councils is that they could serve as a means to circumvent the bureaucratic and top down structure of the major labor unions. While such unions are, even at their worst, a line of working class defense against capital, and even though they are mass organizations that NEFAC works within (as both members and tactical allies), they are by no means revolutionary in and of themselves. In addition, the self-perpetuating and alienating nature of some of these organizations, a number of whom consistently fail to involve rank and file workers in their overall decision making process, is problematic towards our transformative goals. Left unchanged, such unions cannot be expected to evolve into class war organizations; at least not without direct intervention by ourselves, other revolutionary organizations, and/or a radicalized internal workers' movement. And even when some of these unions are challenged from within, they, like the state, have a tendency to structurally maintain themselves and the more moderate politics that they assume.

OK, it should be recognized that it is one thing to say that workers' councils are powerful revolutionary bodies and that we should seek to create them, and it is another thing to actually do it. First of all NEFAC, like most relevant leftwing organizations, is both limited in numbers and resources. While we are workers, and while many of us are currently in labor unions, we on our own are in no position to galvanize the hundreds of shops and thousands of workers necessary to make such a project realistically feasible in the foreseeable future. In addition, each separate collective has differing degrees of practical organizing experience, respect in their community, and clear channels of communication with the mass of workers in their areas. While some collectives, as in Quebec and CAC in Boston, have been actively building good working relations with unions and rank and file workers, others are still trying to find ways to relate to the broader, more outwardly moderate labor movement. Bottom line, if a coordinated campaign to build such councils is done by NEFAC in isolation, we would most likely fail.

Even assuming that we were capable of building such councils, where would we begin? Would we seek to incorporate all workers, both union and non-union? If so, that would place our collectives in the unrealistic position of having to mobilize thousands of workers who have no organizational accountability to the project. Where it may be possible for us to bring together several hundred workers in the beginning, the task of maintaining momentum among so many individuals would be unlikely if they fail to see themselves as the owner of the project. Then what are we to do? Should we look to potential allies from within the already established unions as partners in this project? Do we build councils that are essentially bodies of separate area unions? Should we attempt to form more democratic and localized versions of ALF-CIO Central labor Councils? Recognizing that all of these tasks are daunting in and of themselves, and recognizing that without many conditions already in place, we most likely would fail at all of them, the answer to the question remains both yes and no.

First of all, we would need for participating workers to have a degree of accountability. In this capacity it makes sense to only include unionized workers (including those without official recognition who are in what is called a "minority union" at their specific shop). But this leads to a significant problem: if these councils are to be indicative of a directly democratic workforce, then we cannot shutout the majority of workers who, in actuality, are not union members. In the U.S. approximately fifteen million people are in unions. That is roughly 13% of the workforce. In the northeast those numbers are somewhat higher, but still constitute a minority. A direct workers' democracy cannot be based on such a minority. For this reason it would appear that there are certain preliminary campaigns that would have to be sufficiently accomplished in a locality before it is possible to launch a workers' council. And, as will be demonstrated through the testimony of this text, it is through these preliminary campaigns that the subjective conditions necessary for such a project to shift its chances of success from slim to likely.

Given our social-political context, one preliminary condition must be the creation of unions which are based on small geographic locations, and are open to all workers. This is not to say that the abstract existence of such a union, like the modern incarnation of the Industrial Workers of the World (IWW) exonerates us from building more practical alternatives. While the IWW does good work in some localities, it has almost no resources to carry out sustained organizing drives. Regionally (as opposed to specific localities) it is fairly irrelevant, has a total membership of only 1000+, and officially represents only a half dozen shops across the entire continent. No, the IWW does not fit the bill. We need all-workers-unions which show growth, effectiveness, creativity, and are capable of winning real victories, and of representing many workers. So where does this leave us?

One possibility is that NEFAC begin to build our own all-worker-unions. Something to this effect was proposed by our Quebecois comrades at the 2002 Boston Strategy Summit (The Precarious Workers' Union). While clearly this would be a positive development, we question NEFAC's ability to effectively carry this out. While we have little doubt that NEFAC is capable of building strong independent unions in select workplaces, it is difficult to understand how we could rally the resources necessary to carry such a campaign into the larger public arena. NEFAC has limited legal, financial, and human resources. And such an effective all-workers-union must seek to actively involve hundreds, if not thousands of workers from numerous shops. For example, the Pissed Off Projectionists campaign, while being a great victory for the federation, took all the efforts of one collective months just to build an organized presence among less than a dozen workers. We must be sober enough to accept that the building of such unions in small shops, even given 100 years at the present trajectory, will never constitute a workers' organization large enough to give an organized voice to the people.

Therefore, if we are to build such a movement, and we contend that we can, we will have to seek committed allies, primarily from within the established labor movement.

Lessons From The Green Mountains

The Green Mountain Anarchist Collective (GMAC) has always looked for ways in which dual power can be built. We are not utopian; rather we are revolutionary anarchists who prioritize victory over vague dreams. We have done our best to experiment with different strategies, and have met both relative failure and success. With this being said, we have been working with the United Electrical, Radio, and Machine Workers of America (UE) and the Vermont Workers Center (VWC), and dozens of community members for well over six months on creating a democratic workers union, for all workers, in Vermont's capital city of Montpelier (The Montpelier Downtown

Workers Union-MDWU). This experience has taught us some valuable lessons and has helped illuminate ways in which such duel power can be achieved.

It is our contention that the experiences of the Vermont working class has a direct and relevant bearing upon struggles in other regions. We also contend that the experiences of the Montpelier Downtown Workers Union, as well as the context out of which it emerged, has direct ramifications for the movement towards direct democracy and socialism throughout the northeast. In the following section of this document we will discuss and analyze these developments, giving an accurate history of the struggle, as well as discuss the broader social-political context out of which they emerged. It is our claim that the thus far successful advances of the Vermont working class can, given reasonable modification to suit the particularities of different regions, be replicated throughout the northeast. Therefore, following the below history and analysis of Vermont's experience, we will propose concrete steps that NEFAC should take in order to build all-worker-unions and workers' councils.

Building A Workers' Center & Launching An All-Workers-Union

The launching of the Montpelier Downtown Workers' Union could not have been possible without the pre-existence of the Vermont Workers' Center. In was the VWC Director James Haslam (previously a supporter of the anarchist Northern Spy Collective) who began to push for the idea of creating a general union of workers in Vermont. This idea was presented as a means to organize those within the service sector and other employees who labor in shops historically too small for the established unions to spend time and resources to individually organize (*in Vermont only 11% of the workforce is unionized — nationally it is 13%, down from a high-water mark of 35% in 1960). Developing an effective means to bring such workers into the organized camp is pivotal to the future of the labor movement and the left generally in Vermont, as it also is to the northeast and North America as a whole. Without organization, this most strategic segment of the American population, the working class, will inevitably fail to resist the continuing and escalating attacks of the wealthy ruling class against the masses of poor and working people. Vermont, like much of the industrialized world, has lost thousands of decent paying, often union, manufacturing jobs as a result of the free trade policies of NAFTA, the WTO, and the general trends of global capitalism (factories to Mexico, China, etc.). While many workers in the manufacturing sector are fighting back through their unions, and while a small a small amount are seeking to form worker-owned factories 9i.e. Island Pond Wood Workers), the reality is that this sector of employment is quickly disintegrating while the service and retail sectors are expanding in order to partially fill this employment vacuum. Again, in 2003, while Vermont lost manufacturing jobs it gained 6000 new service and retail jobs (bringing down the net job loss for 2003 to a still unacceptable two thousand). The contradiction of the domestic manufacturing sector and the expansion of the domestic service and retail sectors translates into thousands of Vermont workers having to survive on poverty wages, little or no benefits, and, as things stand, no job security, no union protection, and little or no organized means of economic and political self-defense. This situation is driven by the fact that service and retail jobs rarely pay anything close to a livable wage (which today, 2004, in Vermont is $11.60 an hour). With the exception of certain wait-staff bartending positions, the vast majority of service and retail jobs pay closer to the minimum wage, which in Vermont is presently $6.75 an hour — and in no way comes close to a dignified, sustainable income, decent enough to support a family on. The growth of these sectors commonly translates into the weakening of the labor movement. For most such employers hire no more than between three and twenty-five workers. In this way Vermont's economy is quickly becoming strikingly similar to that of a colony to the greater U.S. nation. The service and retail jobs are largely driven by tourism, and the larger employers are often owned by corporate out-of-state interests (i.e. the American Ski Corporation — who owns the Mount Snow and Killington resorts and employs over 2000 workers, most at poverty wages). Even in other sectors such as large logging interests and the IBM plant in Essex Junction (which is Vermont's largest private employers at 9000 jobs), etc., the ownership class comes from the corporate culture and is based out-of-state. On the other hand, the majority of businesses (most very small), are owned locally and still fail to provide decent living standards for its employees.

Large, more established unions tend to not spend time and energy organizing such individual small workplaces, as the energy to secure union recognition is not normally proportionate to their size. As the manufacturing base disappears, the unions, who commonly held recognition at such plants, dwindle in size as their membership base decreases, and along with it, so does their accrued revenue through dues. As their resources dwindle, the potential arises for them to become even less apt to spend time and money organizing small shops. While this situation, as felt all across North America, unfolds, it is tempting to view the social-political context in terms of a downward spiral, with the end result of the strengthening of capital over labor. However, this situation, which is indicative of the new western capitalism, also carries with it new possibilities for radical resistance and socialist emergence.

Correctly recognizing these objective conditions, Mr. Haslam began to discuss his ideas with VWC founders, trade unionists, other leftist community supporters, and personal friends within GMAC. Most of all, he and others began to discuss the possibility of forming such a union with local Montpelier service workers, with whom he held friendships. Montpelier was identified as a potential battleground because of the symbolism it brought with it as the capital of Vermont, because of the strong presence of labor in the area (the VWC officers as well as that of the VT AFL-CIO and Vermont State Employees' Association are located there), and because a recent victory there (at the largest city grocery store) would give the new drive early momentum.

After several months, Haslam (having gained the endorsement for the project by the democratically run VWC Steering Committee) arranged a series of meetings with representatives of the UE. There he discussed the possibility of launching such a campaign in the capital city (population 7800) with the aid of that union. Here much of the above discussed reasons for union hesitation was overcome by the idea that they would not so much seek to unionize individual small shops (each requiring formal NLRB-mediated elections and individual labor contracts), but that they would seek to build a citywide union of the estimated 800, mostly service and retail oriented workers from small shops. They would provide a simple, relatively short universal contract that could better guarantee protections against unjust firings, a grievance procedure, and modest wage increases with the eventual goal of establishing livable wages for all workers. So instead of seeing the struggle in terms of gaining union recognition in a series of very small shops, the UE was made to understand the potential of creating a local of all 800 workers. And finally, the potential for an active VWC/UE alliance was furthered by a Workers' Center offer to pay half the salary (the other half coming from the UE) of one full time organizer for the project. With all this in place, the UE accepted the offer, and in a matter of weeks the campaign was launched.

The UE was approached, as opposed to other allied unions, for three primary reasons. 1.) The UE is a very democratic union and would be unlikely to co-opt the democratic outcome of the organizing drive. 2.) The UE, in the months prior and with active support of the Workers Center, successfully helped the employees of the Hunger Mountain Food Co-op gain union recognition and a decent contract (*the co-op is the largest grocery employer in the city). Here it was argued that those 70+ newly unionized workers (who overwhelmingly joined the union) would act as a kind of advanced guard for the general organizing drive. In other words, it was thought that these workers would help with much of the preliminary actions which would have to be done before the union could publicly establish itself, and that their recent victory would help instill a sense of impending victory among yet to be unionized workers.[44] 3.) The UE was formally a strong force in the region in the manufacturing industry, and with its collapse, the union was seeking creative ways to organize workers among emerging industries (in the months prior, it was the UE who successfully organized the Montpelier based Hunger Mountain Co-op, as well as the Burlington based City Market — also a food co-op).

What is apparent from these beginnings is that it is very unlikely that this project could have got off the ground without it being advanced by Workers' Center. This is due to several reason. 1.) The VWC, then five years old, had gained a good deal of respect from within the Vermont labor movement, the broader left, as well as among the working class as a whole. In fact the VWC in recent years evolved into a kind of hybrid between Jobs With Justice and a center seeking to aid in the struggles of non-union laborers. This confidence did not manifest overnight. Jason Winston, a co-founder of the VWC, former Love & Rage #10 Collective member, and current VWC President recalls that in the early years the established Vermont labor movement was very apprehensive about their involvement in union struggles. "Back then it was a big deal if we received permission to table at their events." For many years the center diligently worked to build solidarity for strikes, contract drives, union drives, etc., without pushing an overt leftwing ideology upon those it aided and worked with. Rather, it battled alongside labor on concrete issues, and in the process helped win concrete gains. From its humble beginnings, it also established a statewide, 24/7 workers' rights hotline. This 1-800 number was distributed across the state in flyers, publications, and by word of mouth, and through it workers can discuss instances

---

44 As the effort unfolded, these co-op workers were not engaged in the campaign at the levels optimistically expected to organizers.

of discrimination, unfair labor practices, etc. with trained VWC personnel (often such volunteers are rank & file union members). Such personnel, in turn, can inform the workers of their rights, refer them to legal aid, or unions if they wish to organize. This hotline, which continues to this day, is confidential, yet contact information is entered into an internal database, and complaints about employers are also logged and catalogued. To date, more than one percent of the state's workforce has used this free service.

It was through such diligent and relevant solidarity work that the center began to win over the active support of hundreds of workers and the unions themselves. In time, the center took on more and more responsibilities for statewide workers' campaigns and local struggles, and as it did it began to focus, in part, on the bigger picture and articulate it back to the individual unions. In other words, it did not limit itself to solidarity work centered around separate specific issues. Rather it sought to build a broader labor movement which valued class-wide (cross-union) mutual aid and respect. It sought to link specific issues with bigger issues, and attempted to draw popular attention to these links and logical ends.

In 2000, it launched a campaign called "Justice For Healthcare Workers." Coming off the heels of union recognition for workers from a private nursing home provider (Berlin Health & Rehab), and in the midst of a contentious union drive for the nurses at the state's largest hospital (Fletcher Allen of Burlington[45]) This campaign sought to build a network of solidarity between all healthcare workers, publicly link certain workers' issues such as short staffing and mandatory overtime with the inherent dangers they caused to maintaining quality public care, and finally, to link the entire campaign with the broader demand for universal healthcare.

The VWC has more recently announced their "Good Jobs For Vermont" campaign, which seeks to bring together the different building trades in order to gain class power and better pay/working conditions for such workers across the state. For the last several years the center has also organized an annual Labor Day march and picnic in Burlington. This event regularly draws 300-400 mostly union workers in a demonstration of class solidarity. Tellingly, in 2001, the Vermont AFL-CIO recognized the organizing efforts of VWC Director James Haslam with the Labor Leader of the Year award.

---

45 Not only did the nurses win, but they achieved a contract which has significantly raised the statewide standard for wages, benefits, and working conditions.

By 2002, the 8000-strong Vermont AFL-CIO, the 7000 strong Vermont State Employees' Association (VSEA), the UE, the Teamsters, and numerous other labor unions, as well as other mass organizations were official members of the center. The VWC's official membership constituency now numbers over 15,000 (in a state with a total population of just over 600,000).[46]

Without this earned respect, the major unions (who have economic, legal, political, and personnel resources that most leftwing organizations — including NEFAC — no not have) would not have taken the proposal to form an all-workers-union seriously. It is unlikely that any of them would have committed themselves to the project. And without their resources — without a fulltime organizer, and without the confidence that, for better or worse, these established unions bring to the workers, it is unlikely that such an ambitious project as the Montpelier Downtown Workers' Union would have gone as far as it thus far has.

Origins of The Vermont Workers' Center and Internal Structure[47]

The Vermont Workers' Center opened the doors to its first office space in the spring of 1998. The mission of the center reads: "we seek an economically just and democratic Vermont in which all residents have living wages, decent healthcare, childcare, housing and transportation. We work to build a democratic, diverse movement of working Vermonters that is locally focused and coordinated on a statewide basis. We work with organized labor in moving towards economic justice and in strengthening the right to organize. We are committed to taking action on the full range of issues that

46 Organizational members of the Vermont Workers Center include: Alliance at IBM/CWA Local 1701, AFSCME Local 1369, AFSCME Council 93, Champlain Valley Central Labor Council, GCIU Local 745, IBEW Local 300, Machinists Local 2704, VT National Writers Union (UAW Local 1981), Plumbers and Pipe Fitters Local 693, Teamsters Local 597, UE District 2, UE local 221, UE Local 234, UE Local 254, UE Local 267, United Nurses and Allied Professionals Local 5086, United Nurses and Allied Professionals 5109, United Professions of Vermont-AFT, United Steelworkers of America Amalgamated Local 4, United Steelworkers of America Local 518, Vermont Federation of Nurses and Health Professionals Local 5221, Vermont State College Faculty Federation AFT Local 3180, Vermont State Employees' Association, Vermont State Labor Council AFL-CIO, Washington-Orange County Central Labor Council, Older Woman's League (Vermont Chapter), Anti-Racist Action Team, Woman's International League for Peace & Freedom (Vermont Chapter).

47 The next thirteen paragraphs, with only minor alterations, were written by Lady (a member of the Green Mountain Anarchist Collective) and first appeared in the article *Class Struggle in The Green Mountains: Vermont Workers Center*, which was published in the Northeastern Anarchist, fall 2003.

concern working people, and to building alliances nationally and internationally." The VWC seeks to build an effective and meaningful labor movement within the particularities of Vermont.

The overarching goal of the VWC is to empower those persons within the working class who are normally shutout of the political and economic systems that, time and again, pursue policies that do not uplift the worker, but rather pushes them closer to the precipice of poverty and ignorance. To quote from their outreach pamphlet: "by organizing public hearings, forums, publicizing people's stories, and taking part in direct action, we support workers throughout the state who are trying to improve their wages, benefits, rights on the job, working conditions, and their communities."

This is not to say that the sole focus of the VWC is centered on piecemeal issues that are perpetuated by the basic internal dualities of capitalism (which can be seen as the idea that the rich get richer, and the poor get poorer). In a word, the VWC is not simply running around sticking their fingers in leaky dams. The center also makes the connection to, and is actively working towards, long term, more comprehensive solutions to the problems of capitalism and the oppressive contradictions between worker and owner, labor and management, the common person and the boss, the voter and politician.

The founding membership of the VWC came from a community group founded in 1896 called Central Vermonters For a Livable Wage. This group was made up of welfare recipients, activists, labor union people, community affiliated people, and one-quarter of the group's membership was the #10 Collective (formerly Love & Rage Revolutionary Anarchist Federation members). Central Vermonters For a Livable Wage did solidarity work with labor struggles, and got people together to talk about economic justice. Tanya Waters, a former member of the #10 Collective, founding member of the Vermont Workers Center, and Vice President of her local nurses' union recalls: "Many of the members began talking about raising the minimum wage, which meant legislative work. We were effective in earning another $1 an hour, but we wanted to do work that was more focused around working with the community; whereas legislative work was a disempowering experience."

The first projects of the VWC were a statewide workers' rights handbook and hotline that still functions today, solidarity with the Bennington Potters, Solidarity with Capital City Press workers in Barre, raising the minimum wage, and presentations on workers' rights at adult education programs, churches, union shops, several high schools, and a few colleges.

The VWC was an evolution of three years of work and tactics that organized as an issue organization (Central Vermonters For a Livable Wage). Issue organizations are harder to keep together than a workers' center that organizes around several of the concerns working class people have. A workers' center is an organization that people will self-identify with, a place where people can find others who share similar experiences they have had to deal with. It serves as a place with resources that the community can access, such as writing press releases, phone banking, and a meeting space. It organizes campaigns that try to improve wages, benefits, rights on the job, working conditions, and ultimately the community.

Functionally the VWC has a steering committee and a coordinating committee made up of unions, community organizations, religious groups, and individuals. Organizations and individuals are accepted as members of the steering committee after they have been nominated by a member organization or person. Following this, the steering committee votes to accept the nomination, or not. Political parties are not allowed to become members. It is also worth mentioning that since the VWC accepts both organizations (usually unions) and individuals as members, it sometimes serves as a place where left union dissidents are able to democratically take part in the organized class struggle alongside the union which, although they may be a member, effectively shuts them out of the internal decision making hierarchy due to their political convictions and workplace actions. In this way the VWC acts as a democratizing body despite the participation of some unions that are not known as being internally democratic as would be desirable.

The steering committee (composed of both organizational delegates and individuals) meets four times a year to democratically decide on projects they will work on, and the coordinating committee, which is elected by the steering committee, meets monthly to focus on more day-to-day issues. The VWC is funded through foundation grants, individual donations, and union donations. The first year it started with an annual budget of $11,000 and the ability to pay one staff person at $100 per week. Currently, through display of successful work to union and community members, their budget has increased to $65,000 a year and the ability to pay one fulltime, and two part time staff persons. At the onset, the VWC was able to solicit such funding through the use of the Burlington Peace & Justice Center's

501C3 tax exempt status. In 2003 the VWC gained independent tax exempt status and no longer holds any formal ties with the Peace & Justice Center.

The VWC differs in some regards from other workers' centers across the continent. One way it is unique is because Vermont is traditionally different than areas where workers' centers primarily exist. This difference is reflected in two areas: race and population. The population of Vermont is 620,000 and with rural living comes a higher real-unemployment rate[48] due to economic flight (i.e. the effects of free trade) and a minimal amount of jobs employing a large number of people, such as factory work. Eighty-five percent of businesses in Vermont employ 9 workers of less. "Vermont is unique because there are no models where you can organize 85% of the businesses. You really have to pull your resources together," says Tanya. "We build rights and power for people who might not work in a large factory and have the minimal protection of a union."

Most workers' centers in the U.S. are located in immigrant communities. However, in a state that is 97% European-American, there is no prevalent immigrant community or larger minority population for such a center to connect with. "Our analysis early on was really about finding the power to make change. Early on we recognized race was not going to be our rally point. Gender has always been an issue, and economics is what we found to be most powerful because it is something people here can relate to." (Tanya)

The VWC was founded by a large proportion of class struggle anarchists, and currently those who do a lot of the organizing identify to one degree or another with anarchism or left socialism. While the volunteers involved with the center do not all identify as such, a number of those who do are known to the community as anarchists. However, their personal politics are not front and center. It is about the work they are doing. The VWC prioritizes its work by first building a movement around people and what their issues are. Then, the need to figure out how to build that into a more radical democratic movement, emerges. "We are far from being revolutionary," says Jason Winston, a VWC co-founder and former #10 Collective member. "But we have the strategy of starting where people are at. People only joined because of what we are doing, not because of what we said.

---

48 Official unemployment estimates run low. Presently [2004] they claim to have less than 4% unemployment. However, this statistic is based on the number of people who qualify for unemployment insurance. Unfortunately many thousands of people do not qualify for such and are therefore ignored by the official statistics. In reality portions of Vermont such as the Northeast Kingdom commonly see seasonable real unemployment rates of 15% or higher.

We don't act like we could tell them what they want to hear. It is not a theoretical relationship. You build trust with people because you stand on their picket line," says Winston. Through the course of the last five years of doing diligent, nonsectarian solidarity work, the VWC (with the VT AFL-CIO & VSEA & other major unions as participating members) was able to pass an official resolution against the imperialist invasion of Iraq during a 2003 Steering Committee meeting, officially endorsing the two million strong U.S. Labor Against the War..

It is important to note that many VWC organizers recognize the historical limitations of bureaucratic trade unions (of which they work closely with). Often these organizations fail to see beyond their limited (and immediate) self-interest. In the current union model, the labor unions are not the all-powerful defenders of the working class they have the potential to be. Due to the collaborative nature of many unions between their official leadership, party politics, and cooperation with the bosses, numerous labor organizations are compelled to traverse undemocratic paths, and this often stifles attempts of direct action in the workplace. Acknowledging these flaws, we know that mainstream trade unions in the U.S. are not currently revolutionary organizations, and most unions today fail to promote radical worker self-activity and serious class warfare. The issue is not whether unions are revolutionary, rather it is how anarchists work within unions towards a revolutionary end.

Karl Marx once referred to the unions as 'the universities of the working class.' While this may have been clearly more true during his time, we should understand the potential that unions retain today for such educating to occur. Through participation in labor unions, workers acknowledge class interests and develop class consciousness. The union movement is the most important mass movement the working class has built. Based on the numbers of people represented by unions, anarchist groups and other radical organizations must have a program that addresses and relates to these organizations and the workers who participate in them.

Bottom line, it took eight years of hard work (three within the parameters of Central Vermonters For a Living Wage, and five more organizing as the Vermont Workers Center) to get to the point where major unions could realistically be approached about the possibility of starting an all-workers union in one trial area. This was done through nonsectarian solidarity work on behalf of the working class and their imperfect organizations, and through the eventual gaining of working class respect and the respect of the established union leadership. Additionally, the Green Mountain Anarchist Collective is currently able to maintain relatively good and productive relationships with the established mass labor movement because those doors were diligently opened to us by those class struggle anarchists who came before, and are still active in the VWC and as union members and organizers. Even so, it is worth noting that it has taken us a good part of two years of concerted effort to build these relations to where they are today. And of course this too was achieved through diligent solidarity work, a willingness to engage in militant and non-militant picket lines, and generally demonstrating that we are committed working class organizers.

State of The Montpelier Downtown Workers Union

As of print, the union drive, which seeks to organize all workers in the capital city, includes about 100 of the 800 employees of small downtown shops. Official union recognition has been won at the Savoy Theatre & Downstairs Video shop (14 workers), a majority has been reached at six other shops, and workers from more than fifteen separate shops have joined the union. A workers' organizing committee meets regularly in order to discuss strategy and to coordinate worker solidarity actions. Recently this committee has begun the publication of a monthly newspaper, the Downtown Workers' Journal (funded by the VWC and UE), which discusses the union drive and other worker issues. The workers distribute them on the street to other area employees and send them in the mail to core VWC activists. Within this organizing committee there is also a sub-organizing committee of five workers from one of the large and more contentious shops in the city. These are workers from J. Morgan's restaurant (40 workers), and they meet on their own to discuss the direction of the specific union drive in their shop. In addition to these committees, community support meetings are held every other month at which community members are able to come together in order to discuss how they think the general strategy should go, and to further coordinate their own support activity among the broader population. These meetings regularly draw 25 or so people from diverse left perspectives. These include union members (including the President of the Vermont AFL-CIO), Vermont Progressive Party members (social democrats), peace activists, and of course members of the Green Mountain Anarchist Collective.

The formal decision making process of the entire campaign is far from perfect. While the UE is a very democratic union, they do not believe that democracy should necessarily be practiced until after a shop wins official recognition.[49] The official stance of the union aside, high degrees of direct democracy have been achieved. It is common for general and specific tactics and strategies to be discussed at both the workers' organizing committee meetings and at the community support meetings. If a general consensus, or strong majority position is not reached at both these meetings, plans are often modified, delayed, or changed. Furthermore, the union, both paid staff (of which there are three) and workers, do not undertake any action targeting a specific shop without the plans first being approved by the union workers at that shop. All told, internal democracy, especially during these phases where workers are not officially incorporated into a recognized union, is something that must be guarded. GMAC, as well as others, have maintained vigilance in this sphere. Here it is helps that a number of the people directly involved in this drive, including a minority of workers on the organizing committee, identify with anarchist.

In regards to official recognition, the strategy from the beginning has been to demand card check recognition, and to avoid filing for any National Labor Relations Board (NLRB) monitored elections. The reasoning behind this is that the lapse of time between the filing for an election and the date of the vote leaves too much space for the bosses to intimidate the workers. This is thought to be more of a problem than in larger shops (like factories and grocery stores) because the boss (who often is the owner) tends to work with the employees, and in such small, isolated spaces the obvious and subtle threats of this person can have a serious impact upon the workers combative stance. Also, the union does not wish to become bogged down in countless elections in dozens of separate shops. Finally, the structure and legalities of such elections are consistently tilted in favor of the bosses and tend to weaken the motivation of the workers.

This strategy has thus far had mixed results. On the one hand, filing for so many elections could have resulted in a draining of much of the energy of the overall drive. Each election would require a concerted campaign to maintain confidence and momentum in each shop leading up to the vote. And recognizing that the drive, even with the backing of the UE and VWC, has limited resources, such a

---

49 There are exceptions to this within the union, especially in instances of 'minority unionism', wherein internal democracy is practiced.

course could have translated into the overall campaign being bogged down in legalities, shortsighted efforts, etc.. On the other hand, after six months of organizing we only have official recognition at one shop. With NLRB monitored votes, we could have two to four more shops officially recognized. As the successful Cambridge Pissed Off Projectionists union drive demonstrated (CAC, Boston-NEFAC), there are pros and cons to both sides of this question. Any similar union drive in the U.S. will have to decide this one on their own.[50]

In general, the union has fought for recognition by adapting a two-prong strategy. First, they have attempted to convince bosses to recognize through a highroad public recognition campaign. Second, they have used direct action and public demonstrations as a means to force an anti-union boss to relent to their demands.

Concerning the highroad approach, the union has launched a pro-union letter writing drive to the two local mainstream newspapers (both independent — one a weekly the other a daily). To date dozens of pro-union letters have been printed (as have a smaller number of anti-union ones). They have also gained 700 signatures on a pro-union petition (no small feat in a city of only 7800 residents). Hundreds of these signatures were from Montpelier residents. The petition also stated that the signatories would frequent union shops for business. The most important part of this petition effort was the hundreds of working class people who union members and supporters were able to talk to while gathering signatures. One GMAC[51] wet door to door in a working class Montpelier neighborhood, and discovered that most working people (who work outside the city), who presumably do not read the papers, were unaware of the drive. Many of these people invited this person into their home in order to discuss the campaign, and in that neighborhood only three people refused to sign. In turn the VWC and UE paid to have the petition published as a full page ad in a local newspaper. The union has also sent community delegations to a number of shops where a majority of the workers have joined — especially those where the boss had been publicly supportive of the organizing activities of the employees. These delegations were made up of respected community members, workers, and union officials (include those from outside the UE). There the delegations requested that the boss/owner voluntarily recognize the union. Finally, the union also organized a union buy-in day, where maybe 100 supporters frequented shops, wearing union pins, and told the boss that they

---

50 In Quebec, Ontario, and Canada generally, card check recognition is recognized as a legally binding form of gaining official union recognition.
51 2017 note from the author: That was me.

were spending money there because of their apparent willingness to recognize the demands of the workers.

All told, this high road approach, with one exception, has not seceded in gaining recognition at any shops. However, this approach is being conducted in conjunction with a more confrontational campaign at one shop, J. Morgan's restaurant, and its combined effectiveness will not be fully known for perhaps another six months.

At J. Morgan's the union drive has taken much more confrontational turns. The restaurant is owned by one of the wealthiest families in the city. This family also owns a movie theatre (not the Savoy), a dry cleaners, a laundromat, and a hotel. As such they are able to spend large sums of capital fighting the union drive. In this capacity they have hired a union busting firm and have chosen to intimidate, interrogate, threaten, and spy on workers. Management even fired one worker for her union activity. In response, the union, upon invitation from the shop's organizing committee, has disrupted restaurant business through various means during peak hours. These methods have been diverse and have included the holding of a coffee-in (where union supporters take up all the tables for several hours and spend no more than the price of a cup of coffee while leaving a large tip and pro-union messages on the bill), the presenting of a Grinch-of-the-year award in front of patrons, the holding of large pro-union demonstrations outside the business, the organizing of regular informational pickets, and encouraging of organizations to pull business from the establishment until they recognize the union. These actions have cost the owners untold thousands of dollars, as has the hiring of union busters (which costs are currently estimated at over $250,000). While the owners have thus far been able to absorb these losses, it is hoped that they are wearing management down. In addition to these actions, the union has also filed twenty Unfair Labor Practices (ULPs) with the NLRB. Tellingly enough, the assigned NLRB investigator decided to file these, plus eight additional charges, some very serious. While we cannot say with confidence that this shop will become union, it appears that the negative publicity that they have accrued, the loss of respect from elements of the community in regards to the owners, the loss of revenue, and the difficulty that direct actions and pickets have had on the normal operations of the business may result in other shops accepting union recognition as a means to avoid the type of struggles not witnessed at J. Morgan's. While the richest family in town may be able to hold out against continuing losses, most businesses would fail if subjected to such pressures over an extended period of time. Any small business owner in Montpelier, who is not a fool, knows this and is forced to contemplate this reality.

At present, Bob Kingsley, the National Director of Organizing for the UE, based out of Pittsburgh PA, has met with the organizers of this drive on several occasions, and is now advocating that the union move beyond the immediate goal of signing up members and gaining shop majorities, and instead begin to "act like a union." What is meant by this is that the union is moving in the direction of organizing actions in support of the demands of the workers, whether or not they have official recognition or even a majority in a particular shop. From the beginning some organizers argued that this would be the best way to launch the union, as opposed to simply signing people up (which sometimes, without context, can seem a bit too abstract). One of the first efforts has been to post signs around the city letting workers know that it is against the law for bosses to subtract from one's hourly wage for breaks that last less than thirty minutes (union contact info is included on the flyer). In this same vein, organizers plan on working with employees of targeted shops that are known to break this labor law in order to get such practices discontinued. It is further thought that making an example out of one or two shops will indirectly have the effect of bringing a number of other shops inline. Here it is hoped that the union will be successful, and with success they will be able to point to a small but real victory won by the union against the bosses. As the union takes part in more and more of these sub-campaigns it is anticipated that more workers will come to view the union as a democratic force that is both on their side, directly relevant, and an arm of their class defense. And with that it is hoped that the union's numbers will begin to swell.

Union organizers have also put together a questionnaire for workers to fill out. With this the union intends to ascertain the basic democratic wishes of the majority of workers. From this the union will produce a document provisionally named "The Montpelier Standard", which will demand that certain basic workers' rights and shop standards be recognized by all bosses in the city. A workers' Town Meeting is currently scheduled for April 22nd, 2004, where this document will be discussed, debated, amended, and hopefully ratified through directly democratic means. What comes out of this workers' Town Meeting will inform the tactical direction of the union's efforts. Whatever the workers demand as their top priorities will be what the union fights for in the coming months. And here, the union will not just carry the fight to shops with union majorities, but they will seek to widen the arena of struggle across the entire city. The workers will set the common standards, and the organized force of the union will facilitate a campaign around these standards.

In essence this overall tactic should be understood as an attempt to apply the functioning concept of minority unionism to an entire (small) city. Like in a factory where one thousand out of a possible eight thousand workers organize a union, and then persists in acting like one, the Downtown Workers Union is viewing their 100 members as a minority within a potential pool of 800. And if they can exert their power throughout the capital and in doing infuse the unorganized workers with a sense of excitement and hope, it is more likely that a momentum can be built and maintained that can propel them even further down the road of building a powerful dual power. With this in place, it is unclear as to whether or not this move towards minority unionism will result in the UE officially recognizing the democratic integrity of the union (as UE local 221), or if they will continue to officially uphold their institutional right to direct the drive above the authority of the workers. Here it is important to recall that the drive, thus far, has been run very democratically. The only question is whether or not that democracy will become the guaranteed right of the workers. It is expected that this question will be formally answered in a matter of days.

Since the union drive does not seek to negotiate separate contracts with each shop, and since the contract is much less comprehensive than is usually the case (only three pages), the union is only requiring a flay $3 a week sum from each unionized worker. If an employee works only eight hours or less, the weekly sum is only $1.50. If a worker works at multiple shops (as many downtown workers are compelled to hold several jobs to make ends meet), they are not required to pay additional amounts above the standard $3. From the start of the drive it was understood that workers would not pay any dues until their workplace wins official recognition. As the union begins to exert itself in regards to concrete issues in the city, it is hoped by some organizers that union members from shops that are not officially recognized will begin to pay regular dues voluntarily from each weekly paycheck. Such money would go into supporting such projects as the Downtown Workers' Journal. This approach may or may not prove effective. On the one hand, if the workers come to see the union as both theirs and as a real counter force in the community, they may be ok with supporting it to the tune of three bucks a week. On the other hand, if the union does not demonstrate its relevance in a timely manner, many workers will be turned off by the prospect of giving it even a dollar of their hard earned money. In either case, as this change becomes formalized, it is likely that the union will suffer at least a temporary decline in membership.[52]

During the beginning of the union drive most activity was driven by VWC and UE organizers. However, one of their initial goals was to build a workers' organizing committee representing employees of at least ten different shops. After several months of effort, and after talking to dozens and dozens of workers, this was achieved. Today the honest truth is that without the paid staff and/or volunteer staff the entire drive would likely fall apart. While clear leaders have been emerging out of the rank and file, most still lack the experience of organized struggle necessary to carry the torch on their own. Still, much progress has been made, and as the fight continues, it would appear that certain workers will develop into outstanding strategists and tacticians. While rank and file leadership development can be aided through workshops, trainings, etc., it is mostly by walking through fire that one learns how not to burn the feet. And as the campaign wears on, the signs are there that things are moving in a positive direction.

During the course of the last two months, the workers' organizing committee has begun the writing, layout, and distribution of their own monthly newspaper. They also organized a rapid response delegation to the workplace of one union member (also a member of the organizing committee) in order to confront her boss.[53] This boss, the day before, cut her hours, most likely because of her outspoken support of the union. The delegation confronted the boss and demanded that she be given her hours back. The boss, obviously intimidated, relented. Victory. More recently a number of workers attended a Montpelier Business Association meeting where they were allotted time to speak before the owners in regards to why they demand recognition of the union. Their goal was to try and help foster natural spits among the small owners, neutralizing the potential venom of some, winning support of the very few, and separating these from the rabid anti-union camp. By doing so it is hoped to stifle attempts by owners to organize a front against the drive and to further pool their collective resources in order to stamp it out. All told the meeting went well from the point of view of the workers. But revealingly enough, the workers decided

---

52 2017 note from the author: The UE ultimately decided to *require* weekly dues from all members regardless if they had recognition in their shop of not.

53 2017 note from the author: The delegation was headed by Sean West, a union member and a member of the Green Mountain Anarchist Collective.

amongst themselves afterwards that next time they would not invite the paid organizer with them, as it was felt that her presence (as she has been very visible from the beginning) immediately turns off small owners that may naturally be riding the fence in regards to their active position on the union. The workers decided by themselves that attempts at dividing the owners would be more effective if carried out by them alone. This event is significant as it shows that the workers are beginning to develop their own collective identity as something, not distinct from the union, but as something that constitutes the legitimate existence of the union. The union, in their minds, is developing into an expression of their democratic will, as opposed to a separate organization which has their interests in mind.

The more such worker self-activity can be fostered the better. For it is such activity which points to a maturing in class consciousness, and it is just such a mass of workers which is necessary if we are to build a movement which is eventually capable of escaping the ideo-religious confines of authoritarianism and capital.

As has previously been discussed, a small number of anarchists, and others sympathetic to anarchist ideals, were involved in the union drive since its conception insofar as certain anarchist persons who helped form the Workers' Center continued to maintain an active role within it. Specifically, the Green Mountain Anarchist Collective sought ways to support the drive from the start. Still, in the early months, GMAC participation was very limited. At that stage the primary work was around collecting intelligence (i.e. cataloging all the separate shops, finding out how many workers each had, what they were paid, and whether or not they received any benefits). This task was performed by a paid union organizer and a worker from the recently unionized Hunger Mountain Food Co-op. Later the tasks moved to drafting agitational material which described the idea of forming an all-workers union, and clandestinely getting these materials to the workers. Here again GMAC was minimally involved, as this was easily handled by a few involved people, and primarily relied upon workers passing them out to each other.

As the union drive began to mature, and as more and more workers signed union cards, GMAC decided to commit its members to support roles in different elements of the drive. One member, who was also a downtown Montpelier worker, joined the workers' organizing committee (this member was recently voted in as Treasurer of the Local). This member was also instrumental in the production of the agitational Downtown Workers' Journal. Two other members immersed themselves in the drive as non-paid staff volunteers with the VWC.[54] These two have recently begun to act as a team in support of winning union majorities in targeting shops and carrying out other support tasks. Another member continued to help produce GMAC/anarchist specific agitational material which was distributed to the workers, and posted around the city. Towards this end, GMAC produced a four page pamphlet entitled "Union + Town Meeting = Democracy." Several hundred of these were given directly to workers and posted everywhere possible around the capital by the GMAC member on the workers' organizing committee. This pamphlet, using accessible language which incorporates imagery that is reflective of the regional culture and history, sought to demonstrate the link between building such a union and achieving direct democracy in Vermont. GMAC's newspaper, Catamount Tavern news, also committed itself to providing coverage of the union drive from an anarchist perspective.

Generally speaking, GMAC members have made an effort to publicly separate their roles in the drive. Those members that have committed themselves to signing up workers alongside the UE and VWC staff maintain their public identity with that of these organizations. This is not to say that any GMAC member ever lies about their political beliefs and/or affiliations when asked. We don't, and any worker or organizer who asks, or who is around for any length of time knows exactly what those beliefs and affiliations are. All we are here doing is not confusing the union and the VWC with that of NEFAC. In addition to being arrogant and misleading, it is possible that claims of NEFAC/anarchist control of the drive, or even the over stating of our role, could result in the UE and the VWC being red baited by opponents. While the actual result of such a red baiting campaign is uncertain[55], we see no need to test the waters at this time. Our immediate goal is to build a democratic organization of workers (who are commonly not in workplaces that possess unions) that will be capable of adding to the overall class struggle in the region. As to what name it is done under, or who publicly gets credit, those are questions that have no real bearing for us. Besides, the political identity of the union will have to be defined by the workers themselves, not by ideological lines.

---

54 One of these GMAC members recently became employed in a downtown Montpelier shop and has recently joined the workers' organizing committee.
55 Red baiting campaigns have consistently failed to diminish the popularity of Vermont's self-described socialist, Congressman Bernie Sanders.

All told, GMAC's duel role as both non-sectarian supporters/ Workers' Center organizers, and that of producing explicitly anarchist oriented agitational literature, has done nothing but help the drive. While many workers join the union because of bread and butter issues (which the VWC and UE staff are good at articulating), many have also joined because of the basic issue of democracy. And here GMAC's anarchist perspective has aided in bringing over such workers. At the end of the day our role as an organized anarchist presence in the campaign is both to help the drive along however we can, and to publicly articulate (through our writings and appropriate conversations with workers) how the specifics of the campaign relate to the broader goals of direct democracy and socialism. Internally within the drive we also try to suggest tactical directions that we feel could be effective, and try to encourage as much democracy as possible. Finally, we see our long term role as a force that can potentially effect the direction of the union after the campaign reaches certain levels of success and self-sustainability.

Any similar union drive in different regions would benefit from such a mix of official bread and butter unionism (as determined through official organizing staff), and radical, pro-direct democracy, pro-socialism agitation on behalf of anarchist groups. Furthermore, by making connections to workers' democracy from the near onset, seeds are planted in the minds of interested workers that in future years can only make the struggle to achieve a radical class consciousness among the population that much more successful.

From Montpelier Downtown Workers' Union To A Montpelier Workers' Council

This unique union drive has had a positive effect in bringing together area unions (non-UE) and individual union members in a common support role. At community support meetings it is common for representatives from the state AFL-CIO to be present, as well as individual members unions such as the Teamsters, Vermont State Employees' Association (VSEA), Iron Workers, National Writers Union, National Educators Association, etc.. The VSEA, who for years held their union events at Capital Plaza (which includes J. Morgans), pulled their business from the establishment in solidarity with the union drive. Other union members have offered help on the drive ranging from phone banking, to talking picket lines, to collecting relevant intelligence. In a word, this effort has galvanized many different branches of labor, adding to the growing sense of inter-union solidarity in the region.

It is not a huge leap to believe that the Montpelier Downtown Workers' Union will have official recognition in maybe five shops, a total membership of 150 workers, in maybe a year and a half. At that point, when the union becomes a legitimate and stable force in the city, a real union presence will be represented in the capital that is potentially inclusive of all workers. Already utility workers, librarians, firefighters, teachers, state workers, some tradesmen, postal workers, etc., have their own unions. Only now *all* workers will have access to organized labor.

When this time comes, in maybe two years-time, we can conceive of an issue coming up in the city which affects all, or a significant segment of the working class population on the local level. When such occurs, it is possible, given the general context outlined above, that all unions could be brought together in a general assembly of union members in order to address the issue.[56]

We can foresee a situation where such a meeting was called for by the rank and file of the Downtown Workers' Union, and/or by organizers from the Workers Center — maybe through GMAC prompting. Here a few volunteers could physically go to dozens of shops in the city personally giving invitations and other related information directly to shop stewards with the intension of them distributing these to their fellow workers. We could reach out across union lines to the teachers (NEA), the utility workers (IBEW), the state workers (VSEA), the service and retail workers (UE), the postal workers, the librarians, the firefighters, the tradesmen, etc.. And if such a general meeting of unionized workers was called for from elements within organized labor, and because of the ten year history above discussed, we could feasibly imagine a large and diverse number of workers attending the meeting.

One potential stumbling block for any such attempt would be opposition on the state level from within the different unions to these meetings. Without a strong and tested history of inter-union mutual aid and trust, certain union officials, from the county level up, could view this as a threat to the integrity of their larger, separate, apparatus. This may not prove to be a problem with the unions such as the NEA

---

56 The current [2004] contract fights going on in Boston, leading up to the Democratic National Convention, immediately comes to mind as a perfect spark to ignite such a project. We must understand that the contradictions of capitalism will time and again lead to such opportunities. Only we must build the effective channels through which this class anger can be brought together as a far reaching, organized force.

(who vest a good deal of autonomy within the Locals), but within the AFL-CIO it is always a possibility that should be thought about. And again, if such a negative intervention is pursued by Executive Councils and even local Labor Councils, the tragic history of organized labor being held back by a built in bureaucratic and centralizing tendency could easily repeat itself and potentially doom such an all-worker meeting before it even began. But because of the positive environment of labor solidarity brought about through the five years of effort on the part of the Workers' Center, we have reason to believe that if the right circumstances presented themselves, such a meeting could be called for in Montpelier without having to fight tooth and nail against failure. And again, this is thought to be possible also because of the changing conditions within the pre-existing labor movement itself.

The effective solidarity work and inter-union coordinating efforts of the Workers' Center has also helped to raise the level of political and organizational activity of the different unions. In some cases these emerging dynamics have helped to motivate more of the rank and file, and in turn this motivated rank and file has further motivated the unions. With this, many leftists and reformers have been elected to high ranks within the Vermont unions in the last few years. Dan Brush, a print worker from Capital City Press, was recently elected President of the Vermont AFL-CIO on the reform ticket. Ed Stanak, who is supportive of many left leaning initiatives, is President of the VSEA. This past fall Jerry Colby, of the Burlington area, was elected national President of the Writers' Union (UAW Local 1981) also as a reform candidate. In addition, many progressive union members have been elected to posts within their Central Labor Councils. Tellingly, Hall Leyshon[57], President of the Washington County Central Labor Council (under whose jurisdiction is Montpelier) has taken to inviting unions other than those in the AFL-CIO (VSEA, UE, NEA, etc.) to their meetings.[58] It would seem that the tide is turning in our favor.

If we could get as far as successfully holding such a democratic all-workers meeting, and if this body voted to take action in response to the issue at hand, and if that action resulted in some level of immediate success, it is possible that a new sense of class empowerment could reverberate through the ranks of the workers. Here it may be possible that the assembly of workers would be invigorated in such a way as to indefinitely extend the tenure of the assembly. And if this were to happen, NEFAC collectives/members (which inevitably will include

---

57 2017 note from the author: he later changed his name to Traven Leyshon.
58 Central Labor Councils are typically composed AFL-CIO unions exclusively.

local union members) would be in a very good position to see that the new body adopt an internal structure which is in line with direct democracy.

For example, if the spark issue that brought this meeting together was a desire to organize solidarity work for several unions which were out on strike, is it not conceivable, given a pre-existing inter-union atmosphere of respect, trust, and mutual aid, that such an all-workers assembly could, in solidarity, vote to call for a one day general strike? And if such a strike was successfully carried out with positive effects, it is also conceivable that the assembly would recognize the benefits of coming together in such a grassroots, united, fashion. With this realization it is only a very short step to the permanent formation of a formalized all-workers organization. As soon as the local rank and file of separate unions begin to organize their own activities in the general interest of the entire class (as opposed to just their particular shop), and as soon as this is expressed through directly democratic means by the mass of workers (of which NEFAC should strongly encourage), the workers' council is born! And if such an organization was to form through a similar evolution as outlined above, there is a good chance that it would develop into a directly democratic body with effective structural means to take positions, actions, and to coordinate basic struggles. This is true insofar as basic values of union democracy, class solidarity, and respect will have presumably been infused throughout a great number of the most outspoken and influential workers through the long trials, tribulations, and campaigns which presuppose these new councils. In this sense, even if a short cut could be used to foster such workers' councils, it is uncertain if such a road should be trusted. Maybe, maybe not. This, in that it will be the very process of building the conditions necessary for their rational appearance which will not only make them likely, but also subjectively sustainable.[59]

Finally, we recognize that the transformation of all-worker unions to that of workers' councils is uncertain. These are waters that we not yet swam in. However, because of where we now sit, we can see such possibilities looming on the not so distant horizon. The Green Mountain Anarchist Collective contends that the recent history of the Vermont labor movement, and specifically the long term strategies carried out by class struggle anarchists (namely that of the former #10 Collective) can serve as a partial model for NEFAC activities across the northeast. If we keep our eye on the prize we assert that NEFAC can

---

59 Here it is worth noting that achieving a directly democratic structure within such bodies will be a more natural direction throughout the areas of New England where a Town Meeting culture still exists.

move to create the necessary conditions for, and then build workers' councils in all our areas of operation. Too speculative to base our federation's strategy on? We would say 'no.' If we are successful, we have much to gain. And if this transformation is not pulled off? Well, we still will have lost nothing and will have gained the continuing victories of stronger labor movements in our areas of activity. Emma Goldman once said "to the daring belong the future." Comrades, the future is at hand. Let us, NEFAC, venture into the unknown that is tomorrow, and let us risk victory as the bet against failure!

Proposal

Each member collective, individual, or, where it pertains, local federation unions of area collectives, individual members and supporters who are not presently engaged in activities that relate to building of directly democratic peoples' assemblies, or building of directly democratic farmer organizations:

1.) Pursue the creation of area workers' councils as the overall strategy of how, in part, we intend to build both duel power and real revolutionary potential within our class — the working class!

NEFAC, to the best of its abilities, will see that these councils are directly democratic, and will incorporate all unionized workers within the selected geographic area.

NEFAC, to the best of its abilities, will also see that they meet (a minimum of) twice a year, at which all unionized workers will be invited to decide all major policy and campaigns that the council shall pursue until the next general meeting. Votes will be made by simple majority opinion, unless the question is to call for a general strike, or any additional activity that can be considered as or more militant, in which case a two thirds majority is required. At this meeting a workers' select board of five persons shall be elected from (when and where possible) separate shops and separate unions. The election of this workers' select board shall be done by a public hand count of all assembled workers. The workers' select board shall be tasked with facilitating the general, voted on, council policy.

Recognizing that it is less likely that such a council can form without the official approval of effected unions (be that on the local, state, or provincial level), such an approval shall be vigorously sought by NEFAC collectives, and area union members. Where such approval cannot be reasonably attained, and where it appears that such formations are still possible, NEFAC shall continue to pursue the formation of such councils.

2.) In order to meaningfully achieve this end it will be necessary to build democratic unions in all these areas that include as members all the small shops that traditional unions do not seek to organize. NEFAC shall work towards, and prioritize the building of these unions. These unions should be made up of any non-union workers that seek to join. This union should seek to gain legal recognition in individual shops in which a majority of the workers join the union. This union shall not be considered even partially effective until it has official or effective recognition in a minimum of three different shops in the specific targeted geographical area.

3.) In order to build these unions, and recognizing the limited resources of NEFAC, each member collective, or, where it pertains, local federation union of area collectives and individual members and supporters form an alliance with a progressive, proven, union, and work with them on creating such unions, where necessary under that union's name.

4.) In order to make such alliances both possible and likely each member collective, or, where it pertains, local federation union of area collectives and individual members and supporters should develop a way to form strong and trusted ties with the labor unions in their vicinity. They will do this by committing themselves to doing consistent and effective solidarity work on behalf of strikes, union drives, contract drives, etc.. In doing so they will be free to express their honest thoughts and critiques to both the rank and file, the elected officials, and the union staff. Such critiques shall be done good naturedly, and the severity of the critique shall depend on the severity of the complaint. This relationship shall be pursued in the earliest phases (or until mutual respect is achieved) with little or no attempts at large scale ideological conversion. From the onset, such relationships shall entail the full knowledge by all pertinent parties that we are anarcho-communists, members of NEFAC, and workers.

5.) In order to achieve effective social-political avenues for such conversations to take place it may be necessary for each member collective, or, where it pertains, local federation union of area collectives and individual members and supporters to facilitate the building of an area workers' center. These workers' centers shall not be sectarian, and will encourage the official membership of individuals and labor and social justice organizations. These workers' centers shall be democratic as possible, while still retaining a broad base of support and potential support. While this may not be necessary in some regions, it may prove to be in others. The decision as to whether or not to implement point #5 will be left to the directly democratic discretion of the related parties in distinct areas. However, these related parties will seek advice of the federation as a whole, and will seriously take that advice into account in their decision making process.

6.) In some regions pre-existing workers' centers, Jobs With Justice chapters, Central Labor Councils, or other union based organizations may prove themselves to be a viable place from which to implement the above strategy. Where that is the case, each member collective, or, where it pertains, local federation union of area collectives and individual members and supporters should seek to immerse themselves in these organizations in order to carry forth the above strategy. The decision as to how point #6 is implemented will be left to the directly democratic discretion of related parties in distinct areas. However, these related parties will seek advice of the federation as a whole, and will seriously take that advice into account in their decision making process.

7.) In order to be able to realistically build strong relationships with unions, and/or to be able to realistically build a workers' center, each member collective, or, where it pertains, local federation union of area collectives and individual members and supporters shall work diligently to build their local unions and collectives into strong, well organized, self-disciplined, politically knowledgeable, tactically effective, and respected units. The means by which this should be achieved as well as the decision as to when they reach an acceptable level, shall be left to these units themselves. However, in regards to the above, these units shall diligently listen to the advice of the federation as a whole.

8.) Each member collective, or, where it pertains, local federation union of area collectives and individual members and supporters will include a detailed written account and analysis of the progress made in carrying out the above strategy in their monthly reports to the federation. We must all learn from the struggles and experiences of each other!

9.) Individual members of NEFAC who are not attached to NEFAC member collectives or local NEFAC unions, and who are operating in general isolation from NEFAC bodies will diligently disseminate agitational information throughout the ranks of the local working class about the progress of the related campaigns taking place in other towns and cities. In doing they will seek to sow the seeds of such organizing methods among their local population.

10.) NEFAC shall officially bring this proposal to the Federation of Revolutionary Anarchist Collectives —Great Lakes Region, the Pacific Northwest Anarcho-Communist Federation, and any other regionally based North American anarchist federation which forms in the future, with the encouragement that they too consider this strategy for the advancement of the class struggle in their regions.

SOLIDARITY AMONG THE WORKING CLASS !
THE GREEN MOUNTAIN
ANARCHIST COLLECTIVE,
NEFAC-VERMONT, SPRING 2004

Montpelier Downtown Workers Union:
Building Working Class Democracy, One City At A Time[60]

FORWARD! THE DAY IS BREAKING!"

Montpelier VT, February 2005 — Under the shadows of the Green Mountains workers in Vermont's capital city (population 7900) have been building direct democracy and power on the job for more than a year and a half. The City of Montpelier, whose downtown shops are largely composed of independently owned businesses, is the site of a new innovative labor union known as the Montpelier Downtown Workers' Union, UE Amalgamated Local 221 (MDWU). Unlike a traditional union, the Downtown Workers' are organized geographically, effectively incorporating people employed in the service, retail, and nonprofit sectors in different shops all throughout the city. The union legally represents workers in a number of contracted shops as well as workers in minority shops. In addition, the union claims a number of majorities where they have not yet won legal recognition and a contract.

---

60 2017 note from the author: This article was first printed in the *Northeastern Anarchist*, 2005.

Through this union, all of these workers are brought together under one big tent where their collective voice can no longer be ignored by the bosses, and where their power is felt even by the elite and those that follow. With or without a contract, this union fights for the rights of all downtown employees and is building real working class power in this northern capital city, and all by practicing directly democratic means.

Origins, Necessities, and Eventualities

As Vermont's once powerful manufacturing base (which formally included highly productive towns from Brattleboro to Springfield[61] to Newport) has increasingly jumped ship for the super-exploited labor markets of Mexico and China, the economy in this small New England state (Pop. 621,115) has become increasingly reliant upon an expanding service and retail sector to offset massive job loss. The vast majority of these jobs pay a fraction of what they are replacing and carry little to no benefits. In addition, 79% of Vermont businesses employ nine or less workers. Because of the separateness and sheer quantity of these jobs, and because of the small number of employees who labor in each individual shop, most of the traditional unions have not been interested in expending their limited resources in order to organize these workers. This stands true throughout the nation. For many unions such endeavors represent an untried gamble that they are currently not willing to take, even if that is where the majority of the labor force is increasingly situated.

Finding themselves isolated from the organizational power of the more established labor movement, it is extremely difficult for such employees to win a collective voice at work, much less effect positive long-lasting change in their working conditions and create local democracy. Ironically, as this mode of labor becomes more and more of a numerical majority of Vermont's (and elsewhere's) workforce, and as the traditional unions refrain from organizing these workers, the overall union base has become more tenuous. With that, organized labor has risked becoming outpaced by capitalist interests and losing what political clout they maintained for the last century. In a word, it is becoming increasingly clear to all who pay attention that if the class struggle in the Green Mountains (and the rest of

---

61 As late as World War II, the U.S. Department of Defense listed Springfield, Vermont, as one of the most likely places Nazi Germany would bomb, if and when it had the opportunity, because of the industrial output from its machine shops.

the developed world) is not to lose ground and instead is to move forward, something has to be done. And again, as long as the larger more conservative unions sit on the sideline, it is possible that those unions and workers who do step forward will be in a better position to create locals devoid of arbitrary hierarchies and bureaucracies. In other words, in the near virgin territory of small service and retail shops opens the possibility of organizing workers through a truly democratic and self-empowering means.

Enter the Vermont Workers Center

In the spring of 2003, James Haslam, the Director of the Montpelier based Vermont Workers' Center (VWC), began to float the idea of establishing an "all-workers' union" in the capital city in order to empower those who work in small shops and as a way to begin organizing those in the fastest growing (and lowest paying) sector. This idea sprang out of numerous conversations with area employees about working conditions, as well as the many negative calls the center received in the previous five years on their workers' rights hotline relating to shops in that city.

By the summer of 2003 the independent and rank & file oriented United Electrical, Radio, and Machine Workers of America (UE) became interested in the project, and before long these two organizations (VWC & UE) agreed to split the cost of the project and move forward towards concrete organizing. It was not by chance that this project was being launched by these two organizations. The Vermont Workers' Center is a coalition of unions (including the UE, Vermont State Employees' Association, and the entire Vermont AFL-CIO), rank and file workers, and allied organizations representing a staggering 25,000 Vermont workers (out of a total labor force of just over 330,000). It was founded six years ago, in a large part by anarchists formerly in the Love & Rage #10 Collective.[62] Today the center remains committed to building real working class democracy and the fulfillment of basic social needs. Internally the center operates through a democratic means.[63]

---

62 While the former Love and Rage Revolutionary Anarchist Federation is now increasingly the topic of books, pamphlets and articles, it is ironic that one of its two most lasting and effective legacies (The Vermont Worker's Center — the other being the building of the Anti-Racist Action network) receives little to no attention. Unfortunately, writers have tended to make the less dynamic story of its internal ideological conflicts the main strain of the often-told narrative.
63 See the Northeastern Anarchist #8, Class Struggle in the green Mountains, by Lady (NEFAC-Vermont.)

The UE, for its part, is a democratically run leftwing union traditionally based in the industrial sector. Presently UE officially reports have 30,000 total members across the United States. Known to include many members of the old Communist Party-USA, the UE has recognized the new reality of the consumer based economy for some time, and has been experimenting in finding ways of getting a foothold in the growing service and retail sectors. In the months prior to agreeing to this new project, they successfully organized the two largest downtown supermarkets in the Vermont cities of Burlington and Montpelier (both co-ops).

Eventually the VWC and UE decided to pare down the target population to focus on the estimated 800 service, retail, and (later) nonprofit workers employed throughout the Montpelier city limits. Here it deserves mention that although the UE is a democratically run union, such democracy does not formally take effect until after a shop or a group of workers are constituted as their own local or are merged into an existing local. Until that time, the lead organizer, who in this case was Kim Lawson, has final say in regards to tactics and strategy. It would not be until the spring of 2004 that the Downtown Workers' Union, who at that time became part of local 221, would gain absolute authority over their direction and policy.[64] Even so, the workers exercised a considerable amount of democratic power during the early and middle phases of the campaign. This can be accredited to the commitment to internal democracy on the part of key organizers as well as the persistent voice of workers themselves.

What made the union drive different from others was the fact that the goal was not to target a single specific shop, but instead to attempt to bring together workers from dozens of small individual shops into one citywide local and seek, among other things, to implement one unified labor contract for all workers in these sectors: geographic unionism. Montpelier was picked as the location for three reasons:

> (1) As the capital, a successful organizing campaign here would carry with it a higher degree of statewide media attention and symbolism. This could eventually lead to similar projects being launched in other Vermont towns and cities.

---

64 2017 note from the author: This turned out not to be true. Later in 2005, the UE and Vermont Workers' Center staff decided unilaterally to end the organizing campaign. This was not the decision of MDWU members. For a time an effort was made to keep the union going through an affiliation with the IWW, but in the end it proved unsustainable. For a good description of the fall of the union, and lessons that were learned, see Precarious & Pissed Off, by Sean West, 2006: https://theanarchistlibrary.org/library/sean-west-green-mountain-anarchist-collective-precarious-pissed-off .

(2) Months before the UE successfully organized the largest retail shop in the city (the Hunger Mountain Food Co-op-75 workers), and it was therefore hoped that those workers would voluntarily lend a hand in the early phases of the new drive.[65]

(3) The headquarters of both the Vermont Workers' Center and the Vermont AFL-CIO [and the Vermont State Employees' Association] are located in Montpelier, and therefore it would be easier to organize on-the-street support for the new union than in other locations.

The First Strategy

The initial strategy adopted by campaign organizers was to quietly sign up as many workers to the union as fast it could, and seek as many specific shop majorities in as short a time as possible. After majorities were reached in a significant number of shops the union would publicly announce itself and demand legal recognition from affected shop owners. In turn these shops would seek the implementation of a basic uniform contract. This basic contract would: (1) Require a fifty cent raise; (2) Require employers to work towards a livable wage; (3) Establish a formal grievance procedure on the shop floor whereby workers' concerns could not be ignored by management; (4) and protect workers against unjust firings. Armed with one full time organizer (Tenaya Lafore), and financed jointly by the Workers' Center and UE, the part-time efforts of Kim Lawson (the UE lead organizer), James Haslam (of the Workers' Center), a small core of sympathetic workers and volunteers (including a small number of Vermont Progressive Party and NEFAC-VT members), and others from the community, the organizing drive took off with speed and promise.

Within the first few months of the drive, an Organizing Committee of fifteen workers from ten separate shops was formed. Soon after, pro-union majorities were reached at six different shops, which totaled seventy-five. Upon reaching these half dozen majorities, the Workers' Center, UE, and rank & file union members held their first press conference announcing the existence of the union and demanding recognition and contracts at these shops. The mood among workers and organizers was optimistic. It was believed that the union could

---

65 Unfortunately this did not pan out, other than a couple of union members who helped create a preliminary demographic map of downtown shops (how many workers, what the starting and average pay is etc.) and a couple more who eventually had limited involvement on the Community Solidarity Committee, the co-op workers offered little concrete support to the project. Today one co-op worker serves on the Worker's Defense Squad.

pressure the businesses into voluntary recognition, and quickly move to win at additional shops.

Here it should be noted that early on it was decided that the union would not pursue recognition through formal federally monitored elections. This decision was reached in light of the fact that the National Labor Relations Board (NLRB), which monitors and regulates such elections, tends to work hand and glove with management, and in opposition to union/worker interests. The NLRB is run by appointees of President George W. Bush, is notorious for allowing bosses varying degrees of advantages, and has even gone so far as putting election results under wraps (in a kind of limbo) for years —thereby effectively tabling concerted union activity indefinitely. Therefore, it was instead decided to seek voluntary recognition, if need be, through public pressure.[66]

Capitalist Backlash

In the wake of this early success came an immediate backlash from a large segment of the bosses. Within weeks of going public a significant number of business owners circled the proverbial wagons and began a sustained campaign of reactionary, anti-union propaganda through the capitalist media, and intimidations and scare tactics on the job. The worst of these shops was J. Morgan's. Others included the Coffee Corner diner, Capital Grounds Coffee Shop, and M & M Beverage and Redemption Center. Of course, the activity of the owners was not uniform. A minority of the smaller shops (primarily those that could not afford to employ anyone, those that employed only occasional or limited help, and those where the owners still were compelled to hold a second job as a common worker) voiced support for the union. These included The Book Garden and La Pizio shoes. In sociological terms, certain Marxist predictions proved themselves true. The wealthier owners (those who owned multiple businesses and/or controlled large portions of property i.e. the local bourgeoisie) stood firmly against the workers. On the other hand the allegiances of the petit-bourgeoisie became split with a minority of this subclass identifying with the workers

---

66 This is not to imply that this strategy should be employed at all times and in all places. For example, if recognition were being sought at corporate chain stores, it is unlikely that such could be had without one of these elections. It is conceivable that the MDWU can and will choose to go such legalistic routes when and if they gain union majorities at such shops, or whenever circumstances demand.

At J. Morgan's Steakhouse (an upscale restaurant), the owners, the multi-millionaire Bashara family, quickly moved to hire the union-busting law firm Gallagher and Flynn. There, waitress Val Tofani, an outspoken union supporter, was fired for dubious reasons. Other union members had their hours cut and were taken off the more lucrative shifts. Management also harassed and threatened union supporters, installed security cameras to spy on workers, and had employees followed home after work.

Workers in other shops also began to feel the pressure. As the hammer began to come down, many began to distance themselves from the union. Although one in eight (100 total) from the service and retail sector signed a petition making themselves union members, the effective public strength of the organization was beginning to decline. Of the original six majority shops, only one, the Savoy, recognized the union and signed a contract. At the others, workers began to retreat from their public support of the union as bosses began to threaten and intimidate those who they suspected of signing union cards or even considering signing union cards.

The union attempted to retaliate in several ways. To build broader support for the organization, a Community Solidarity Committee was formed which included more than 20 people from within non-UE unions (NEA, VSEA, Teamsters, Carpenters, Iron Workers, Nurses etc.), retirees, and others. These folks, alongside downtown workers from within the Organizing Committee sought various ways to maintain the union's momentum despite the bosses' counter attack.

At J. Morgan's a number of informational pickets were held. The largest picket drew 200 people from the labor movement (both Downtown Workers and those from other unions). Union members and supporters also held a 'coffee in' at the restaurant where most if not all the tables were filled up, and nothing but coffee was ordered. Here servers were delivered encouraging pro-union messages and large tips, while the owners made pennies on what would have otherwise been a lucrative dinner rush. The message was clear.

In December 2003, a union member also gained entrance to the restaurant dressed as Santa Claus, where he made a public scene announcing that the owners were being delivered the "Grinch of the Year Award" for their union busting activities and unfair treatment of workers. In addition to losing thousands of dollars in business due to the bad publicity and pickets, many organizations, such as the Older Women's League and VSEA pulled their plans to hold events there and at the adjoining hotel. Finally, the union filed 28 'unfair labor practice' charges with the federal government on behalf of those workers and union members that bore the wrath of management. With this, what began as periodic pickets at the steakhouse became organized weekly events. These pickets and the unofficial boycott continued until the 28 charges were settled in the summer of 2004.[67] In a word, the union busting owners lost tens of thousands of dollars in revenue and were compelled to spend an estimated quarter of a million on attorney fees; all of this to avoid paying 40 employees fifty cents more an hour, and allowing shop floor democracy from gaining a foothold.

Beyond the actions targeting J. Morgan's, workers and community members circulated a petition throughout the community voicing popular support for the union. Here workers and volunteers went door to door collecting signatures, and also sought them out at the weekly Farmer's Market. This proved to be an important activity because in many cases the person collecting signatures was the first person to inform folks of the struggle being launched downtown; after all, not everyone reads the newspapers and not everyone works in the city they live in. In one working class neighborhood (Barre Street), every single person who was home signed the petition with the exception of three. Eventually more than 700 people (the majority being Montpelier residents) signed it, and the UE and VWC had it printed as a full page ad in the local newspaper (The Montpelier Bridge). Dozens of union supporters also wrote solidarity letters to all the area newspaper (The Barre-Montpelier Times-Argus, The Bridge, and the Burlington based Seven Days). One organizer from the National Educators Association (and Vermont Progressive Party), Ellen David-Friedman, recorded a pro-union, pro-MDWU commentary which was broadcast statewide on Vermont Public Radio.

In addition, the union printed a small pamphlet which included the photos of a dozen downtown workers and their statements as to why they decided to join the union. This "speak out" was widely distributed all across the city. By February 2004, the Organizing Committee (and later the Steward's Committee) published a regular newsletter called the Downtown Workers Journal in which the specific union struggles, perspectives of downtown workers, and other related news was disseminated throughout the local community. This journal was and continues to be utilized as an organizing tool. It was and remains available in pro-union shops, and is handed out

---

67 The union was able to claim victory with the settlement. Management had to post notices that they would not interfere with union activity and all the union members who had been penalized by management were awarded relatively large sums of money.

to workers by workers both on the job and in the streets. For it or against it, the union drive manifested as a real force, as well as a topic for tavern discussion and debate.

While the overall effect of all these actions clearly helped the union survive the initial counter attack, and to a limited extend helped recruit a number of strong new members, these actions on their own were not enough to propel the organization to acceptable levels of growth in numbers and power. And again, it should be noted that a huge portion of the union's energy was being used fighting the counterattack at J. Morgan's. This was being done at the expense of adequately focusing resources on the other, smaller shops that also had achieved an unrecognized union majority. Ultimately, it could be argued that this was a significant mistake. While the union's inclination of "going after the biggest dog first" (J. Morgan's) had a degree of validity, the end result of not winning recognition there or, with the exception of the Savoy, in the other majority shops clearly represented a lost opportunity for quick success and long term stability. In short, by the late winter of 2004, it was becoming clear that the union needed to change its course if it were not only to survive, but gain a stronger more active membership and win more contracts. But what course should it take?

At this point workers and organizers decided to reevaluate their strategy. Here it was decided to begin a new dialogue with downtown employees. To facilitate this discussion the union drew up a simple survey which sought to ask workers what the most pressing issues were on the shop floor and among their class generally. Over the course of several weeks the Organizing Committee, union/Worker Center staff, and community supporters stood on street corners asking people to fill out the survey. One eighth of those in the service and retail sector made their voice known. The top priority: protection against unfair discipline and firings. Number two: the desire to establish an effective grievance procedure to deal with issues which arise at work. Now all that remained was to find a way to tap into these priorities that could demonstrate the power and relevance of a citywide worker's organization.

It was at this point that the UE Director of Organizing (the Pittsburgh based, Bob Kingsley) made the decision to pull funding for the fulltime organizing position. With the UE funding being cut, the Worker's Center was compelled to cut the bulk of their funding as well. It was further decided that the time had come for union members to be officially incorporated into Local 221 in order to gain the democratic link to the larger organization, and to start paying dues. The time had come for the union to start making progress to become a self-sufficient organization or risk being dissolved.

To many workers, this seemed a mixed blessing. On the one hand being officially incorporated into a local would mean that they would formally gain the right to democratically direct their organization, but on the other hand, losing a fulltime organizer is a hard pill to swallow. After all, massive amounts of organizing remained to be done, and now the great bulk of that work would fall on the shoulders of people who were already working 40-60 hours a week to pay the bills. Again, the decision to require dues from all members, in conjunction with the bosses' anti-union campaign, resulted in the union effectively retaining only 25 workers, not including the 15 protected under the union contract at the Savoy. With these developments in place, the union's Organizing Committee decided to call for their first Worker Town Meeting.

A Worker Town Meeting

Vermont has a 250 year history of participatory democratic Town Meetings. From the times of the first European settlers through the present, communities have relied upon the coming together of people in order to discuss, debate, and publicly vote on pressing issues as they arise. To this day, towns still gather on the first Tuesday of every March to pass resolutions, debate local budgets, and set priorities for the coming year. Given this context it only seemed natural to seek the extension of such a tradition to apply to the class struggle in a given location. Therefore, the Organizing Committee decided to call together its larger membership in order to unveil the survey results and see what folks wanted the union to do about it.

The meeting, held in April 2004, was well publicized and attracted workers from a dozen separate shops. After the survey results were unveiled, a long conversation ensued which resulted in the unanimous passage of two strategic resolutions. First, the Organizing Committee would in effect be transformed into a Steward's Committee, whose role it would be to facilitate a new citywide grievance procedure and to carry out the day-to-day operations of the union between Worker Town Meetings.[68] Second, this committee would also set up a new body of workers to be called the Worker's Defense Squad. It would be

---

68 This committee is empowered to carry out the general directives of the membership, and itself operates according to an internal democratic process.

the role of the former to provide workers (both union members and non-union members) a means to resist unfair treatment on the job, and the role of the latter to back up this procedure in shops where the union would not have the legal rights allotted with a signed contract. In a sense, the collective will of the membership at this meeting was that the union should start to act like a union regardless of whether or not the bosses chose to recognize it.

Beyond these specific resolutions, this meeting was significant in that it set the precedent for union policy being democratically set by the membership as a whole. The organization had made the leap into direct democracy. Sine that meeting, it has become the unwavering stance of the union to seek general direction and policy from the base, allowing officers such as the stewards no more power than the ability to carry out the collective decisions of the whole. This event produced the sentiment that such empowered Worker Town Meetings would be held a minimum of twice a year in order to guarantee the direct control of the organization by its members.

Citywide Grievance Procedure

The citywide grievance procedure which came out of that meeting was and remains structured as follows:

> If and when a worker feels that they have been unfairly treated by their boss, they are encouraged to contact the steward responsible for the section of the city where they work.

> The steward will then launch an investigation into the grievance to ensure that it is valid. This includes providing the boss a request of information form that asks management for whatever files and information that may help in the investigation

> If the grievance is found to be valid, the steward delivers an official written grievance to the offending boss. This grievance will document the basic findings of the investigations, and will also include potential resolutions to the conflict (*such proposed resolutions have a lot to do with the desires of the grievant and often includes requests for back pay, a letter of recommendation, the changing of certain work rules, reinstatement following a firing, etc.). The steward will then request a meeting with the boss in order to resolve the situation.

> If the boss refuses to negotiate in good faith, a second written grievance is delivered by the elected Chief Steward, who then attempts to negotiate with the offending boss.

If the boss still refuses to deal, the Chief Steward can request, in writing, supportive action on the part of the Worker's Defense Squad. This grievance procedure differs from those employed by other labor groups in that it does not concern itself with contracted shops alone, and it was made readily available to all downtown workers, not just union members.

Once this process was drawn up a brief description of it (along with photos and phone numbers of area stewards) were put to paper and distributed to workers all across the city. To facilitate this, stewards committed to give out these informative flyers to workers in their areas of responsibility. Similar to when we conducted the initial survey, this process had the secondary benefit of again creating a forum for worker/organizers and other downtown employees to discuss the union, how it functions, and what it intends on winning.

Worker's Defense Squad

The other innovation that came out of the Worker's Town Meeting was the Worker's Defense Squad. Here the Steward's Committee was given the go ahead in organizing a body of people from the Montpelier area that would help give teeth to the grievance procedure. Their primary mission is to organize actions targeting bosses who failed to negotiate with the stewards in good faith. In principle, such action could include any number of ways which would result in disrupting the business of the offending boss. It was decided to sign up a contingent of people, a core belonging to the MDWU (excluding stewards), and the others coming from other labor unions. Within eight weeks, a squad was formed which included four people from the Downtown Union, and twelve more from other sources.

When the Stewards Committee requires the intervention of the Defense Squad, they must make a formal request in writing, and provide them with all related grievance documents. At that point the Chief Steward and the grievant are required to meet with the squad in order to explain the situation and answer questions. After this, the squad itself determines what supporting action to take. This grouping also concluded that it would not necessarily limit its activity to the grievance procedure. By a unanimous vote, it decided that it would, in principle, make itself available to other workers and other unions in Montpelier in order to further the struggle of laboring people against the bosses. While the squad has two elected Chairs, one coming from the MDWU[69], the other from the Vermont Worker's Center Steering Committee, all collective decisions are made through the directly democratic means of the squad's membership. The MDWU Chair also sits on the union's Steward's Committee.

This new group was quickly made known to the business community. Its very existence has made the bosses more willing to deal with the union than could otherwise have been expected. In brief, they either deal with the cool headed stewards, or they face the concerted efforts of a group who has no choice other than to aggressively pursue them.

A New Contract and Citywide Elections

As the union began to reorient itself, Steward Kristin Warner, a 22-year-old Montpelier native, not only signed up the majority of workers at her shop, Mountain Cafe, but reached an agreement with the owner on voluntary recognition. Within weeks the union won its second contract, this one giving protection to ten more workers. The contract at the Mountain Cafe made it the only unionized restaurant in the State of Vermont.

Also at this time, and in accordance with the new directives set forth at the Worker Town Meeting, a citywide election open to all union members in good standing was held for the position of Chief Steward. In a tight race, which involved 75% of eligible voters, Kristin won the position. From this moment on, the organization began to unquestionably direct itself, and the age-old reactionary claim that the MDWU was no more than a puppet of unseen labor officials was forever crushed. The Montpelier Downtown Workers' Union clearly became an organization of the workers, for the workers, and by the workers.

Street Victories

Even before the official procedure was set up, the union had won at least two grievances. In one instance, Amanda Lyon, a member of the Organizing Committee and La Pizzeria employee of four years, had her hours drastically cut by management. It became clear that the motivation for his came from the boss' anti-union, sexist worldview. Upon hearing this, a delegation of workers went down to the restaurant and confronted the boss. Within 72 hours of this intervention, the boss called union organizers and informed them

---

69 2017 note from the author: I served in this position.

that he would give Amanda back much of her time. The other early victory came when Kristen Warner, prior to gaining employment at Mountain Cafe, was turned away from a job at Capital Grounds because of her public support for the union. In this instance, Dave Kazinski of the Iron Workers sat down with the offending boss, Bob Watson, and informed him that such actions were both illegal and morally reprehensible. The boss caved and offered to hire Kirsten. These actions, although coming before the establishment of the more formalized system, gave the union confidence that they were capable of winning real victories, even without contracts.

After the official system was in place, it was not long before workers began calling their stewards in order to lodge grievances. At Shaw's Supermarket, a worker (who was not a MDWU member) was taken off the schedule because she refused to remove an anti-George W. Bush pin while other workers were allowed to wear pins that supported the war, certain religious beliefs, and other causes. After her steward, Ellen Thomson, presented the boss with a "request of information form", management immediately gave her hours back and rationalized the pin rule. This worker joined the union.

At J. Morgan's union members again became the target of what appeared to be dubious written warnings in regard to alleged infractions. It was feared that these actions were the prelude to terminations. Union Steward Jessie Rosado filed a grievance, and management agreed to state, in writing, that the documents in questions should not be perceived as disciplinary measures.

At Julio's, a bartender (who was not a MDWU member) was fired for telling her boss that she may need time off because of an illness. Her Steward Kristin Warner investigated the matter and found that the boss's action was in violation of the Family Medical Leave Act. Upon delivering a formal grievance, the steward came to a negotiated settlement with the boss that, among other things, resulted in the worker getting her job back. This person also joined the union.

At Mountain Cafe, which is a contracted shop, the owner fired a number of cooks for reasons not relating to their job performance. Stewards Kristin Warner and Sean Damon were able to get compensation for those cooks who wanted it, and got one person his job back with back pay.

Most recently the union won a big victory at Coffee Corner. There, owner/boss Brian Mitosky, fired a waitress. She contacted her steward, Nick Robinson, and the subsequent investigation resulted in the union verifying the validity of her grievance. This was put in writing and delivered to the boss. After being briefly side tracked by meetings with attorneys (representing the grievant and the boss), the union was able to help negotiate a very good settlement involving a letter of recommendation and monetary compensation. This worker is now a member of the union.

However, not all grievances turn out perfectly. In these circumstances, the union has still managed to inflict punitive damages upon the offending bosses. In one instance, a Capital Plaza Hotel (owned by the Bashara family) worker was fired because of a mistake made by the boss, Laura Bashara. While the union was unable to negotiate a reasonable settlement with management, Chief Steward Kristin Warner was able to convince the Vermont National Educators Association not to hold a large event there. This cost the hotel thousands and thousands of dollars. In another instance, a bartender[70] was fired from Charlie O's for no apparent reason (other than being an identified union member). Like before, Steward Nicole Schaeffer and Chief Steward Kristin Warner were unable to negotiate a settlement. However the union did help the worker win his unemployment claim, and did organize a retaliatory action at the establishment. This action consisted of 70 patrons showing up on a Saturday night wearing stickers in support of the fired bartender. As part of the action, patrons refused to tip the offending manager, Stacey Shibly; one could consider it a tip strike. Also, a former bartender (Mo) took it upon herself to give the manager a piece of her mind. This resulted in her smashing a glass (aimed at the manager's head) against the wall behind the bar.

Even in these situations where the union failed to win clear victories, they demonstrated their willingness to fight, and their ability to disrupt business as usual. This clearly put pressure on the bosses to deal with us, regardless of whether their shop has legal union recognition or not.

As of print, stewards are fielding additional grievances across the city, and we suspect that we will win more victories and more union members as the year goes on. No matter how one looks at it, the fact that the MDWU has won clear victories in seven out of nine grievances (6 of them in non-union shops) is a damn good track record, even when compared to locals that operate exclusively in shops that possess binding union contracts. The union and the citywide grievance procedure has established itself as an important weapon in the local class struggle.

---

70 2017 note from the author: That bartender was myself.

Union Holds Public Hearing at City Hall

In late June 2004, not long after the citywide grievance procedure was established, the union organized a public hearing on the wages and working conditions in the local service and retail sector. The hearing, held at City Hall, included testimony on patterns of unjust firings, suspect pay practices, and the lack of respect given to workers by the bosses. Testifying were workers from Aubuchon's Hardware, the Thrush Tavern, J. Morgan's, Mountain Cafe, Brooks Pharmacy, Hunger Mountain Co-op , as well as many other shops. Present in the audience were more than 70 community members. Also in attendance was an official listening panel composed of the Mayor, Democrat Mary Hooper, two City Councilmen, Jim Sheridan and Chris Smart, and a number of well-respected activists from the community. The hearing received newspaper coverage and was broadcast on a cable access TV station.

This hearing allowed workers to tell their stories to the broader community. As these stories were told, a clear picture began to emerge as to why it was necessary to build such a union in Montpelier. By bringing so many people to the event and by making the event even more accessible via media coverage, the union was able to galvanize their efforts in the ongoing organizing campaign. The success of the hearing said to the public, "the union has arrived: and is here to stay."

Union Expands Organizing Scope

In the summer of 2004, union members held a strategy retreat, where among other things, it was decided to expand the scope of the union to include not only service and retail workers, but also those from within the nonprofit sector. In addition, the definition of the service sector was made to include those working in health and childcare related shops. If any worker in the Montpelier city limits who labored in such shops sought to join the union, they would be allowed to on the spot. However, the union also recognized that a number of workers who did not labor in these sectors, but who worked in other small shops, may seek membership in the MDWU. It was decided that their membership would have to be approved by a majority vote of the rank and file.

The decision to seek the inclusion of the nonprofit sector was spurred by the proposed incorporation of a number of employees of the Vermont Center for Independent Living (VCIL). VCIL, a nonprofit organization that seeks to help handicapped persons live a dignified independent life, were themselves seeking to win union recognition with the UE for some months. Being one vote short on a clear majority, they and the MDWU decided that rather than hold off on forming a union, they would merge with the Downtown Workers. With their joining of the MDWU, and with the further decision to accept workers from other sectors, pending approval from the membership, the union began to come full circle. The original idea of an "All Worker's Union" could again be seen on the horizon.

To what extent workers from these other sectors will be represented by the MDWU is a question that only time will tell. However, as the struggle continues, it is likely that the union will take up the fight with those being exploited by the bosses whenever they are asked to. The union is about building overall class power as much as it is about building specific power in any one or two sectors.

A Force in City Politics

Up until October of 2004 the union stayed focused on the symbiotic tasks of building a stronger membership base and protecting workers from unfair discipline and firings. However, all of that was soon to change. Leading up to the November 2nd elections, it came to the union's attention that a special resolution would appear on the city ballot. This resolution would give the City Council the authority to begin discussions with the state, aimed at creating a local 1% tax on all services and goods.

After researching the effects that such a tax would have on the community, the union discovered that the only people to directly benefit would be property owners who make over $40,000 a year. These select few would receive a reduction of their property tax in the ballpark of $200 a year. Most downtown employees are renters and tend to earn close to the minimum wage. They would not gain anything from this new tax. The only effect it would have on them would be that they would be paying 1% more for every sandwich and cup of coffee they bought. As such, the tax seemed to effectively amount to no more than a pay cut for our members. The Steward's Committee called a special general membership meeting to discuss the issue and to see what if any position the union should take. There it was unanimously voted to publicly oppose the tax and to encourage workers to vote against it.

Following this decision, the union with the support of the Worker's Center held a public discussion on the issue at city Hall. There a number of workers, officials from the state tax department, and the Mayor listened to the reasons the union opposed the measure.

In addition, "Workers, Vote No on the Local Option Tax!" flyers were posted all around the city. Oddly enough, by opposing this tax, the union, for the first time, ended up on the same side of an issue as the business owners (though for different reasons). On November 2nd, the union's fist sortie into city politics ended in a resounding victory. The measure was soundly defeated.

Second Worker Town Meeting

In late fall, 2004, the union, now protecting 25 workers in two contracted shops, and claiming an additional 25 members in more than a dozen other shops, held its second Worker Town Meeting. Like before, workers from twelve different shops were present. The meeting sought to review and evaluate the work of the organization since the last gathering. It also sought to ask the membership what direction it should take in the next six months. Here it was decided that the union would develop a new survey that would seek the general opinion of downtown workers as to what the minimum standards in working conditions should be in Montpelier. It was further resolved that the aim of this survey would be the creation of "The Montpelier Standard". After this standard is developed, the union will seek to have area shops endorse it. By endorsing it, management will be expected to treat their workforce according to this basic criterion. In return, the union will encourage community members to bring their business there. While the details and even basic outline of the standard are still being worked out, one thing is clear: the basic goal of The Montpelier Standard will be to pressure area businesses into uplifting the basic working conditions of the downtown employees.

As of print, the Steward's Committee has produced the basic survey, and is in the process of fine-tuning it. The stewards have also committed to getting 200 workers to fill them out. It is expected that this project will serve as a means to actively involve a second tier of union leaders: those not willing or ready to serve on the labor intensive Steward's Committee, but still desiring to be active. Finally, the survey will again serve as a means to open up a new round of discussions with those who may not yet be members of the union, but are employed downtown. It is expected that this process will lead to a further growth in the overall membership.

This second Worker Town Meeting also witnessed an official proposal to incorporate certain bylaws. The union functions through directly democratic means. It was therefore proposed to formalize these practices. One union member presented the organization with a set of concrete proposals. These included maintaining the biannual Worker Town Meeting system, formalizing the means by which workers and stewards can call for additional Worker Town Meetings, requiring a citywide vote (of dues paying members) on the overall citywide contract, etc. The adoption of any finalized bylaws will require the participation of the entire membership. It is not foreseen that the larger UE will oppose any of these proposals. After all, in the UE, the members, for better or worse, really do run the union.

The proposal was made available to all present at the Worker Town Meeting. In the coming weeks it will be sent out to those members who were not present. After this, members will be encouraged to come to a special meeting where the proposed bylaws will be discussed and amended. Finally, any such amended version will again be made available to the entire membership and again voted on. This participatory process will dictate that no finalized set of bylaws will come into being until this spring, at the earliest.

The Struggle Today and in the Future

As of February, 2005 the union includes 25 workers in two businesses protected by a contract, as well as 25 more who are members in other shops. While this may seem small, one should keep in mind that the total population of Montpelier is over 1000 times smaller than New York City. In a word, 50 workers in more than a dozen different shops is a significant presence in this small New England city. Even so, it is our hope to win more contracts, and increase the at-large membership over the course of the coming year (Note: organizing drives are currently underway in new shops). This will be done by virtue of our continuing victories, using the citywide grievance procedure and by making new contacts through the survey.

Over the course of the last year and a half, The Montpelier Downtown Worker's Union has proven that geographic unionism using directly democratic principles is possible. It has demonstrated the way forward for workers in other towns, neighborhoods, and cities. In the coming decade, we hope to be able to export the model across the Green Mountains and beyond. We recognize that in order for working people to build real power, we must continuously organize afield and afar. In Vermont, that means in the smallest rural towns, as well as in cities like Burlington and Rutland. Furthermore, we recognize that the ultimate power of the working class cannot be limited to any single state or region. Working folks must rise up wherever they labor.

We are proud to report that since the MDWU has formed, other similar unions have begun to come together in different place. The most advance of these is the South Street Workers (IWW), in Philadelphia. Comparable to Montpelier, NEFAC members are playing an important role in the forming of this union. What makes the South Street Workers significant is the fact that they are demonstrating that such a model is possible in a large urban setting. Recently, workers in Madison, Wisconsin have contacted the MDWU and have informed us that they too are preparing to build a similar geographic union. NEFAC members in Montreal have also been discussing forming a Precarious Worker's Union in that city. As more and more of these democratic, geographic unions form, it will be increasingly important that we keep the dialogue open. We must never forget that it is imperative to not only learn from each other's victories, but also from our mistakes. Together we have the potential to transform the future.

The formation of such unions should not be understood as an end in itself. Rather, it is one step down the road of delivering an overall directly democratic, socialist society. First we must create a forum where workers can empower themselves. Starting a union for those that labor in small shops, such as the Montpelier Downtown Workers' Union, is a necessary step in that direction. Inevitably, such organizations begin by seeking bread and butter victories for their constituencies, thereby proving their power and raising the expectations of those workers it uplifts. It is reasonable to expect that such unions will begin to branch out and take on broader social issues such as the establishment of universal healthcare and an ending of imperialist war.

In addition to building these organizations, we must seek ways of bringing the rank and file members of the different unions together, geographically, in directly democratic bodies. As a prelude, we must foster an overall sense of class unity and common cause between the different trades and sectors. In Montpelier where many sectors are already organized into unions, we see this potentially beginning through the formation of the Worker's Defense Squad. Eventually, as the struggle continues, we must not settle for merely the creation of working class organizations which tackle the symptoms of capitalism, but we must create larger democratic bodies of workers who are ready and willing to establish a dual power that is fundamentally at odds with the forces of capital; we must establish local Worker's Councils.

Such worker organizations, along with democratic community organizations such as Town Meetings and Tenant's Unions are the seeds of said dual power. It will only be when the workers, farmers, and communities are organized and prepared to fight for their collective self-interest (housing, healthcare, childcare, job security, livable wages, etc.) that socialism and democracy will have the practical means through which to overcome capitalism. The establishment of the Montpelier Downtown Worker's Union is one small step in that direction.

The Role of Anarchists

From the start of the campaign to the present, members of the NEFAC-Vermont had one worker on the Organizing Committee. Currently, there are four NEFAC members and supporters on the Stewards' Committee and two additional members/supporters also in the union. It should be recognized that of those six NEFAC members and supporters, only four were in the organization before they became union members. The others have recently become involved, in large part, because the basic goals and principles of NEFAC (direct democracy, socialism, class struggle, etc.) dovetail to a certain extent, with those that are emerging organically within the union. With this being said, one should not make the mistake of believing that this is an anarchist lead union. What this small number of anarchists have done in the union, has been through their capacities as workers first, and anything else second. Further, the vast majority of union members would not consciously identify themselves politically as anarchists. However Vermonters have a strong tendency towards direct democracy. This tendency is influenced by their tradition of Town Meeting. As this tradition intersects with the contemporary class struggle it has the potential to evolve into a movement which will seek the eventual transformation of society into something resembling a form of libertarian socialism. It should not be expected that this potential trajectory will reach maturity tomorrow.

NEFAC-Vermont as an independent organization has sought, at times, to consciously inject the larger picture of the class struggle and the logical socialist conclusions of direct democracy into the union movement. Early on, NEFAC-Vermont wrote and distributed to hundreds of Montpelier works the brief pamphlet "Union + Town

Meeting = Democracy".[71] In this work, we endorsed the call for the Downtown Workers' Union, and discussed how such an organization could be a first step in achieving economic and democratic freedom. We have also given the union drive significant exposure and analysis in our seasonal statewide newspaper, Catamount Tavern News. Finally, we have sought to act as the watchdogs of internal democracy whenever such issues arise.

As we are all ourselves workers, we lent whatever hand we could. If we were employed outside the scope of the union, we contributed to the cause with vigor. If we labored in the city, we joined the union and did our duty as working class revolutionaries to strengthen the movement. We have walked side by side with our fellow workers prioritizing the building of this democratic union first and our ideology second. As anarchists, we understand that it will be the workers themselves who must and will eventually lead the movement, and (one day) the revolution. What they call themselves (be it anarchist, progressive, or socialist) will matter not if they remain committed to establishing meaningful forms of democracy that result in a community where the scarecrows of poverty are replaced with bounties of plenty. Here, in this norther state capital surrounded by the wooded mountains, and mindful of the tradition of the Green Mountain Boys, workers are taking the first steps in reclaiming a democracy which has been obscured by 200 years of capitalism. One has to start somewhere and, today, that somewhere is Montpelier.

---

71 See Catamount Tavern News, Fall 2003.

VERMONT SECESSION: DEMOCRACY & THE EXTREME RIGHT[72]

Flag of the first Republic of Vermont

Catamount Tavern News Service, Vermont, March 6th 2007 — Political Independence. Sustainability. Economic Solidarity Power Sharing. "Equal access for all Vermont citizens to quality education, health care, housing, and employment." These are some of the basic points which the Second Vermont Republic (SVR) organization lists as their binding principles. In the past, this organization has also stated that it stood for the further cultivation of democracy on the farm, in the workplace, and at Town Meeting. When the racist Minuteman organization tried to gain a foothold in Vermont, SVR's founder called on Vermonters to resist them (and we successfully did). Honorable? Yes. Many outstanding Vermont leftists have also thought so, and thus SVR has included members such as anti-

---

72 2017 note from the author: This article was first printed in Catamount Tavern News, 2007. The Second Vermont Republic would essentially implode as a rest of this scandal. However, Vermonters' interest in secession has increased. A 2017 poll conducted by the University of Vermont found that supporters of secession now number 21% of the population. In 2007 a similar UVM poll put that number to be at 13%. In 2006 UVM found that 8% supported secession.

Bush anti-war activist Dan Dewalt of Newfane, and Bread & Puppet founder Peter Schuman of Glover. But how can such high principles co-exist with cultivated relationships with persons and organizations that instead cling to xenophobia, religious fundamentalism, racism, and unrestrained market capitalism as their principles of operation? Such is the dichotomy of the Second Vermont Republic. And as such connections have increasingly come to light, SVR's leadership has not adequately sought to distance themselves from such relations, but instead has sought to justify the betrayal of Vermont ideals at the expense of the support of their own constituency.

It is now apparent the Second Vermont Republic organization is not now nor has ever been much more than the political assertions of founder, Mississippi native, former Duke University economics professor, and current Charlotte resident Thomas Naylor. The organization, which until recently counted more than two hundred members has been lead into an absurd and potentially dangerous alliance with forces that have no legitimacy or meaningful social base in the Green Mountains. Without a rank and file vote, without meaningful debate, and without input from secessionist supporters Thomas Naylor and Rob Williams (who has now resigned) appointed themselves to act as co-chairs of the movement. I know both of these men personally. Beyond the serious political disagreements discussed below, I know them both to be good people, anti-racists (when it comes to their personal/local politics), and honest believers in the idea of an independent Vermont. My issues with them stem from deep political differences, not personal antagonism. There was a time when these men served the cause of Vermont secession well by publicizing the idea, and making the issue a focus of common household discussion. However, good people can make very bad decisions. And without democratic oversight such bad decisions can quickly become amplified. Point in case: Naylor willingly, and acting alone, appointed a number of rightwing extremists (all non-Vermonters) to serve an official role in the organization as members of the group's Advisory Board. These include: 1.) Milan Professor Marco Bassani, member of the xenophobic and violent Northern League of Italy — a party who includes a member of the European Parliament who is now in prison for fire-bombing an immigrant camp. The Northern League, in a further demonstration of its extremist tendencies, was also recently a member of the rightwing ruling coalition which included the avowedly fascist Italian Social Movement (this government has since been electorally replaced by the center-left). 2.) Thomas Dirolenzo, the southern quasi economist which sees pro union workers and socialists as "malcontents" bent on the destruction of all things good in society. Dirolenzo instead trumpets Wal-Mart as the economic model which liberty demands and lends his intellectual support to foreign sweat shops insofar as they help to weaken organized labor domestically. And 3.) Jason Sorens, leader of the New Hampshire Free State Movement which, as their laissez faire economics imply, hopes to return our New England neighbor to the times of unfettered capitalism before anti-child labor laws and work safety standards became a 'burden' to industry. In a word he is a radical capitalist masked in a folksy libertarianism; one who contends social programs are no more than a yoke on the free movement of capital. These rightwing extremists have no place in Vermont, or anywhere in the political arena where real democracy and hope of social and economic equality are still held in high regard. For the Second Vermont Republic to provide them with a platform and veneer of legitimacy in the Green Mountains is inexcusable.

Under Naylor's leadership the Second Vermont Republic has ignored the enlightened and reasonable sentiments of most Vermonters and has knowingly and willingly cultivated organization to organization relationships between marginal, misguided, and potentially dangerous separatists groups beyond our Green Mountains. From neo-Confederate neo-racists (known as the League of The South), to Christian fundamentalist separatists in South Carolina, to members of the xenophobic Northern League in Italy, Naylor and others in SVR's leadership have seen no reason to make the moral distinction between a Vermont separatist movement aimed at participatory democracy and social equity and those elsewhere aimed at a reactionary totalitarianism; or at the very least they have failed to build a meaningful firewall between the two. Even though SVR's leadership are not themselves racists (Naylor has a history of anti-racism while living in Mississippi), and even though they do not advocate the authoritarian and/or theocratic models supported by some of their out-of-state counterparts, such cultivated institutional relationships have been condemned by the rank and file Vermont separatist and non-separatist alike as out of step with Vermont values at best, and a harbinger of unseen semi-conscious sympathies at worst. This is not a 'guilt by association' this is guilt through cultivated institutional relationships. If any other political organization in the state held such ties, they too would be brought to task. Even more, it appears that radical models of capitalism, the kind advocated by

Advisory Board members Dirolenzo and Sorens (both of whom hold an economic ideology that would eliminate such popular social programs as Dr. Dinosaur, unemployment insurance, and section 8 housing out of hand), are finding sympathetic ears within the ranks of SVR leadership and its allied groups. This, among a population who just overwhelmingly voted a socialist into the US Senate and who includes 100,000 current and retired union members/dependents, has done nothing but discredit the Second Vermont Republic and the secessionist movement as a whole in the eyes of common Vermonters.

When these factual connections where made public by well documented reports by a Mr. John Odum appearing on the Green Mountain Daily website, Naylor and the SVR leadership chose to dig in and defend their past decisions rather than admit wrong and make corrective moves. Betraying the good faith of most secessionist minded Vermonters (which are currently estimated to number 40,000 persons, or 8% of the population), Naylor refused to admit fault. Instead, in a February 26th press release, he lashed out at those who have dared question his judgment. He termed his detractors "Techno Fascists," speculated that the Vermont Natural Resources Council, John Odum's employer, is backing what he perceives to be an ungrounded and "well-coordinated" smear campaign, called the Southern Poverty Law Center (who categorizes the League of The South as a hate group) a "McCarthy-like group of mercenaries based in Montgomery, Alabama," and, with a hint of irony, simultaneously red baited the publisher of this paper, the Green Mountain Collective (of which, as news editor I am a support member of), charging that the group seeks to establish a Cuban style socialism across New England. (*Note: For the record, unless Cuba is run through a system of decentralized Town Meetings, and directly democratic worker & farmer unions, this is not our publisher's goal. —see CT News' mission statement). Naylor has also lashed out at the (democratic socialist) Vermont Progressive Party, who he alleges are the "clone" of the Democrats, and went on to state that John Odum and the Green Mountain Collective "are all mirror images of what is wrong with Vermont politics." In his mind we "just don't get it." Then who does Mr. Naylor? Thomas Dirolenzo? The so called economist who would have children working in coal mines? Or perhaps the Northern League gets it? Perhaps fire-bombing immigrants is the way of progress? Or is it the League of The South? In a word, instead of viewing the situation with clarity and political savvy, Naylor has responded with paranoia, counter accusations, and by making enemies with any and all respected Vermont political organizations and individuals who dare to be appalled at the company the Second Vermont Republic has chosen to keep? This is not the way to build a movement in the Green Mountains.

Further damning themselves, when numerous people from within the Second Vermont Republic and supporters of secession throughout the state demanded that SVR address these issues and sever all ties to such rightwing extremists they were met with the stone wall of an apparent internal dictatorship. One associate editor of the group's sister newspaper, Vermont Commons, a Mr. Robert Riversong asked the group's leaders to address its errors in an honest and comprehensive manner. Their response? He was quickly and officially expelled from the Second Vermont Republic by that same arbitrary leadership. Meanwhile, Vermont Commons editor and former SVR co-chair Rob Williams publicly stated that it was none of his business as to whether or not certain members of the Advisory Board were racists. Another self-proclaimed sister organization of SVR, the Middlebury Institute (a small think tank supportive of the idea of secession) headed by a certain Kirkpatrick Sale (also a SVR member), publicly proclaimed its intention of retaining ties to separatists groups outside Vermont regardless of the concerns of most Vermonters. One should wonder, does this include groups such as the Aryan Nations, a white supremacist separatist organization? All told, instead of digging out, SVR's leadership dug in. This lack of concern for the moral and political implications of their ongoing organizing efforts not only illustrates the poisoned political leanings of the current separatist leadership (or at the very least of the political naivety of that leadership), but also makes strikingly plain the lack of internal democracy within the current separatist movement. And with that, the Second Vermont Republic, unavoidably and rightly so, imploded. As a result of the unfolding situation, popular support for SVR has dwindled to a negligible few. If SVR continues at all, it will likely do so as no more than a paper tiger; a vehicle for the writings of Mr. Naylor and little more.

This unfortunate turn of events has disheartened many Vermonters who hoped SVR would act as a catalyst for a free and unfettered Vermont. Further, the unfolding situation has highlighted the inherent failures of attempting to create a social movement by the will of the few, alone, as opposed to the democratic participation of the many. Where one person, where a small Junta of leaders are commonly doomed to make fatal mistakes and political misjudgments, the participation of the many guarantees, at the very least, that the right decision will be reached at least more times than not. As imperfect as such odds are, it is the best that history allows for, and as such is the gift of participatory democracy; a gift that has thus far been spurned by the secessionist movement in all but empty rhetoric.

But is the cause of secession itself a worthy cause to begin with? As Vermonters it is true that we, at times, feel an instinct to rebel, an instinct towards independence insofar as we suspect our freedom is marred by the dictates of forces beyond our hills. This is no different than the old motivations of Ethan Allan and the Green Mountain Boys who, by force of arms and through Town Meeting votes, spurned the moneyed interests of the Royal New York Colony and claimed Vermont for the yeoman farmers who worked the fields. And still today it is true that even though we elect a socialist to the US Senate, our common economic and political reality is unavoidably warped by the confines of Wall Street and Washington DC. The truth is, no matter who we send to Washington they alone will never have the power to fundamentally buck the system which keeps many of us living at or below the poverty line. No matter how democratic our Town Meetings are, and no matter how many resolutions we pass against the war, the federal politicians acting in the interests of the big oil companies will continue to send our sons and daughters to be slaughtered in the chaos that is Iraq. And it is no secret that vast amounts of our collective wealth is everyday hauled away; be it our timber which is sent to mills far outside our boarders or tourist money that is transferred to corporate bank accounts that no Vermonter will ever see. And while hundreds of millions of dollars are siphoned out of our collective pockets, many of us cannot afford to send our children to college, or to buy adequate health care for our families. In a word, we are increasingly no more than an economic colony within the American Empire. So is secession a worthy cause? Maybe, but unlike what Thomas Naylor and the Second Vermont Republic proclaim, not in and of itself.

Many of the faulty steps demonstrated by Naylor and the Second Vermont Republic stem from a cheap, undefined logic that secession is sufficient goal; one that by virtue of some distant pantheon of gods will also result in a free Vermont and the disembowelment of all that is wrong with America. While SVR has the right impulse in judging the federal government and its economic backers to be a major cause of strife in the world today, that impulse serves as no blanket justification for secession; be it in Vermont or beyond. History clearly and irrefutably demonstrates this truth. Are we to call the blood bath that was Bosnia noble in and of itself because it was sparked by the act of secession? Do we judge the deadly anti-Semitism of fascist Croatia (backed by the Nazis) of the 1940s as just because it was seeking a demented self determination to slaughter its perceived ethnic others? Are we to understand the great sacrifices of Vermont regiments in the US Civil War as immoral because they sought to put down an act of secession, even if they themselves believed they were at war against slavery? Should Killington have the right to secede from Vermont, as Naylor has publicly asserted they do, because they do not want their tax money to go towards text books for poor children in Hardwick? Few Vermonters would answer yes to any of these questions. Historically, the experience of our own Green Mountain Boys tells us that even these revolutionaries were not apt to accept the validity of secession at all times and at all places. In 1781 Ethan Allen and two hundred armed men set out from Bennington to put down a counter-revolution in the town of Guilford. At the time Guilford was itself in the process of succeeding from Vermont with the aim of joining in political union with New York. To support this revolt the town was actively stockpiling lead, powder, and drilling a militia. After a brief skirmish, Allen entered the town, rounded up the leading citizens and threatened, "I Ethan Allen do declare that I will give no quarter to the man, woman, or child who shall oppose me, and unless the inhabitants of Guilford peacefully submit to the authority of Vermont, I swear that I will lay it as desolate as Sodom and Gomorrah, by God!" The counter revolution was put down, and the first Republic of Vermont (which persisted until 1791) survived the crisis.

The fact is secession is a means, a tool, a lever to be used at specific moments and specific times towards an end which itself must be unequivocally righteous if we are to put any value upon it. So is Vermont's secession from the union justified? Logic dictates that it would depend on the end that it hopes to achieve. If that end is simply to shorten the pond in order for certain fish to feel bigger, than no. That is, if the goal is no more than to recreate the inequities of American Empire in a smaller and more personal form, than no. On the other hand if it is aimed at recreating the social sphere in such a way as to provide an end to alienation, an end to poverty, and an end to the bureaucratic mediocrity of the state, than the answer, perhaps, is yes. Meaning does not exist without context, and any separatist movement would do well to answer the questions that history, and the people, will rightly demand be answered. Separatism, in and of itself, has never put food on the table or shoes on a child's feet.

With all this being said, it must be admitted that the theoretical justification for separatism, or lack thereof, is in many ways no more than an interesting academic debate best left for UVM professors. The fact remains that if the separatist movement fails to offer a social program; if it ignores the real issues that affect Vermonters on a day to day basis than it is very unlikely that many will view the movement with more than a forgetful interest — tavern conversation at best. There is a sharp divide between saying you support secession in a telephone poll, and masses of people actually struggling to see it through. The first Republic of Vermont was not founded on abstractions or passive intellectual leanings. The first Republic was forged in lead and class struggle against the elite of the New York ruling class. If the fight was lost, thousands of small farmers would have been thrown off the fields they cleared, Yorkers would have occupied the cabins they built, and local democracy would have been sacrificed at the altar of the central authority in Albany, New York. In a word, the founding of Vermont was grounded in tangible social and economic forces. It was not an abstraction or a product of academic debate. Hence, any meaningful contemporary separatist movement must learn from history, and not try to create an illusory existence outside of it. A people cannot live off nostalgia alone. The issues that trouble Vermonters today, the modern answer to the Yorker intrusions of old, are bread and butter issues; affording rent, finding a job, putting your kids through school, having health care for your family, retaining dignity in the face of all that is stacked against you. These are some of the real issues that weigh on the majority of Vermonters, and yes the majority of Vermonters are unquestionably working people and small farmers. Thus economic class is the cornerstone of all modern conflict in the Green Mountains (much as it was long ago).

This is born out in a quick survey of the large and dynamic social movements found across the state. It should come as no surprise that the Vermont Workers' Center, a group dedicated to building workplace democracy and uplifting the living standards of common people, has a membership constituency approaching 30,000. Nor should it come as a shock that the Dairy Farmers' of Vermont, who are fighting to stem the tide of farm closings, claims the support one third of all raw milk produced in our hills. Even on Town Meeting day Vermonters have demonstrated time and again that when their voices are heard, they too have cast their lot with meaningful popular movements that aim to bring true social and economic justice to these hills. Least we brush off the fact that out of the 23 towns that voted on health care related issues in 2005, 87% of them overwhelmingly voted in support of a universal single payer system by which all Vermonters would be covered. Thomas Naylor and the Second Vermont Republic state that they refuse to take a stand on how the future independent Vermont will be organized, nor will they toss there lot squarely with the majority, with working people. If they did, there would be no Dirolenzos, no Jason Sorens on their Advisory Board. Instead they say that the ultimate organization of the reconstituted republic will be decided by Vermonters themselves. This sentiment, in part, should be applauded, but it remains another instance of putting the cart before the horse. If truth be known Vermonters have already spoken, and the type of Vermont they hope to build is one of democracy, economic justice, and social equity. Working people cast their vote for such a future every time they sign a union card, every time they form a farmer cooperative, every time they protest for their right to health care, every time they stand up against the failures of the current economic and political system, every time they vote contrary to the policies of the General Assembly and Washington DC in their Town Meeting. So yes Vermonters will decide how best to organize their society and, in fact, the majority of them, that being working people, already have. What stands in the way are the state and federal institutions which act as a bulwark of the privileged few. It is a failure of the Second Vermont Republic that they refuse to recognize this and instead let history pass them by.

Instead of embracing the majority, the small farmer and working class, Naylor and the Second Vermont Republic has sought to retain a so called alliance of left and right, of workers and bosses, of poor and rich. Such a strategy is doomed to fail on many accounts. These groups have no more in common beyond living in proximity of these hills. What, pray tell, do rich men such as Richard Tarrant and Jack McMullen have in common with a line worker at the Cabot Creamery? What do they have in common with a logger, a dairy farmer, a ski lift operator, a cook, a nurse, or a fire fighter? Are not the Tarrants of Vermont no more than an extension of everything that is wrong with the American Empire? Are not the wealthy of Stowe and Killington mere stumbling blocks along the road of social, political, and economic equality? Does not one person's wealth necessitate the poverty of one hundred others? Common sense tells us that it does, and that same common sense tells us that the great mass of Vermonters will no more act in political collusion with such folks any more than they will aid them in any scheme that is seen as a vehicle for the elite minority to implant themselves as the new ruling class in a future Republic of Vermont. Therefore, by refusing to squarely side with the working majority, the Second Vermont Republic has made the blunder of alienating hundreds of thousands of Vermonters. This, insofar as a machine shop worker laboring 12 hours a day is unlikely to sacrifice his limited time or risk anything for a vision of the future in which the economic chains that bind him are still fettered to his wallet and soul. But perhaps this is no more than a straw man argument.

In truth Tarrant and McMullen are not now members of SVR nor have they ever been members. For them, the current political system of federal capitalism suits them just fine. SVR's leadership is not composed of millionaires, but rather, in part, of comfortable middle class intellectuals. And maybe it is the comfort and relative leisure of these persons which act as an anchor against any social platform which would challenge the economics which allow for that security. This is not surprising. Many historical secessionist movements, such as that in Catalonia, Spain, are primarily an upper middle class movement. And here, consciously or otherwise, we return to the motivating factor of the 'small pond.' But this does not have to be. There are also many mass separatist movements that are based largely on class; based on the desire of the exploited to shake off the chains that bind them and experience life as something other than one long kick in the ass. Such is the case, at least in part, in Northern Ireland and Palestine, and initially such was the case with the Quebecoise. This is not to say that middle class intellectuals should not be welcome in social movements of working people. It is only to say that such intellectuals must bend to the majority and must work towards the articulated aspiration of those tens of thousands who feel the crush of exploitation in every callus on their laboring hands.

So where is the Vermont separatist movement today? There are rumblings that a number of former Second Vermont Republic leaders (apparently excluding Thomas Naylor) recognize the democratic shortcomings of SVR. A joint proposal submitted by myself and SVR member Jim Hogue (*see "A Way Forward") calls on the movement to implement a Town Meeting like system where all policy and all committee memberships would be decided by the direct democratic participation of any and all Vermonters who, in good faith, support political self-determination. The preliminary feedback on this proposal has been positive. Factions of former SVR leaders, with this proposal in mind, are reorganizing under the name Free Vermont. However, many of these folks are the same persons who, directly or indirectly, bear responsibility for the past mistakes and failures of SVR. And again, it is likely that some of them are friendly to the reactionary economics of Dirolenzo and Sorens. But IF they invest all movement power within directly democratic Town Meeting like bodies, their biases can be dulled. For the fact is that working people are by far the majority in Vermont, and if we chose to partake in a directly democratic assembly of secessionists, our views, our concerns, our class allegiances will carry the day over those who would demur. There will be no Tarrants, no McMullens, no Dirolenzos, and no Sorens in our movement. Such a popular legislative body would result in the reconstituted secessionist movement finally entering into the mass arena. It would guarantee a progressive, left platform (one congruent with the sentiments of most Vermonters), and would expel the ghosts of the reactionary right in that our concerns, our desires, and our dreams would act as the language through which secession would be understood.

If Free Vermont moves forward with plans to democratize the movement, and if that democracy is at least as free as our Town Meetings, then secession minded Vermonters, working class Vermonters in particular, should engage the organization. For as long as the current organizes of Free Vermont hold democracy in higher regards than the capitalist ideologies that they may or may not harbor, then there is little for us to loose and, possibly, much for us to gain. If Free Vermont refuses to walk the road of democracy, then the organization should be boycotted by working Vermonters and be allowed to die on the vine of fringe isolation. Half measures and rightwing postures can go down on their own ship. They do not need us. And if Free Vermont refuses to be a voice for the working majority of Vermonters, and if it does not reflect the progressive sentiments of those who have long dreamed of an independent Vermont, than perhaps such folks should start their own secessionist organization; one that is in fact democratic; one that embraces the concerns and perspectives of the great majority of Vermonters; that being working people and small farmers. It will only be such a secession organization that will have the ability to draw active supporters in the tens of thousands, and it will only be such an organization which can result in the Vermont secessionist movement being able to lay claim to anything approaching a moral high ground.

Finally, Vermont secession can be a powerful weapon in the arsenal of democracy. But can it deliver a comprehensive freedom? Can it open the doors for a full participatory and equitable economy? Probably not. The chains of authoritarianism and capitalism can only be shattered when they are broken at many links. Vermont is our home, and it serves as the one link that we can access, but it is only one. Any victory here would only be partial. Deliverance to the Promised Land will only come when many more than us rise up against that which holds the many in bondage. Therefore our separatist movement must never succumb to provincialism, xenophobia, racism, or exclusionism. Instead it must be internationalist in spirit, even if it is localist in character. Even while we may struggle for our own self-determination, we must leave the door open to others, like us, who are engaged in the same battle at different points. That battle is not secession per se, but is economic equality and direct democracy. We should never forget the enemy of my enemy is not always my friend. Just as our movement must be principled, we must only build bonds with folks elsewhere who hold such similar principles dear to their heart as well. And again, if secession is not grounded in the material fact of class struggle, than it is no more than a fool's game.

***

This essay must conclude as the sun is now coming up, and today is the first Tuesday of March. But it will be with all of these concerns, hopes, and desires in my thoughts that I soon will make my way to Town Meeting. Freedom and Unity.

CHAPTER 7: ON THE ROAD

WHEN THE LEVEE BREAKS[73]

New Orleans residents try to evacuate, 2005

> If it keeps on rainin', levee's goin' to break.
> If it keeps on rainin', levee's goin' to break.
> And the water gonna come in and we'll have no place to stay.
>
> —The lyrics in this chapter all come from Kansas Joe McCoy and Memphis Minnie, "When the Levee Breaks"

---

73 2017 note from the author: A version of this article was first printed in *Vermont Livin' Magazine*, 2005. I traveled by truck to New Orleans following Katrina with comrades Carrie Cleveland and Bridget Mudd.

New Orleans, LA, September 2005 —It was Friday, September 9th, 3:00AM. I stood on a balcony on Orleans Street trying to piece together a story I was six hours late calling in. I was hunkered down in the only occupied apartment on the entire block. To my left, through the apocalyptic darkness, Johnny White's Sports Bar was still serving drinks to a few of the scattered folks left in the Quarter. Besides the occasional military truck, the only sound came from a battery powered boom box in the bar. Cutting the silence was a rock and roll station; and they were playing *good rock and roll!* It is a travesty that it took a national disaster for the keepers of the airwaves to grant us decent music. I stood and blew smoke to the dark sky. The few lost and/or brave souls looking up tonight would see the beauty of the stars, perhaps for the first time. As I pitched my butt to the street, I heard Keith and Mick coming across the radio. The drums, strange mumbling, then like a knife, *"Please allow me to introduce myself, I'm a man of wealth and taste!"* I thought about the time, years ago, when I lived in the French Quarter. I thought about what strange end of the world visions I had seen these last few days. I thought about what the future held for these battered streets and about all the pain and death this city had witnessed in the last week. I lit another cigarette, and stared into the night. *"Pleased to meet you. Hope you guessed my name!"*

Night Patrol with the Vermont National Guard

> Well, all last night I sat on the levee and moan.
> Well, all last night I sat on the levee and moan.
> Thinkin' 'bout my baby and my happy home.

I arrived in Jefferson Parish, Just across the Mississippi River from New Orleans, on the afternoon of Tuesday, September 6th. I drove down from Vermont in an old red pick-up. In the bed I kept a dozen cans of soup, fifteen gallons of extra gas, and ten gallons of water. From the rear view mirror hung a press pass of dubious value. In the glove box I kept a loaded pistol. Prior to arriving, I arranged to be "embedded" with the 130 Vermont National Guard troops operating in the area. Within minutes of pulling up to Head Quarters, an old middle school, I boarded a truck with ten solders from the 1st of the 86th Field Artillery. It was 6:00 PM, still light. This was to be their first night patrol.

As we left the gates the solders loaded their M-16s. They had no more idea of what to expect than I. All we knew were the images of chaos that flashed upon the network news several days before.

We rolled through the streets of Jefferson Parish. Katrina's devastating power was evident. Telephone poles were snapped like toothpicks. Roofs we ripped from their beams. Electricity, of course, was still out. One gas station was simply flattened. I had never seen anything like it. A soldier turned towards me and said, "Better than we seen in Baghdad."

We reached the sector assigned to the unit. Holms Avenue. The truck drove through the area to get a feel for it. One house had the entire second floor wall torn from its framing. I could see into what was once a person's bedroom. It looked like a giant, postmodern dollhouse, made to appear in a war zone. A mall sat deserted. A large section of it was burnt down. Near the fire damage was an abandoned police station. Local cops allege that they were shot at when they evacuated.

We soon dismounted and began a foot patrol. As we walked Sergeant Cramdon, the squad leader, remarked how strange this felt. All the open windows, all the alleyways; this would be a very dangerous situation back in Baghdad. "Every one of us was over (for eleven months)," said Cramdon. Maybe subconsciously, maybe through intent, the group fell into military formation.

As night drew near the guardsmen converged around the truck. The streets were deserted. Most heeded the dusk till dawn curfew. Standing around with little to do, we talked to pass the time. I asked what they thought about this assignment. Sergeant Cramdon answered, "(Compared with the Regular Army) we're more public friendly." This was a telling statement as it was rumored that tens of thousands of Regular Army troops were heading for the New Orleans area. As it turned out the 82nd Air Borne was put in charge of maintaining order in the French Quarter.

Sergeant Scott, who in the civilian world works as a Burlington auto mechanic, stated, "These guys (some Regular Army) don't understand. You don't want to piss off the people who live in your backyard."

The conversation quickly and inevitably turned to their experiences in Iraq. Oversees they were assigned to protect military convoys passing through the Baghdad area. This is one of the most dangerous assignments in the occupied region.

"One guy (an Iraqi) got shot at the north gate there, and two days later we got mortared," said a soldier in his late thirties."

Sergeant Cramdon added, "You just want to keep the peace in the community. Let them know you're there, but let them know you're not there... When we were over in Iraq we were never proactive, we were always reactive," said Cramdon. If our President operated according to this principle, we would not be in Iraq today.

Many Guardsmen recalled that in Iraq they were compelled to fire their weapons on a near daily basis. One soldier, helmet pushed forward, almost sleeping, said he only fired his gun once in eleven months. The others looked at him, some with disbelief. Still leaning back, hardly bothering to open his eyes he mused, "We threw rocks when other people were shooting bullets."

"Rocks don't do to good when they're shooting bullets at you," countered Sergeant Cramdon. I thought of the Palestinian youth who throw stones as the Israeli Army. Sergeant Cramdon was right; their fate is often death.

As the night wore on, there was little to do but maintain vigilance, smoke cigarettes, and talk. At one point two local cops from the sheriff's department pulled up. In the darkness they did not notice that a member of the press was present. I heard them tell the Guardsmen, "No one on this street is innocent." They went on to encourage the Guard to shoot people, and informed them that they would cover up such events. As they pulled away, they aimed their PA system at area apartments, blaring the sounds of a woman screaming. The Vermont Guardsmen had no interest in following their lead.

The night eventually grew into morning. As the six o'clock hour again approached, we headed back towards the base. I asked when is the soonest the unit can be ordered back to Iraq? "February," came the reply. Someone questioned, "Does this deployment extend that?" Sergeant Cramdon answered, "No."

A soldier announced, "F– that. I'm not going back." Another rejoined, "You'll have to if they call you up." It was left at that. I inquired, "How long will the war last? How long do you think it will go on for?" Someone grumbled "Forever." No one disagreed.

As we pulled into the HQ, the officer gave the order to unload their weapons. "All weapons are cleared." I asked how long they would be deployed in Louisiana. A soldier replied, "No idea. Until they tell us to go home."

Food, Water, and Murder

> Now look here mama what am I to do?
> Now look here mama what am I, I to do?
> I ain't got nobody to tell my troubles to.

Two hours after we returned, I joined a different squad heading out to distribute food and water. The first destination was a housing project in Tarrytown. The apartment buildings were two story structures built in the 1970s. The neighborhood was typically populated by several hundred low income African-Americans. When the Guard arrived with provisions, it appeared that only a few dozen remained. The streets were littered with debris. Many buildings showed signs of Katrina's devastating winds. At the flood's height, waters flowed waist deep through this neighborhood.

As the Guard drove slowly through the streets passing out food and water, I followed, interviewing residents. I approached a group of four adults, three women and one man who all appeared to be in their late thirties-early forties. This group was standing around a car loaded with belongings. They immediately expressed their desire to leave for Texas, but confessed they had no gas.

A distraught woman, mother of three, told me "I'm just trying to look after my children... We got no gas, we got [some] water in jugs... We're trying to keep [our home] clean the best way we can, but it still has the whole filth and smell in it. The damage is real bad... I'm trying to get out of here. I'm trying to get to Texas. I don't care where I go as long as I get the [heck] out of here."

I asked how she assessed the local and federal government's response to the crisis. Her eyes became sharp. "They're not handling it right. They're not doing what they're supposed to do. If they were to do what they were supposed to do, we would be out of here right about now."

Addressing local officials she charged, "People came here and drew guns on us... The police... They were about to beat up my (twelve year old) son on his birthday because he told them not to search his bag... They came out from nowhere, just crept up on us... We didn't know what was going on. They draw guns on us, telling us to raise our hands up, you know — and everything. My little niece was right there, she had her baby and they still was drawing guns."

The woman claimed that police shot and killed local residents without just cause. "People that's dear to us done got shot. People we know got killed. They (the police) got the permission to shoot them on sight."

A strong looking man in his forties stepped forward and said, "They draw guns on all of us. Every last one of my kids, my wife, and my nephew, and everything."

The man discussed the plight of those who were forced to loot food when government aid failed to arrive, "We got a lot of people who go get food for their (family). They (the police) killed them, since the storm, in this neighborhood, on Manhattan (Street) across the river and everything. All down here (The police) have been shooting on the kids. They aren't saying freeze or nothing. They shooting you in the head and that's bad."

Another resident, a woman in her late 30s, attributed the alleged instances of police killings to racism. "We got a lot of racist (White) cops that are taking advantage of this fact that it's supposed to be marshal law, and they're really taking advantage of it."

I kept pace moving behind the Guard. Throughout the day we went to many neighborhoods. Everywhere people expressed anger at the government. Still, this anger did not appear to apply to those Vermont Guard troops who gave them food and water. In many communities this was the first government assistance since the storm hit. Throughout the day, the twelve Guardsmen I traveled with distributed an estimated 900 meals to the people of Jefferson Parish.

Katrina's Heart of Darkness: Into New Orleans

> I worked on the levee, momma, both night and day.
> I worked on the levee, momma, both night and day.
> I ain't got nobody to keep the water away.

The next morning I headed out, leaving the Guard behind. Now armed with a "National Guard Media Affairs" press pass, I decided to make an attempt on New Orleans itself. The city had been blockaded for some days by the military. The entrance to the Mississippi Bridge was manned by the Army. Word had it that only military, emergency, and authorized utility vehicles were being allowed in. I approached. Pulling up to the checkpoint I flashed my "National Guard" pass. To my astonishment I was waved through.

By 9:00AM I found an open bar on the corner of Bourbon and Orleans —Johnny White's. This tavern, one of two open in the French Quarter, was serving as a kind of oasis for many of the 200-300 residents remaining in the area. In addition to whiskey, scotch, and gin, they maintained stockpiles of free food and drinking water. I ordered a beer.

I asked the bartender, Joe Bellamy, 24, what the situation was. He answered, "We are the community center. It started out as just a bar and then people started bringing food here. People started bringing clothes and water. Suddenly, it became a soup kitchen and a homeless shelter." Bellamy, a former para-rescuer in the Air Force and self-described socialist, continued, "It doesn't matter if you're gay, straight, no matter race, religion, no matter what your personal beliefs are, you come in and need some food — you're getting it. You need some water — you're getting it."

After two beers and a shot of whiskey I prepared to push on. I wanted to take a look at the devastated Ninth Ward while it was still early. Before Katrina this was one of the poorest and most neglected sections of the city. When the levees ruptured, the area was submerged under many feet of water. The Ninth Ward was also the location of much alleged shootings. Thousands of Superdome refugees came from this neighborhood.

I asked a bar patron, James La Lon, a 62 year old artist, for directions to the Ward. He told me to head three miles past Esplanade — away from the Quarter. "You can't miss it." In addition to directions I also was given a warning to be careful. He claimed to have been shot at a dozen times while driving through three days before.

I did not set out alone. Accompanying me was Ride Hamilton, 29, a local volunteer first aid provider of Cheyenne descent. I met him less than an hour before. He expressed interest in seeing the Ninth, and I had an interest in someone riding shotgun.

"Do you know how to handle one of these?" I asked, handing him a loaded pistol. He said "yes" and proceeded to put a round in the chamber —just in case. Ride, six feet tall with long black hair, wore a blue "Sioux City" fire department shirt he bought in a thrift store. He found that the uniform helped avoid hassles with the local police. We headed north.

As we drove away from Johnny White's it became eerily apparent that we were the only vehicle on the streets. In this sea of destruction traffic laws no longer applied. We took a one-way street the wrong way for a mile past Esplanade.

As we drew closer to the ward, we began to see large "x"s spray painted on the sides of every house. In each quadrant of the X were written letters and numbers. In the top it read "9-6." To the left, "TX-1." To the right, "NE." At the bottom, "1." We correctly guessed (as was confirmed later) that these symbols were the record of a search conducted by the military or other government agency. The top obviously represented the date of the search. The left, the unit who conducted it. The right was a code for the type of contamination found within. The bottom number told the grim tale of how many bodies were found. Again, these were on every house.

A mile past Esplanade we saw the first other vehicles. Two military trucks rolled past. In the back we could see the sullen faces of haggard evacuees. Nobody bothered to wave. We continued.

The deeper into the neighborhood we got, the more debris littered the deserted streets. "[Curse] Bush. Them Bitches Flood Us," was written in black spray paint across a brick wall.

Heading up Rampart Street we passed a tire garage. A wiry Black man sat out front. The sign said "open." This tire shop represented the last outpost of commerce in New Orleans.

Soon we approached a small bridge crossing a canal deep into the Ninth Ward. A gate sat across our path. Four National Guard troops stood watch with M-16s. We approached. I got out and presented my magic press pass. They opened the gate and let us in. Immediately the flooding began.

The road we drove on, North Rampart was sometimes dry, sometimes six inches underwater. The side streets to our left were under too much water to traverse. The water was black and smelled like rotting meat.

On the corner of St. Clair and Deslonde the water deepened. The wreckage from the flood and winds was immense. Walls and roofs were severed from houses. The tops of abandoned trucks were caked with mud.

We drove a half-mile further and still we saw no signs of the living. The tightly packed houses were left alone. Here, a number of homes were yet to have an 'X' to keep them company. The scene made me think of some kind of evil Venice that had been bombed and left for dead.

The flooding worsened. I saw a boat that had been heaved atop of a four-foot fence. Trees were up-rooted and strewn across the road.

Breaking the strange silence two empty military trucks passed heading deeper into the Ward. Did they expect to find survivors?

Down a side street, still underwater, I saw empty school busses. I assumed they never brought people out.

We turned right down Gordon Street. We had to drive carefully not to be ensnared by fallen power lines. The letters "DEA-OK" were painted on a cement wall. Arrows pointed in both directions. A few blocks away we made out five military personnel on a front porch. They were battering down a door. We drove through the black putrid waters in their direction.

When we reached them I asked, "have you been finding anyone?"

A soldier replied, "No. Just dead bodies."

"Are you going to start clearing out the dead bodies?"

The soldier answered, "No."

He gave me a cold look. The conversation was over.

In silence we headed back up to Rampart, then south out of the Ward. There was little doubt in ether of our minds that thousands were dead.

The People vs. Katrina

Oh, cryin' won't help you, prayin' won't do no good.
Oh, cryin' won't help you, prayin' won't do no good.
Whenever the levee breaks, momma, you got to lose.

We got back to the Quarter and turned left down Esplanade. Taking a right on Decatur I saw a makeshift sign reading "Rebuild The French Quarter HQ." I first heard of the organization earlier in the day. This group, as with a number of other like organizations, was composed of local residents who spontaneously came together after the hurricane.

HQ was previously a bar known as "Oswald's." After Katrina the entire 9000 square foot building was commandeered by local residents for use as a storage depot. Inside tens of thousands of dollars' worth of food, water, and tools were evident. The facility was also equipped with a gas generator, and two fully stocked bars. I was told booze was used to bribe police into not messing with them. This depot, as well as others I visited, was stocked with donated and "looted" goods. More recently, their supplies were bolstered by military rations.

Standing in the inner courtyard were a half a dozen locals. One of them introduced himself as "Steve." Steve, who worked in construction, explained that Rebuild the French Quarter (RFQ) numbered forty volunteers. Their exploits included clearing rubbish and downed trees. One of their first acts was to make Esplanade, a major street marking the border of the neighborhood, passable by vehicle. RFQ went the extra step of stenciling white "RFQ Volunteer" t-shirts, printing professional looking ID badges, and writing and producing a mission statement.

After the crisis began, their first priority was to help distribute guns and ammunition to area residents to use in self-defense. Steve told me of one local who shot a man breaking through his front door. The shot did not kill him. The shooter ran outside, and less than a block away found two New Orleans police officers. He told them what happened, and asked for their help. The officers told him to get lost. The man then returned home, dragged the bleeding intruder into the street, and shot him dead.

However, by the time I spoke with RFQ, the general situation had become relatively stable. As such, the organization was preparing to go forward with modest reconstruction projects. They were in the process of gathering resources to repair a number of area roofs when a rumor stopped them in their tracks. Earlier in the day word got around that either the local or federal government was close to enforcing the mandatory evacuation. This rumor gained validity when a number of Louisiana State Troopers entered Johnny White's and initially demanded that all patrons leave with them to be evacuated immediately. After some heated words, the Troopers were convinced to call their superiors for confirmation. As things went, they left with no one in tow. Even so, the story and fear of a looming forced removal spread like wildfire across the community.

"All of us are... hiding in our residences. Is that stupid or what? There are hundreds, even thousands, of people right here that would be active volunteers (in rebuilding our city). We know this city like the back of our hands. We are not driving around like Mississippi cops that don't know this place. We know what we're doing, where everything is, and how to get resources. We can get this place back up and running. They (the government) need to leave the French Quarter alone, and let us do this," said Steve.

Karen Watt, 61, a small bar owner and RFQ member added, "We are survivors who live here. We can take care of ourselves."

I wondered if RFQ was scared into non-action? The answer was no. I listened as RFQ members planned a massive cleanup starting near Jackson Square (the middle of the Quarter). The action was planned for the following day. It was hoped that this display would convince officials that residents should be allowed to stay and directly partake in the recovery effort.

While at the RFQ compound, I was told that a similar organization was forming in the nearby Marigny neighborhood. I was also informed of another group in the French Quarter known informally as the 'Red Shirts.' The Red Shirts cleaned up Jackson Square and had been providing first aid to those in need. Later I learned that across the river in Algiers the residents were also organizing. It was reported that former Black Panthers were active in those efforts. More recently a community center has been opened up in the Ninth Ward by an organization called Food Not Bombs.

It was clear that people were coming together across the city. However, instead of local officials and/or FEMA working with these groups, they were being pressured to evacuate against their will. While still at HQ I listened as a local sheriff warned RFQ members not to let FEMA know they had stockpiles of food and water. He claimed that if FEMA found out they would confiscate the supplies.

Eventually Ride and I departed for another 'community center,' Molly's At The Market. Molly's, located on Decatur Street, was the other pub opened in the Quarter. Unlike Johnny White's (which literally had not been closed in fourteen years), Molly's kept hours. Their doors were opened 11:00 AM to 6:00 PM. This tavern was two blocks from an apartment I kept years ago. I knew the jukebox by heart. Tom Waits: Small Change. The Clash: Combat Rock. Johnny Cash: Live From San Quinton. On this day it was the only place in the city where you could get a cold beer. Where they got the ice, I did not ask.

Sitting at the bar was Mike Howl, 46, a professional tarot card reader before the storm. I asked him how people were doing. Howl's depiction of events contradicted the media reports of general mayhem.

"I live right off of Rampart Street so I saw thousands of people leaving the Ninth Ward and heading, unfortunately, to the Superdome. I saw people share the only pair of shoes that they had. I didn't see any acts of violence. I saw people just trying to help one another... The people have been good. I haven't seen any problem with violence."

Howl continued, "This whole image of the poor people coming from the Ninth Ward being this uncontrolled mob is absolute BS. Like I said, I was right where the people were coming from, and I didn't have any problems with anyone."

"The main thing (is) how humane the people were... Everybody said, 'hello', 'how are you', 'good luck.' They'd tell you where to go to get things. It was heartwarming, because even people that were in worse shape than I was in, much worse shape, would do things that were helpful, and I'm very thankful for that... I saw the best of people, and that includes people from the Ninth Ward," recalled Howl.

Mike went on to tell me that many more people than one might think were coming together and organizing. He made reference to two "communes" that formed following the crisis. He explained that these communes were households of people who have pooled their belongings and labor in order to provide collective security and basic necessities.

Howl, like so many other people I spoke with in the past four days, expressed anger and frustration with the government. "The government offered us nothing, except misery and threats... Katrina terrorized us for one day. But the government has terrorized us, meaning the people of New Orleans, every day since," he said.

Howl told me that food and water was slow coming into the city. "We had the first five days (after the storm) of waiting... Jackson

Square was dry and they could have had emergency food distribution there from the day Katrina hit. They never did a thing," he asserted.

Outside I talked with a few passersby. One was David Richardson. Richardson, 56, was a carriage driver in the French Quarter. I asked why he had not evacuated? He answered, "This is my home, I want to stay with it. This is my city. I love this city. I love the French Quarter. I want to be here to put it all back together."

As dusk approached, he leaned up against a post and summed up the New Orleans spirit of community and self-reliance; "This is what I call the 'Committee of 75'. Nobody is giving orders. There are enough people that know what needs to be done and we talk it over."

Conscious of the encroaching night, Ride and I headed back to Johnny White's. In our absence, Ride's comrade, Yellow Stray Dog, a Native American woman in her forties, said she had been thrown up against a wall by the cops. She told me the police accused her of being a looter, put a gun to her neck, and threatened to shoot her. Since the crisis she had been administering first aid along with Ride to locals. She had also helped stockpile and distribute food, water, and supplies to the neighborhood. When I talked to her, she was visibly shaken.

Stray Dog recalled, "[The cops] told me 'you're nothing but a cheap looter,' and I say 'no I'm a respectable person. I'm here helping out my people.' They told me they were gonna arrest me, and they pushed me against the wall, and put a gun... around my neck... They were screaming at me."

Fighting back tears, Stray Dog went on, "Right now I'm more afraid of the New Orleans police than any disease that is around or anything else. They really are overpowering and intimidating... There is no need to be treated like that."

After The Flood

> Oh, mean old levee taught me to weep and moan.
> Yeah, the mean old levee taught me to weep and moan.
> Told me leave my baby and my happy home.

The next morning I stopped in White's, met up with two guys I agreed to take north, said my goodbyes, and headed for the causeway across the lake. One last time I had to wave my press pass at men with machine guns, and one last time I looked over my shoulder to see the sky-scrappers with all those shattered windows. Again I was the only person on the road. I lit a bowl, took a drag.

I wondered if such misery was avoidable. Could the Louisiana National Guard have reacted better and faster to the crisis if 4000 of their troops were not stationed in Iraq? Would the levees have held if they received better maintenance? After all, $350 million in federal assistance earmarked for the levees was instead diverted to pay for the war and tax cuts for the wealthy. And again, class played a huge role in bolstering the body count. In a city whose poverty level is akin to the third world, tens of thousands of residents were stranded without the economic means of escape. It is clear that the state and federal governments failed to adequately deal with the situation as it unfolded.

As I drove north, I was also troubled about the political game which would soon be afoot. I suspect the feds will use New Orleans as a vehicle to award disaster-profiteers like Halliburton billions in reconstruction contracts. They will also use the related federal expenditures as an excuse to further cut social services for poor and working people. Still, while this process plays itself out, the drama of daily survival remains for the hundreds of thousands of people adversely affected by the disaster. This should not be forgotten. It will be many years before New Orleans can count the ghosts that walk her wrecked streets. It will be generations before they can be exorcised from the collective memory of the living. After all, we have seen the face of the Devil, and her name is Katrina.

Printed in the United States
By Bookmasters